Rapha's 12-Step Program for

OVERCOMING CODEPENDENCY

Rapha's 12-Step Program for

OVERCOMING CODEPENDENCY

Pat Springle

Rapha Publishing/Word, Inc.
Houston and Dallas, TX

The Twelve Steps of Alcoholics Anonymous*

1. We admitted we were powerless over alcohol—that our lives had become unmanageable.

2. Came to believe that a Power greater than ourselves could restore us to sanity.

3. Made a decision to turn our will and our lives over to the care of God *as we understood Him.*

4. Made a searching and fearless moral inventory of ourselves.

5. Admitted to God, to ourselves, and to another human being the exact nature of our wrongs.

6. Were entirely ready to have God remove all these defects of character.

7. Humbly asked Him to remove our shortcomings.

8. Made a list of all persons we had harmed, and became willing to make amends to them all.

9. Made direct amends to such people wherever possible, except when to do so would injure them or others.

10. Continued to take personal inventory and when we were wrong promptly admitted it.

11. Sought through prayer and meditation to improve our conscious contact with God *as we understood Him*, praying only for knowledge of His will for us and the power to carry that out.

12. Having had a spiritual awakening as the result of these steps, we tried to carry this message to alcoholics, and to practice these principles in all our affairs.

Contents

Step One   1

We admit that our needs to be needed and our compulsions to rescue others have made our lives unmanageable. *But let each one examine his own work, and then he will have reason for boasting in regard to himself alone, and not in regard to another. For each one shall bear his own load* (Gal. 6:4-5).

Step Two   11

We increasingly believe that Jesus Christ can restore us to spiritual, emotional and relational health. *...for it is God who is at work in you, both to will and to work for His good pleasure* (Phil. 2:13).

Step Three   43

We make a decision to turn our lives over to God through Jesus Christ. *I urge you therefore, brethren, by the mercies of God, to present your bodies a living and holy sacrifice, acceptable to God, which is your spiritual service of worship* (Rom. 12:1).

Step Four   61

We make a searching and fearless moral inventory of ourselves. *Let us examine and probe our ways, and let us return to the Lord* (Lam. 3:40).

Step Five   105

We admit to God, to ourselves and to another person the exact nature of our wrongs. *Therefore, confess your sins to one another, and pray for one another, so that you may be healed* (James 5:16a).

Step Six   121

We commit ourselves to God, desiring that He remove patterns of sin from our lives. *Humble yourselves, therefore, under the mighty hand of God, that He may exalt you at the proper time, casting all your anxiety upon Him, because He cares for you* (1 Pet. 5:6-7).

Step Seven   137

We humbly ask God to renew our minds so that our codependent patterns can be transformed into patterns of righteousness. *And do not be conformed to this world, but be transformed by the renewing of your mind, that you may prove what the will of God is, that which is good and acceptable and perfect* (Rom. 12:2).

Step Eight   173

We make a list of all persons who have hurt us and choose to forgive them; we also make a list of all persons we have harmed and become willing to make amends to them all. *And just as you want people to treat you, treat them in the same way* (Luke 6:31).

Step Nine   **193**

We make direct amends to people where possible, except when doing so will injure them or others. *If therefore you are presenting your offering at the altar, and there remember that your brother has something against you, leave your offering there before the altar, and go your way, first be reconciled to your brother, and then come and present your offering* (Matt. 5:23-24).

Step Ten   **201**

We continue to take personal inventory, and when we are wrong, promptly admit it. *Therefore let him who thinks he stands take heed lest he fall* (1 Cor. 10:12).

Step Eleven   **241**

We seek to grow in our relationship with Jesus Christ through prayer, meditation and obedience, praying for wisdom and power to carry out His will. *But if any of you lacks wisdom, let him ask of God, who gives to all men generously and without reproach, and it will be given to him. But let him ask in faith without any doubting, for the one who doubts is like the surf of the sea driven and tossed by the wind* (James 1:5-6).

Step Twelve   **255**

Having had a spiritual awakening, we try to carry the message of Christ's grace and power to others who struggle with codependency, and to practice these principles in every aspect of our lives. *Brethren, even if a man is caught in any trespass, you who are spiritual, restore such a one in a spirit of gentleness; each one looking to yourself, lest you too be tempted* (Gal. 6:1).

Acknowledgments

I want to thank...

...Sandy Ballard, who has an amazing ability to translate my ancient Sanskrit into English.
...Robert S. McGee and Don Sapaugh, for their encouragement to write this twelve-step workbook.
...Dan Sampson, for coordinating the publication of the workbook and
...Susan Joiner, for editing the manuscript to give it clarity and a smooth flow.

Introduction

Family Systems of Behavior and Communication

Significant research has contributed to much of what we now know about family systems of behavior.[1] For purposes of simplification, these systems are identified as the functional family and the dysfunctional family.

The *functional family*, or family which contributes to the overall growth and development of its members, certainly isn't perfect. It does, however, foster open, honest, loving communication. In this environment, both the parents and their children develop a strong sense of "self," or identity. They learn that they can trust, feel and talk about many—if not all—the issues in their lives. The diagram below illustrates a functional family system:

The Functional Family System*

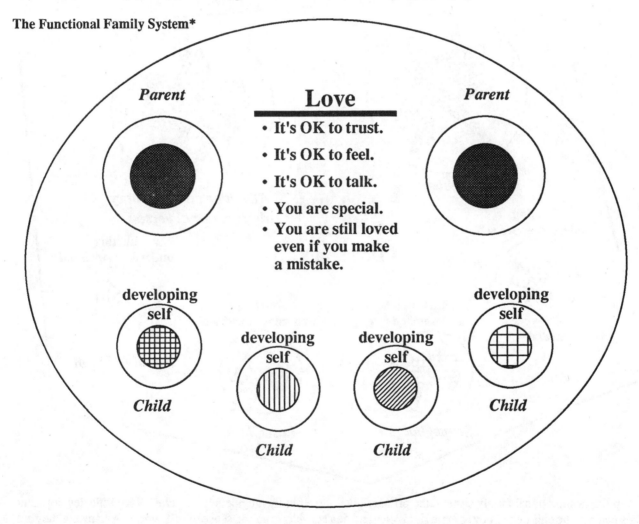

The inner circles represent the development of a person's self-concept. The parents are represented as having healthy self-concepts which are indicated by the darkened inner circles. In the children, various degrees of shading are used to indicate development of the self-concept. The outer circles represent life roles. Examples of life roles are:

- **parent** - wife, mother, teacher, friend, artist
- **parent** - husband, father, businessman, friend, Sunday school teacher
- **child** - brother or sister, student, athlete, dancer, friend

When parents are healthy and there is an environment of love, children are able to develop a positive self-concept. They are able to have positive, productive roles in society and meet life's challenges.

In a *dysfunctional family* system, open, honest, loving communication is thwarted to some degree for one or more reasons: At least one person in the family is emotionally or physically abusive or absent, dependent, handicapped, physically or mentally ill, or manifests some other type of disorder. Resulting problems in family interaction may cause one or more members to feel that something is wrong, but negative communication systems hinder the freedom and ability to be honest about one's feelings. *Denial*, an unwillingness or inability to recognize problems in and around one's "self," promotes more repression and further erodes family trust and intimacy.

The diagram below shows how dysfunctional family systems hinder trusting, feeling and talking. The result is that each family member's growth and development is hindered, resulting in a loss of identity, or "self." Each person then takes one of several roles within the family often marked by codependent behavior.

The Dysfunctional Family System*

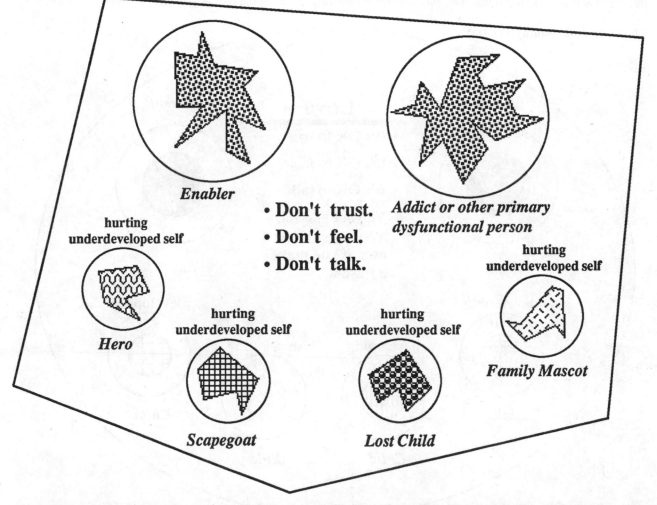

- Don't trust.
- Don't feel.
- Don't talk.

Enabler

Addict or other primary dysfunctional person

hurting underdeveloped self

Hero

hurting underdeveloped self

Scapegoat

hurting underdeveloped self

Lost Child

hurting underdeveloped self

Family Mascot

In the dysfunctional family system, the primary goal of the family members is survival. Very little development takes place in the children. They assume rigid roles and don't develop a strong sense of self-worth. As a result, they are doomed to keep playing these roles in their marriages and other relationships.

In this type of family system, most normal self-development is lost. All of the unconscious focus is on the primary dysfunctional person.

- The **enabler** tries to make everything okay.
- The **hero** thinks that by being perfect, the problems will go away.
- The **scapegoat** rebels against the family problems and ultimately believes that *he* is the problem.
- The **lost child** pulls into a shell, withdraws and isolates himself from meaningful relationships.
- The **mascot** tries desperately to make everyone laugh in the midst of the tragedy of the family situation.

* Adapted from *The Family Trap*, by Sharon Wegscheider-Cruse, and *The Family*, by John Bradshaw.

Children in these systems rarely build healthy self-concepts. They are at great risk for multiple marriages, addiction, codependency and stress-related physical problems.

What Is Codependency?

Codependency was coined in the 1970s in the context of treating alcoholism. Alcoholics were observed to share a somewhat consistent set of behaviors. As therapists treated families of these alcoholics, they observed that the family members also exhibited a fairly consistent pattern of behavior. The alcoholic was *dependent* on alcohol. The family was affected, too, so they were called *codependent*.

Originally, *codependent* was applied only to families of alcoholics. Later the term was given to families of those who were dependent on any kind of drug, including alcohol. Today the word is used to describe anyone in a significant relationship with a person who exhibits any kind of dependency (alcohol, drugs, sex, food, work, gambling, perfectionism, success, etc.) or who is abusive, absent, or physically or mentally impaired. Those who are adversely affected by this other person's behavior, and who have an imbalanced sense of responsibility to rescue, fix and/or help this other person are codependent. This person either consciously or unconsciously deprives the codependent of needed love and attention, which provokes rescuing as a means of obtaining that affirmation.

There are many definitions of codependency. In her best-selling book *Codependent No More*, Melody Beattie defines a codependent person as *one who has let another person's behavior affect him or her, and who is obsessed with controlling that person's behavior.*[2] Sharon Wegscheider-Cruse describes codependency as a...

"...preoccupation and extreme dependence (emotionally, socially, and sometimes physically) on a person or object. Eventually, this dependence on another person becomes a pathological condition that affects the co-dependent in all other relationships. This may include ...all persons who (1) are in a love or marriage relationship with an alcoholic; (2) have one or more alcoholic parents or grandparents; or (3) grew up in an emotionally repressive family...It is a primary disease and a disease within every member of an alcoholic family."[3]

We will define codependency this way: *Codependency is a compulsion to control and rescue people by fixing their problems. It occurs when a person's God-given needs for love and security have been blocked in a relationship with a dysfunctional person, resulting in a lack of objectivity, a warped sense of responsibility, being controlled and controlling others* (three primary characteristics); *and in hurt and anger, guilt, and loneliness* (three corollary characteristics). These characteristics affect the codependent's every relationship and desire. His goal in life is to avoid the pain of being unloved and to find ways to prove that he is lovable. It is a desperate quest.

Some who study family systems of behavior and communication believe that within the dysfunctional system, only the person who plays the role of "enabler" is codependent. Certainly the enabler does control and rescue others within the family. However, the "hero" also acts as a rescuer by calling attention to his successful accomplishments. The "mascot" also rescues. His strategy is using laughter to detract from family pain and discord.

The roles above relate directly to rescuing. Roles which do not exhibit rescuing tendencies outright, but which may well demonstrate overreactions to a compulsion to rescue are the "scapegoat" and the "lost child." The scapegoat typically has given up on rescuing. His rebellion is an adverse response to a sense of over-responsibility within the family. The lost child also escapes from the burden of taking care of others by withdrawing into a shell. (We will examine these reactions more closely when we look at the "savior" and "Judas" characteristics of codependency later in this workbook.)

Just as it's true that the many roles operating within the dysfunctional family system are comprised of codependent behaviors, it is also true that those within the system often change the roles they play. One teenager changed from serving as the family hero to acting as the rebellious scapegoat when her sister moved from the scapegoat role into that of the enabler. Family roles are not static. When one person changes his role, it often forces others to change their roles, too.

This is not to suggest, as some assert, that almost any relational problem or desire to please people is a sign of codependency. The problem is more specific than that: It is a *compulsion* to rescue others, a sense of *having to* get other's approval at all costs and a *need* to control the emotions, attitudes and behaviors of others. Still, many are codependent! Of the millions of alcoholics and their families in this country, Dr. Joseph A. Pursch, of the Family Care Clinic in Santa

Ana Heights, California, observed, "We know that the average affected family consists of 1.8 alcoholics/addicts and four codependents."

Children from divorced homes often develop codependent characteristics. In her article, "Bouncing Back Slowly," Judith S. Wallerstein asserts that caretaking by "overburdened" children probably "runs much higher than the 15 percent we saw in our study."[4] When we add those from other dysfunctional homes characterized by addiction, eating disorders, sexual disorders, an absent father or mother, or by verbal, physical or emotional abuses, we can see that codependency is a widespread problem in our society.

The important point is not how narrowly or broadly we define a term like codependency. The crucial point is to understand why we feel, think and act as we do so that we can begin to get the help we need. For the sake of this book, we can define *codependency* rather narrowly and apply it broadly.

As codependents, we...

- feel responsible for others' behavior, but often don't take responsibility for our own.
- need to be needed.
- expect others to make us happy.
- can be demanding or indecisive.
- can be attentive and caring or selfish and cruel.
- often see people and situations as wonderful or awful, "black or white," with no room for ambiguity, or "gray."
- often overreact to people or situations which we can't control.
- seek affirmation and attention or sulk and hide.
- believe we are perceptive, and sometimes are, but often can't see reality in our own lives.
- see others as being "for us" or "against us."
- get hurt easily.
- use self-pity and/or anger to manipulate others.
- feel like we need to rescue people from themselves.
- communicate contrasting messages, like "I need you. I hate you."
- don't say what we mean and don't mean what we say.
- are deeply repentant but commit the same sins again and again.

We can change. Our lives can be different. We can experience freedom from the compulsion to rescue and control. We can learn to develop deep, healthy relationships.

The goal of this workbook is found in 1 Tim. 1:5:

> *But the goal of our instruction is love from a pure heart and a good conscience and a sincere faith.*

Our goal, then, is *love*, not manipulation, from a *pure heart*, not absorbing dependence; a good conscience, not guilt, morbid introspection and condemnation; and *a sincere faith*, which provides room for both intimacy and independence— for you and for the other dysfunctional person(s) in your life.

By its nature, there are many complexities and variables in codependency. A person's background, personality, relationships with his parents, current relationships, immediate needs and many other factors are important contributors to the mosaic of a person's life.

This twelve-step workbook is based on the book, *Codependency*. Though extensive excerpts have been taken from the book (especially in steps 3, 4, 6, 8 and 10), I recommend that you read the book in conjunction with this workbook. You'll find that the book offers additional insights and illustrations that can aid your understanding.

For those who have previously read books about codependency, this workbook can benefit you in several ways. It can give you...

- more depth about the complexities of codependency.
- more information and reflection about the biblical solutions for codependency.
- a format for discussion and application in a group setting.

This workbook also pulls from other Rapha resources, including *The Search for Significance*, *Rapha's Twelve-Step Program for Overcoming Chemical Dependency*, *Your Parents and You* and *Helping a Friend or Relative Conquer Codependency*. These materials are woven together to form a consistent, effective tool to help someone deal with the deception, complexities and pain of codependency.

The Necessity of Relationships

A person can take several steps of progress toward recovery from codependency by studying and applying the principles in this material individually. I am convinced, however, that one cannot experience significant growth and health apart from honest, affirming relationships.

We need two kinds of relationships in order to develop emotional, relational and spiritual health: a strong relationship with God and strong relationships with people. Volumes have been written about man's need for God. We are desperately deceived people, desperately sinful people and desperately needy people. We need a Savior. We need Jesus Christ. He alone is the source of forgiveness, life, hope, love and peace.

To communicate His character and purposes to us, God has provided two primary sources: the Bible and the Holy Spirit (though government, law and nature also are factors to consider in relationship to God); and two primary environments: the family and the body of Christ. God intends for the family to model and impart His nature during the critical formative years. When that fails, other believers can help us overcome the deficiencies and deceptions of the past so that we can experience the reality of God's presence and purposes.

We need one another. We each need the encouragement, reproof, exhortation, comfort, teaching, love and prayer that others can provide for us. Paul described both the intricate workings and purposes of our relationships with one another in his letter to the Ephesians:

> *...until we all attain to the unity of the faith, and of the knowledge of the Son of God, to a mature man, to the measure of the stature which belongs to the fullness of Christ.*
> *As a result, we are no longer to be children, tossed here and there by waves, and carried about by every wind of doctrine, by the trickery of men, by craftiness in deceitful scheming;*
> *but speaking the truth in love, we are to grow up in all aspects into Him, who is the head, even Christ...*

Eph. 4:13-15

Our goal—for ourselves and each other—is maturity in knowing Christ. A hindrance is the deception that comes from immaturity, but "speaking the truth in love" stimulates growth and development so that we can relate to each other in healthy, productive, stimulating, Christ-honoring ways. The issue of our relationships in the body of Christ is so important that Paul devotes large sections of each of his letters to instruction about enhancing these relationships.

People from dysfunctional families know less about healthy relationships (and need them more) than other people. Deception, abuse, neglect and manipulation have scarred their lives. In an article about the need for authentic relationships in *Christianity Today*, James M. Houston wrote:

> *When authentic spiritual guidance reveals the reality of human sin, and the relevance of Christ's lordship and redemption to our emotions and our minds, then it will help expose the intrinsically self-deceiving character of sin in our lives...*
> *If sin is self-deceiving, then I need a soul friend to give me insights into the ways I am deceived, or insensitive, or hardened by sin within me. I cannot do it alone. Self-examination can only take me so far. I need others to help expose and help me understand where sin would deceive and confuse me.[5]*

Houston describes these authentic Christian relationships as "soul friends." He wrote that these relationships can bring the power and insight needed to change lives:

...often our soul friends can show us the ecology of evil within us, how a particular childhood wound, or fixation of emotion, or emotional frame of mind, have brought the addictions that now enthrall us, coloring and distorting all we do and are. It may be that only the courage and wisdom of true soul friends can expose the ambitions and compulsions that lie behind our addictions to ministry, to pleasing everybody, or to "being in the limelight." [6]

The process for effective, lasting change has four components: cognitive, relational, spiritual and temporal, or time.

Cognitive: As you gain a better understanding of your background, feelings and thoughts, you will be able to apply specific biblical truths to your deepest needs, hurts and desires.

Relational: Again, personal reflection and application are most effective in an environment of affirmation and encouragement. It is extremely difficult—if not impossible—to overcome the painful causes and effects of codependency alone. You need the support of others who have gone through (and are going though) this program of healing. This is especially important! Those who have been where you are now understand. Let them help you!

Spiritual: As you examine God's truths and begin to experience His forgiveness and strength, you will grow in your understanding of His character and purposes in your life. You also will gain a new attitude about accepting others and sharing yourself with them.

Temporal: Recovery is a process. Lasting change won't occur overnight. You may experience flashes of insight occasionally, but the process of real growth is long, slow and steady. Expecting too much too soon may cause you to become disillusioned and pull out of the program completely. Be patient. Work through the exercises carefully. Growth and health will come.

As you begin to practice these "steps of progress," your behavior will begin to change. But more importantly, your perception of yourself, your perception of God and your relationships with others will improve, providing a strong foundation for a lasting recovery, and a healthy and productive life.

God be with you.

Step One

*We admit that our needs to be needed and our compulsions
to rescue others have made our lives unmanageable.*

*But let each one examine his own work, and then he will have reason for boasting in regard to
himself alone, and not in regard to another. For each one shall bear his own load.*
Gal. 6:4-5

Codependents thrive on being needed. We get our sense of value and significance by meeting others' needs. The greater the needs, the more our "rescuing" gives us importance and approval, or so we hope.

Codependency is cultivated in families with great needs. Such families may be characterized by at least one person who is alcoholic, drug dependent, physically, mentally or emotionally ill or very needy in some other way. Other members may be rescuers, but they may be so busy taking care of the other person(s) that they need (and expect) to be rescued by another caretaker in the family—like you.

Relationships and self-esteem in families like these are based on *denial*, an unwillingness or inability to recognize problematic issues in one's life. This denial breeds still more denial:

- We are controlled by others, but think we are in control of them.
- We smother and manipulate others, but think we are providing a loving environment for them.
- We believe we have deep relationships, but nobody is honest about how he or she really feels.
- We thrive on being needed, but rescuing only satisfies us for a short time. Then we feel compelled to rescue again.
- We take care of others, but neglect our own needs.
- In the desire to be somebody, we give up our own identity (our own thoughts, beliefs, feelings and decisions) and develop an identity that pleases others.

Unmanageable

"Unmanageable? Who, me?"

Codependency has led most of us to be highly controlling in several areas of our lives. Those areas are our safe havens. We feel secure if they are in order, even if the rest of our lives are falling apart. If someone were to mention that our lives are unmanageable, we could proudly(!) point to those areas of perfectionism and decry the absurdity of the accusation. We focus our overresponsibility in those aspects of our lives, but fail to see the superficiality, the chaos and the pain in other areas.

For instance, a woman, whose husband is an alcoholic and has lost his job regularly over the past dozen years, is a perfectionist about her clothes and her home. However, she has never talked to her husband about the insecurity, hurt or fear she feels because of his irresponsible behavior.

A young man from a divorced home keeps a meticulous schedule, but his relationships are shallow. He controls his time, and he also controls people by not letting anyone get too close to him emotionally.

One of the most tragic traits of codependency is the loss of identity. In his dysfunctional family, the codependent learns that he has to please others to gain their approval. Therefore, he gravitates to one extreme or another. He may give up his identity by thinking what he believes others want him to think, feeling what he believes others want him to feel and acting the way he believes others want him to act. Or, he may defiantly defend his separate identity. He may argue over the smallest point because he feels threatened, or he may hold to a point of view even after he realizes it is wrong or unreasonable. He may childishly demand his own way. Both of these extremes are common at some time in the lives of most codependents.

This step is the first step into reality. It is not the end; it is only the beginning. (You've probably already taken the first step or two, or you wouldn't be reading this workbook now!) Learning to see clearly is a long, slow process. We will see only a little at first, and most of us will be confused by what comes into view! If you reach a point in the workbook which you don't understand or where you can't identify yourself, that's okay. You may understand much more as you discuss it with a group of people; you may understand it months later or it may be a sub-point that may not relate to you or your situation at all. Be patient.

◼ Write a paragraph answering these questions, using additional paper if necessary.

• Whom do you feel responsible for? (In what ways do these people need you? What would happen if you didn't meet their needs? How do you feel and act when you *do* help them? How do you feel and act when they need you but you *fail* to help them?

_____

_____

_____

_____

_____

_____

_____

• In what ways have you lost some of your identity by feeling, thinking, and acting the way others want you to feel, think and act?

_____

_____

_____

_____

• What aspects of your own life have you neglected as you have focused on the needs of others (consider emotional health, physical health, financial well-being, your schedule, relationships, relaxation, fun, etc.)?

_____

_____

_____

_____

■ The following questions are taken from a helpful analysis of adult children of alcoholics, but they are applicable for all codependents. Answer the following:

	Yes	No
1. Do I often feel isolated and afraid of people, especially authority figures?	_____	_____
2. Have I observed myself to be an approval-seeker, losing my own identity in the process?	_____	_____
3. Do I feel overly frightened of angry people and personal criticism?	_____	_____
4. Do I often feel I'm a victim in personal and career relationships?	_____	_____
5. Do I sometimes feel I have an overdeveloped sense of responsibility, which makes it easier to be more concerned with others than with myself?	_____	_____
6. Is it hard for me to look at my own faults and my own responsibility to myself?	_____	_____
7. Do I feel guilty when I stand up for myself instead of giving in to others?	_____	_____
8. Do I feel addicted to excitement?	_____	_____
9. Do I confuse love with pity, and tend to love people I can pity and rescue?	_____	_____
10. Is it hard for me to feel or express feelings, including feelings such as joy or happiness?	_____	_____
11. Do I judge myself harshly?	_____	_____
12. Do I have a low sense of self-esteem?	_____	_____
13. Do I often feel abandoned in the course of my relationships?	_____	_____
14. Do I tend to be a reactor instead of an initiator?	_____	_____

• Write a paragraph to describe what your responses to these questions tell you about yourself:

_____

_____

_____

_____

We rescue and control others because we hope that our efforts will win the love, stability and approval that we desperately want. Often, our rescuing is appreciated by others. That appreciation then reinforces our compulsion to rescue and control, but we fail to see that it only meets our needs for love at the surface level. It doesn't meet our deepest needs, and in fact, it is insidiously destructive because superficial appreciation and love sink us deeper into the mire of the controlling and rescuing patterns of codependency.

God, God's people and God's Word are the sources of the love, forgiveness and acceptance that can genuinely meet our deepest needs. Any other sources leave us empty, hurting and confused.

■ Paraphrase these passages of Scripture:

> *For My people have committed two evils: They have forsaken Me, the fountain of living waters, to hew for themselves cisterns, broken cisterns, that can hold no water.*
>
> Jer. 2:13

_____

_____

_____

> *Now on the last day, the great day of the feast, Jesus stood and cried out, saying, "If any man is thirsty, let him come to Me and drink.*
>
> *"He who believes in Me, as the Scripture said, 'From his innermost being shall flow rivers of living water.'"*
>
> *But this He spoke of the Spirit, whom those who believed in Him were to receive; for the Spirit was not yet given, because Jesus was not yet glorified.*
>
> John 7:37-39

_____

_____

_____

• What do these passages say about our thirst and God's provision to quench that thirst?_____

_____

_____

_____

The Scriptures speak clearly about our identity in Christ. As we learn more about His love for us and His plan and purpose for our lives, our compulsion to rescue and control will gradually diminish. The fear and shame that energizes our compulsions will gradually be replaced by contentment, peace and joy.

■ Paraphrase these passages about our identity in Christ:

> *Blessed be the God and Father of our Lord Jesus Christ, who has blessed us with every spiritual blessing in the heavenly places in Christ,*

just as He chose us in Him before the foundation of the world, that we should be holy and blameless before Him. In love

He predestined us to adoption as sons through Jesus Christ to Himself, according to the kind intention of His will,

to the praise of the glory of His grace, which He freely bestowed on us in the Beloved,

In Him we have redemption through His blood, the forgiveness of our trespasses, according to the riches of His grace...

In Him, you also, after listening to the message of truth, the gospel of your salvation—having also believed, you were sealed in Him with the Holy Spirit of promise,

who is given as a pledge of our inheritance, with a view to the redemption of God's own possession, to the praise of His glory.

Eph. 1:3-7, 13-14

_____

_____

_____

_____

There is therefore now no condemnation for those who are in Christ Jesus.

Rom. 8:1

_____

_____

See how great a love the Father has bestowed upon us, that we should be called children of God; and such we are. For this reason the world does not know us, because it did not know Him.

Beloved, now we are children of God, and it has not appeared as yet what we shall be. We know that, when He appears, we shall be like Him, because we shall see Him just as He is.

1 John 3:1-2

_____

_____

_____

But you are a chosen race, a royal priesthood, a holy nation, a people for God's own possession, that you may proclaim the excellencies of Him who has called you out of darkness into His marvelous light;

for you once were not a people, but now you are the people of God; you had not received mercy, but now you have received mercy.

1 Pet. 2:9-10

_____

_____

• Write a paragraph to describe how you feel and think about these passages. (Are they hard to believe? Does reflecting on them make you encouraged, happy, sad, angry...? How would your life be different if you really believed them?)

_____

_____

_____

_____

_____

_____

_____

■ The Bible speaks clearly about other issues concerning codependency. In Gal. 6:5, Paul writes: *For each one shall bear his own load.* In what ways have you neglected to "bear your own load"? (That is, how have you failed to be responsible to make your own decisions, be yourself and set limits in your responsibilities to others?)

_____

_____

_____

_____

■ Paul also encouraged the believers in Corinth to give cheerfully: *Let each one do just as he has purposed in his heart; not grudgingly or under compulsion; for God loves a cheerful giver* (2 Cor. 9:7). Codependent people may give cheerfully for a while, but we expect (demand) a positive response in return. When our "selfless giving" is not appreciated, we feel used. We become resentful.

• In what ways are you a cheerful giver?_____

_____

_____

• In what ways have you been resentful when people don't appreciate your serving and helping them? Give examples.

_____

_____

_____

■ As codependents, we usually deny the hurt inside. We learn to put on pleasant facades to hide the reality of our anger, pain, bitterness and depression. Or, we live from successful rescue to successful rescue, feeling really good about ourselves, but again, seldom seeing even a glimmer of the painful cause of our compulsive rescuing. Looking inside is painful but necessary if we are to experience genuine love, warmth, meaning and intimacy.

Christ dealt strongly with the Pharisees, who looked like they were stable and mature on the outside, but who had not dealt with the painful realities on the inside of their lives. He told them:

> *"Woe to you, scribes and Pharisees, hypocrites! For you clean the outside of the cup and of the dish, but inside they are full of robbery and self-indulgence.*
> *"You blind Pharisees, first clean the inside of the cup and of the dish, so that the outside of it may become clean also.*
> *"Woe to you, scribes and Pharisees, hypocrites! For you are like whitewashed tombs which on the outside appear beautiful, but inside they are full of dead men's bones and all uncleanness.*
> *"Even so you too outwardly appear righteous to men, but inwardly you are full of hypocrisy and lawlessness."*
>
> Matt. 23:25-28

• What are some ways that you appear strong and healthy on the outside? (What do you do or say to appear that way?)

_____

_____

_____

• Why is it so hard to be honest about the pain inside?_____

_____

_____

_____

• Why is it so necessary?_____

_____

_____

■ Paul wrote to the believers in Galatia about the compulsion to please people: *For am I now seeking the favor of men, or of God? Or am I striving to please men? If I were still trying to please men, I would not be a bond-servant of Christ* (Gal. 1:10). Codependents want to please people at all costs! That's why we serve and fix and rescue and enable. That's why we allow ourselves to be so easily manipulated. That's why we daydream about someone saying something nice to us or about us. And that's why we are so deeply hurt when someone doesn't appreciate us. Approval means everything to us!

• What are some things you do or say to win others' approval?_____

_____

_____

_____

_____

_____

_____

- How do you respond when you are not appreciated? _____

_____

_____

_____

    Almost twenty years ago, Elisabeth Kübler-Ross wrote a book about the process that terminally ill patients experience as they come to terms with their diagnosis. The process of coping with grave illness closely parallels that of dealing with emotional difficulties. The authors of several books have used this process to describe how a person comes to grips with emotional trauma. Kübler-Ross does not come from an orthodox Christian perspective (and her most recent book has a New Age slant), but her insights into the grief process are very insightful nonetheless. We will apply this process, or a variation of it, to a person's emergence from the blackness of codependency.

    Dealing effectively with traumatic difficulties includes five stages: denial, bargaining, anger, grief and acceptance.[1] This is not a push-button, 1-2-3 kind of process. A person may move quickly through one phase, but very slowly through another. He may go back and forth from time to time, re-entering a stage he has already gone through as he becomes aware of other pains and hurts he has not previously seen. Generally speaking, however, a person will not progress to the next stage until he has more or less fully experienced that which he is in. The following diagram may be helpful. Objectivity is the door which opens into the process. Acceptance is the door leading out of it and into health. In the middle are three vats, or containers, representing bargaining, anger and grief. A person will not progress to constructive anger until he is through with bargaining, and he will not experience grief until he has spent his anger. (This, of course, does not mean that the person does not experience anger or grief except in that phase. It only means that these emotions will be dominant during that time.)

Codependency is a deep wound that requires a lot of attention for a while. Even the emotional bandaging and medication seem to hurt, but if it is well-treated, scar tissue will gradually form as the healing process continues. Though the scar may remain, the pain will gradually be replaced by healing and health. This process isn't pleasant, but it is essential if the wound is to heal.

Step Two

We increasingly believe that Jesus Christ can restore us to spiritual, emotional and relational health.

..for it is God who is at work in you, both to will and to work for His good pleasure.
Phil. 2:13

Dysfunctional families are a breeding ground for wrong assumptions, wrong thinking and wrong choices. Rescuers in these families make the assumption that fixing others' problems and controlling people and situations will buy peace, love and happiness. But this assumption is false and only leads to more spiritual, emotional and relational pain.

This step is designed to help us *identify* codependent characteristics in our lives. Later in this workbook, we will examine how we can *detach,* or objectively reflect on what is going on in our lives, and then *decide* on the best course of action in each relationship and situation.

Let's briefly examine the six characteristics of codependency.

Characteristics of Codependency

A Lack of Objectivity - Despite the highly perceptive nature of most codependents, members of dysfunctional families usually believe that their family is "normal." They simply cannot see the unhealthy ways in which their family members relate to one another because they never have experienced emotionally healthy relationships. Also, coming to grips with the pain, hurt, anger and manipulation they've suffered can be very threatening, so they deny the existence of most problems and their unhealthy patterns of relating continue.

A Warped Sense of Responsibility - Common synonyms for codependency are: rescue, help, fix and enable. The codependent sees himself as a savior; he is driven to help others, especially the needy people in his family. At least one person in the family is unwilling or unable to take care of himself, and may use both self-pity and condemnation to evoke a helping response from the overly responsible codependent. The codependent wants to be loved and accepted, and he wants to avoid conflict, so he does whatever it takes to make that person happy. The codependent is so busy taking care of others, however, that he neglects to care for himself by making his own decisions and determining his own identity and behavior.

Controlled and Controlling - Like everyone else, codependents need love and respect. Having been deprived of these precious commodities, they determine to do whatever it takes to win the affirmation they crave. Their means to that end is to make people happy. Their chief fear is that people will be unhappy with them. Those around the codependent often learn how to use praise and condemnation to manipulate him or her as artfully as a marionette maneuvers a puppet.

Hurt and Anger - Dysfunctional families often foster a system of communication that may include words of love and acceptance, but the actions demonstrated by family members often hurt deeply. Hurt and anger go hand-in-glove. Hurt results from feeling abandoned, used and condemned rather than loved and valued. Anger is a reaction to the source of the hurt.

Guilt - Codependents often feel guilty. They feel guilty for what they've done and haven't done, for what they've said, haven't said, felt and haven't felt. They feel guilty for just about everything. Often such guilt produces feelings of worthlessness and shame.

The codependent gets his worth—his identity—from what he does for others. He rescues, he helps, he enables, but no matter how much he does for others, it's never enough. That's the trap of living in a dysfunctional family: he rescues but is rejected. Lacking objectivity, he concludes: *It's my fault; if I were a better person, they would love me.* He spends his life trying to be good enough to earn the love and acceptance he so desperately wants, but fears he never will have. And he's haunted by the shame of feeling that he hasn't—or can't—measure up.

Loneliness - Codependents spend their lives giving, helping and serving others. They may appear to be the most social people in the world, but inside they are lonely. Their attempts to please others by helping and serving are designed to win affection. Though they may occasionally see a glimpse of love and respect, it usually fades all too quickly. Then, thinking they have been abandoned by both people and God, they feel empty and companionless. They distrust authority, believing that anyone above them is against them, and they build elaborate facades to hide their painful feelings of loneliness.

Blinders

Numerous other factors, perceptions and defense mechanisms prevent the codependent from seeing the truth. Among them:

Selective Filtering of Information - The codependent's mental "grid" filters out a substantial amount of the truth. For example, when her bulimic sister says for the umpteenth time, "It's over; I'm never going to binge and purge again," the codependent wants to believe it so badly that she feels great relief and joy even though her sister's record of keeping promises is abysmal. Or, he may hear and see only what he dreads. If a codependent is given a performance review at work, there may be twenty things he has done with excellence and efficiency and one area in which he needs to improve. But he will be heart-broken. His mind will be consumed by the one area that needs some improvement instead of the report of his great work in the vast majority of his job.

Defending the Offender - Instead of honestly feeling the hurt of betrayal and experiencing the anger of being abused or neglected, the codependent will usually defend the offender. *It's not really her fault*, she surmises. *She couldn't help it, and besides, it doesn't bother me when she curses me like that. I'm used to it by now.* Or, *Yes, it hurts when he treats me that way, but I feel so sorry for him. He wants to stop drinking, but he just can't.*

Redefining the Pain - Being objective about their deep hurt and seething anger may be painful and/or guilt-inducing for codependents, but repressing these emotions often causes psychosomatic illnesses. Many people who experience the tremendous stress of pain, anger and guilt develop severe tension headaches, but instead of admitting to their stress, they say that they are having "migraine headaches." One man told me about his "migraines." When I asked him to describe the pain, his description was not of a one-sided, light-sensitive, throbbing pain at all. It was tension, but calling it a migraine shifted and redefined the pain to make it less threatening. A tension headache means he has stress to deal with. A migraine is a vascular problem—no culpability there! A host of other labels are given to ailments that shift the source of the problem from repressed emotions to a purely physical cause. (This, of course, does not mean that every sickness experienced by a codependent is caused entirely by repressed emotions. Buried emotions do, however, lower one's resistance to all kinds of physical problems.)

Pronouncements of Perception - A codependent will often make pronouncements of his acute understanding of life's situations, even though he may not see them clearly at all. It's as if his proclamations somehow make his perceptions accurate. He may say, "Oh yes, I see it all now!" Or she may proclaim, "I don't need his love and acceptance. It's never bothered me that he doesn't care about me." These kinds of statements are both the result of poor perception and the means for further denial in the future. If a person feels like his perception is accurate when it's not, then that inaccuracy acts as a defense mechanism which prevents him from seeing reality and feeling pain.

Peer Pressure - The intense peer pressure that adolescents face is difficult for even the most stable teenager to cope with. The added pressure felt by a codependent teenager is indeed intense. Dealing with both peer pressure and objective reality is a double whammy! It is almost as difficult for young adults who experience the peer pressure of entering the "real world" after high school or college. Too often, objectivity doesn't come until a codependent is in his thirties, forties or fifties, and the formative, wonderful years of youth have been wasted in the oppressive combination of peer pressure, denial, rescuing, guilt and pain.

Diversions - Codependents use all kinds of activities to keep themselves so busy that they don't have time to reflect and feel. Working seventy to eighty hours a week, participating in clubs or sports, watching television and many other diversions keep them preoccupied. I've heard it said that "activities are often the anaesthetic to deaden the pain of an empty life." Most codependents are unaware that the reason their lives seem empty is because they hurt. They may have a vague, diffuse sense that something is wrong, but they have no idea what it is and reject any suggestion that they may be dealing with repressed emotions.

Exchanged Emotions - Because codependents haven't experienced very much true love and intimacy or genuine support and encouragement, they often substitute one emotion for another. For instance, one woman (the wife of an alcoholic) equated worry with love. She always seemed to be *worrying* about her son, but she very seldom expressed genuine affection for him. She had substituted the intensity of her worry for the love that he actually needed. Some may use condemnation and praise to manipulate others rather than simply loving them, and some may substitute anger with a stoic calm that has the appearance of peacefulness, but which in reality is denial.

Euphemisms - To avoid objectivity about their emotions, codependents often use words that don't accurately reflect how they really feel. The classic example of this is the use of *frustrated* instead of *angry*. People seem to think that it's okay to be frustrated with someone, but real anger is a different story. Real anger is too threatening to the codependent, so he alters his words to make his emotions seem less severe. Though the word *frustrated* is a perfectly legitimate word to describe a mildly negative emotion, it is much overused. In our office, we have agreed not to use the word frustrated, and to go ahead and say that we are angry. People found this to be difficult at first, but after a few days the honesty was very refreshing!

The "glasses" worn by a codependent distort the truth and obstruct his view of reality. Objectivity is a most important first step and the beginning of healing.

■ Examine each of the "blinders" described previously in this step. To what degree does each of these block your perception of reality and enable you to avoid pain?

Selective filtering of information

Never	0	1	2	3	4	5	6	7	8	9	10	Always

Defending the offender

Never	0	1	2	3	4	5	6	7	8	9	10	Always

Redefining pain

Never	0	1	2	3	4	5	6	7	8	9	10	Always

Pronouncements of perception

Never	0	1	2	3	4	5	6	7	8	9	10	Always

Peer pressure

Never   0   1   2   3   4   5   6   7   8   9   10   Always

Diversions

Never   0   1   2   3   4   5   6   7   8   9   10   Always

Exchanged emotions

Never   0   1   2   3   4   5   6   7   8   9   10   Always

Euphemisms

Never   0   1   2   3   4   5   6   7   8   9   10   Always

■ How would increased objectivity affect your life?_____

_____

_____

_____

■ Name several ways and several people that can help you to be more objective. Be specific:_____

_____

_____

_____

_____

_____

_____

_____

_____

Your Parents and You

Our views of God, our self-concepts and our abilities to relate to others are primarily shaped by our parental relationships. If our parents were loving and supportive, we will probably believe that God is loving and strong. If, however, our parents were harsh and demanding, we will probably believe that God is impossible to please. Either way, the foundation of our emotional, relational and spiritual health is usually established by parental modeling, and the results can be wonderful or tragic.[1]

In order to gain a better understanding of this "shaping" process, it is helpful to examine the characteristics of our parents and our relationship with them. The following is an exercise to help you evaluate your relationship with your father as you were growing up.[2] Check the appropriate squares as you recall how he related to you when you were young. Here is an example:

EXAMPLE:

Characteristics	Always	Very Often	Some-	Hardly Ever	Never	Don't Know
Gentle			✓			
Stern	✓					
Loving			✓			
Aloof			✓			
Disapproving		✓				
Distant	✓					

WHEN I WAS A CHILD, MY FATHER WAS...

Characteristics	Always	Very Often	Some- times	Hardly Ever	Never	Don't Know
Gentle						
Stern						
Loving						
Aloof						
Disapproving						
Distant						
Close and Intimate						
Kind						
Angry						
Caring						
Demanding						
Supportive						
Interested						
Discipliner						
Gracious						
Harsh						
Wise						
Holy						
Leader						
Provider						
Trustworthy						
Joyful						
Forgiving						
Good						
Cherishing of Me						
Compassionate						
Impatient						
Unreasonable						
Strong						
Protective						
Passive						
Encouraging						
Sensitive						
Just						
Unpredictable						

Evaluation of Your Relationship with Your Father

■ What does this inventory tell you about your relationship with your father?_____

_____

_____

_____

_____

_____

_____

_____

_____

_____

_____

■ If you were an objective observer of the type of relationship you have just described, how would you feel about the father?

_____

_____

_____

_____

_____

_____

_____

_____

_____

_____

■ About the child?_____

_____

_____

_____

_____

_____

_____

■ How would you respond to the father? Be specific._____

_____

_____

_____

_____

_____

_____

■ To the child?_____

_____

_____

_____

_____

_____

_____

Now complete the same exercise, this time to evaluate your relationship with your mother:[3]

WHEN I WAS A CHILD, MY MOTHER WAS...

Characteristics	Always	Very Often	Some-times	Hardly Ever	Never	Don't Know
Gentle						
Stern						
Loving						
Aloof						
Disapproving						
Distant						
Close and Intimate						
Kind						
Angry						
Caring						
Demanding						
Supportive						
Interested						
Discipliner						
Gracious						
Harsh						
Wise						
Holy						
Leader						
Provider						
Trustworthy						
Joyful						
Forgiving						
Good						
Cherishing of Me						
Compassionate						
Impatient						
Unreasonable						
Strong						
Protective						
Passive						
Encouraging						
Sensitive						
Just						
Unpredictable						

Evaluation of Your Relationship with Your Mother

■ What does this inventory tell you about your relationship with your mother?_____

_____

_____

_____

_____

_____

_____

_____

_____

_____

■ If you were an objective observer of the type of relationship you have just described, how would you feel about the mother?

_____

_____

_____

_____

_____

_____

_____

_____

_____

■ About the child?_____

_____

_____

_____

_____

_____

_____

_____

■ How would you respond to the mother? Be specific._____

_____

_____

_____

_____

_____

_____

_____

■ To the child?_____

_____

_____

_____

_____

_____

_____

Evaluating Your Relationship with God

We can begin to see how our relationships with our parents have influenced our perception of God when we evaluate our present relationship with Him. The inventory on the following page will help you to determine some of your feelings toward God.[4] Because it is subjective, there are no right or wrong answers. To ensure that the test reveals your actual feelings, please follow the instructions carefully.

■ Answer openly and honestly. Don't respond from a theological knowledge of God, but from personal experience.

■ Don't describe what the relationship ought to be, or what you hope it will be, but what it is right now.

■ Some people feel God might be displeased if they give a negative answer. Nothing is further from the truth. He is pleased with our honesty. A foundation of transparency is required for growth to occur.

■ Turn each characteristic into a question. For example: *To what degree do I really feel that God loves me? To what degree do I really feel that God understands me?*

TO WHAT DEGREE DO I REALLY FEEL GOD IS...

Characteristics	Always	Very Often	Some-times	Hardly Ever	Never	Don't Know
Gentle						
Stern						
Loving						
Aloof						
Disapproving						
Distant						
Close and Intimate						
Kind						
Angry						
Caring						
Demanding						
Supportive						
Interested						
Discipliner						
Gracious						
Harsh						
Wise						
Holy						
Leader						
Provider						
Trustworthy						
Joyful						
Forgiving						
Good						
Cherishing of Me						
Compassionate						
Impatient						
Unreasonable						
Strong						
Protective						
Passive						
Encouraging						
Sensitive						
Just						
Unpredictable						

■ What does this exercise tell you about your relationship with God?_____

_____

_____

_____

_____

_____

_____

_____

_____

_____

■ Are there any differences between what you know (theologically) and how you feel (emotionally) about Him? If so, what are they?

_____

_____

_____

_____

_____

_____

_____

_____

_____

Your Father's Influence on Your Relationship with God

Now that we have examined your current relationship with God, let's look at how your relationship with your earthly father has influenced your perception of your heavenly Father.[5]

To make a comparison, transfer all of the check marks you made for your own father on page 16 to the *shaded columns* on page 26. When you have completed this, transfer the check marks you made on page 23 which relate to your relationship with God. To make them more obvious, use an "✗" for this category. Put them in the *white columns* in the appropriate places.

EXAMPLE:

Characteristics	Always	Very Often	Some-times	Hardly Ever	Never	Don't Know
Gentle		✗	✓			
Stern	✓	✗				
Loving		✗	✓			
Aloof		✓		✗		
Disapproving			✓			

Instructions: Transfer all check marks from page 16 to the SHADED columns. Transfer all check marks from page 23 to the WHITE columns.

Characteristics	Always	Very Often	Some-times	Hardly Ever	Never	Don't Know
Gentle						
Stern						
Loving						
Aloof						
Disapproving						
Distant						
Close and Intimate						
Kind						
Angry						
Caring						
Demanding						
Supportive						
Interested						
Discipliner						
Gracious						
Harsh						
Wise						
Holy						
Leader						
Provider						
Trustworthy						
Joyful						
Forgiving						
Good						
Cherishing of Me						
Compassionate						
Impatient						
Unreasonable						
Strong						
Protective						
Passive						
Encouraging						
Sensitive						
Just						
Unpredictable						

■ Which characteristics are the same for both your father and your heavenly Father?_____

_____

_____

_____

_____

_____

_____

■ Which characteristics are quite different (two or more boxes away from each other)?_____

_____

_____

_____

_____

_____

_____

■ What patterns (if any) do you see?_____

_____

_____

_____

_____

_____

_____

■ Write a summary paragraph about how your perception of God has been shaped by your relationship with your father:

_____

_____

_____

_____

_____

_____

_____

_____

_____

_____

_____

_____

_____

_____

_____

_____

_____

_____

_____

_____

_____

_____

Your Mother's Influence on Your Relationship with God

How has your mother influenced your perception of your heavenly Father?[6] To get a comparison, transfer all the check marks you made for your mother on page 19 to the *shaded columns* on page 30. Use a check mark for this category.

When you have completed this, transfer the check marks you made on page 23, which relate to your relationship with God. To make them more obvious, use an "✗" for this category. Put them in the *white columns* in the appropriate places.

EXAMPLE:

Characteristics	Always	Very Often	Some-times	Hardly Ever	Never	Don't Know
Gentle		✗	✓			
Stern	✓	✗				
Loving		✗	✓			
Aloof		✓		✗		
Disapproving			✓			

Instructions: Transfer all check marks from page 19 to the SHADED columns. Transfer all check marks from page 23 to the WHITE columns.

Characteristics	Always	Very Often	Some-times	Hardly Ever	Never	Don't Know
Gentle						
Stern						
Loving						
Aloof						
Disapproving						
Distant						
Close and Intimate						
Kind						
Angry						
Caring						
Demanding						
Supportive						
Interested						
Discipliner						
Gracious						
Harsh						
Wise						
Holy						
Leader						
Provider						
Trustworthy						
Joyful						
Forgiving						
Good						
Cherishing of Me						
Compassionate						
Impatient						
Unreasonable						
Strong						
Protective						
Passive						
Encouraging						
Sensitive						
Just						
Unpredictable						

■ Which characteristics are the same for both your mother and your heavenly Father?_____

_____

_____

_____

_____

_____

_____

■ Which characteristics are quite different (two or more boxes away from each other)?_____

_____

_____

_____

_____

_____

_____

■ What patterns (if any) do you see?_____

_____

_____

_____

_____

_____

_____

■ Write a summary paragraph about how your perception of God has been shaped by your relationship with your mother:

_____

_____

_____

_____

_____

_____

_____

_____

_____

_____

_____

_____

_____

_____

_____

_____

_____

_____

_____

_____

_____

Your Family Portrait

In many situations, it has been very helpful for a person to draw a picture of his family when he was a child. Some of us love to draw. Some of us laugh at the idea. And some of us are afraid our stick men will be laughed at. However, drawing the facial expressions of family members and specific situations from childhood memories helps many people unlock the past so they can express their hurt and anger in ways they never have done before. This promotes the healing process.

Take some time to draw your family in the space below and on the following pages. You may think of particular situations that stand out in your mind—situations that have had a profound impact on your life. Draw how each person related to you (or failed to relate to you). Add captions, buildings, furniture or whatever is appropriate to help you see yourself in the physical and emotional context of your family. When you have finished, describe to a friend or members of your support group *what* you have drawn and *why* you have drawn it that way.

Your Family Portrait

Learning More About God from Psalm 139

Some passages in Scripture highlight certain aspects of our relationship with God. Psalm 139 is a perfect example of this because it describes the character of God in a number of ways. Studying it can help you understand how His *omniscience* (being all-knowing), *omnipresence* (being ever-present) and *omnipotence* (being all-powerful) can apply to you and your circumstances.

We will examine a few verses from this psalm at a time. Then we will ask questions to promote reflection.[7]

God Knows Me Thoroughly

Verses 1-4 (NIV): *O Lord, you have searched me and you know me. You know when I sit and when I rise; you perceive my thoughts from afar. You discern my going out and my lying down; you are familiar with all my ways. Before a word is on my tongue you know it completely, O Lord.*

■ God always knows everything about you. You can keep no secrets from Him, yet He loves you unconditionally! How does this make you feel?

_____

_____

■ In what ways does God's omniscience give you courage and strength?_____

_____

_____

_____

_____

_____

_____

_____

He Protects Me

Verses 5-6 (NIV): *You hem me in—behind and before; you have laid your hand upon me. Such knowledge is too wonderful for me, too lofty for me to attain.*

■ God's perfect knowledge about you enables Him to protect you (to hem you in). From what do you need His protection?

_____

_____

_____

_____

_____

■ Is it difficult for you to understand the Lord's omniscience? Why or why not?_____

_____

_____

_____

_____

He Is Always Present

Verses 7-12 (NIV): *Where can I go from your Spirit? Where can I flee from your presence? If I go up to the heavens, you are there; if I make my bed in the depths [Hebrew Sheol], you are there. If I rise on the wings of the dawn, if I settle on the far side of the sea, even there your hand will guide me, your right hand will hold me fast. If I say, "Surely the darkness will hide me and the light become night around me," even the darkness will not be dark to you; the night will shine like the day, for darkness is as light to you.*

■ The most important assurance to one who has strayed is that he is not lost! How close is God to you?

_____

■ How close does He seem to be?_____

_____

_____

■ How far can you get from Him?_____

He Is a Sovereign Creator

Verses 13-15 (NIV): *For you created my inmost being; you knit me together in my mother's womb. I praise you because I am fearfully and wonderfully made; your works are wonderful, I know that full well. My frame was not hidden from you when I was made in the secret place. When I was woven together in the depths of the earth. . . .*

■ Who is responsible for the creation of your body?_____

• Do you believe that the One who created you can also restore you? If so, why?_____

_____

_____

• Can you rejoice that you look exactly the way the Father wants you to look? If so, why?_____

_____

_____

- If not, why not?_____

_____

- How do you normally respond to your appearance?_____

_____

_____

- How does your perception of your appearance affect your self-image?_____

_____

_____

■ Do you think (or worry) about what other people think of your appearance? Why or why not?_____

_____

_____

■ How could this psalm help free you from the fear of what others think of you?_____

_____

_____

God Has a Plan for You

Verse 16 (NIV): *Your eyes saw my unformed body. All the days ordained for me were written in your book before one of them came to be.*

■ Describe any comfort you gain from knowing that God has a plan for your life:_____

_____

_____

■ What types of plans do you suppose God might have for your future?
Examples:
He wants me to have a relationship with Him through His Son, Jesus Christ (John 3:16-18).
He wants to provide for my welfare, and give me a future and a hope (Jer. 29:11).
He wants to give me things that will be good for me (Matt. 7:7-11).
He wants to strengthen me (Is. 40:29).
He wants me to spend eternity with Him (John 14:1-3).

_____

_____

_____

_____

_____

_____

God Is Constant and Consistent

Verses 17-18 (NIV): *How precious to me are your thoughts, O God! How vast is the sum of them! Were I to count them, they would outnumber the grains of sand. When I awake, I am still with you.*

■ The Lord is infinite and He is thinking about you all the time! How does that fact comfort and encourage you?

_____

_____

_____

_____

_____

Our Response

Verses 23-24 (NIV): *Search me, O God, and know my heart; test me and know my anxious thoughts. See if there is any offensive way in me, and lead me in the way everlasting.*

Openness to God's correction and guidance is the way the psalmist responds to the secure position he has with God. You also can have a secure position with God through Jesus Christ, who died to pay for your sins and rose from the dead to give you new life.

■ Are you open to God's correction and guidance?_____

• Why or why not?_____

_____

_____

For Additional Reflection and Application

■ Read Matt. 9:12-13.

• What comfort does this passage give you?_____

_____

_____

• Do you believe that God, through Jesus Christ, can restore you to spiritual, emotional and relational health?

_____

■ Read Mark 9:23-24.

• If you do not believe that God can restore you to spiritual, emotional and relational health, how can you follow the father's example in this passage?

_____

_____

• Are you willing to ask God to help you in your unbelief?_____

Belief Systems

By completing this step, you are on your way to becoming familiar with both your perception of God and what Scripture tells us about His ways. Understanding the truth of God's Word is the beginning of our restoration. Throughout the four gospels, Jesus repeatedly emphasized the importance of *believing* Him. Why? Because our actions are usually based on our beliefs!

In his book, *The Search for Significance*, Robert S. McGee identifies four false beliefs which distort our perception of both God and ourselves. All of these lies are based on the primary belief that our **self-worth = performance + others' opinions**. In other words, we suffer from a misconception that our significance, or worth, is determined by what we do and what others think of us. Each of these four false beliefs (listed below) results in a specific fear:

False Belief: *I must meet certain standards to feel good about myself. If I fail to meet these standards, I cannot really feel good about myself.* This belief results in the **fear of failure.**

False Belief: *I must be approved (accepted) by certain people to accept myself. If I do not have the approval of these people, I cannot accept myself.* This belief results in the **fear of rejection.**

False Belief: *Those who fail are unworthy of love and deserve to be blamed and condemned.* This belief leads to **the fear of punishment and the propensity to punish others.**

False Belief: *I am what I am. I cannot change. I am hopeless. This means I am simply a total of all my past performances, both good and bad. I am what I have done.* This belief leads to a **sense of shame.**

For each of these false beliefs, there is a corresponding truth from God's Word, the Scriptures:

SATAN'S LIE Your worth = Your performance plus others' opinions	GOD'S TRUTH Your worth = What God says about you
I must meet certain standards to feel good about myself. If I don't... (Fear of Failure)	Justification (Rom. 3:19-25; 2 Cor. 5:21): *I am completely forgiven and fully pleasing to God.*
I must be approved (accepted) by certain others to feel good about myself. If I'm not approved... (Fear of Rejection)	Reconciliation (Col. 1:19-22): *I am totally accepted (by God).*
Those who fail are unworthy of love and desrve to be blamed and condemned. (Fear of Punishment/Punishing Others)	Propitiation (1 John 4:9-11): *I am deeply loved (by God).*
I am what I am; I cannot change; I am hopeless. (Shame)	Regeneration (2 Cor. 5:17): *I am absolutely complete (in Christ).*

Renewing our perception of God, ourselves and others by changing our belief system will take time, study and experience. It has taken years to develop patterns of behavior that reflect a false belief system. It will take time to change. We will continue to examine these beliefs throughout this workbook. The process of learning to apply God's truth to our lives may be painful at times, but it is also rich, rewarding and exciting!

Scalpels and Hugs

A child desperately wants and needs a stable, loving environment. When warmth and stability are lacking to a certain degree, the foundation of the child's life is shaken. In addition, because he is a child, he is unable to view his parents' failures and his own pain objectively. He doesn't have the perception, emotional strength or relationships with others that are needed to cope with the reality in his family. So, he learns to believe that his family is "normal," that his parents and siblings are "the way they should be" and that problems occur in these relationships because something is wrong with him, not them. Day after day and year after year, this learned perception is reinforced. Seeing reality, feeling the pain and anger and talking about these issues are condemned, not encouraged. It is a tight web. A strong grip. A deceptive blindness.

Of the many and varied reasons that people who grow up in these families remain in denial, two seem to stand out most: a lack of knowledge and fear—usually both.

Two factors which seem to be instrumental in the early stages of one's growth (and indeed, throughout the growth process) are truth and love. Truth about God, others and ourselves can cut like a scalpel through the tough layers of defense mechanisms we have erected so that we can begin to see and feel the reality in our own lives. The warmth of loving relationships provides the acceptance and encouragement needed for us to be honest and to begin taking the next steps toward recovery.

There are many good books, Bible studies and teachers that can help us see the painful truth in our lives and the wonderful truth of God's love and strength. Over the past several years, a number of people have begun to see these realitites through a study of *The Search for Significance*. God has used this book to help many expose the lies they've been believing about themselves with the corollary truths from God's Word.

In response to the book, one man told me, "Until I saw it in black and white, I never realized how much I live for other people's approval."

A college student remarked, "I've tried to get all the honors I could so that my family and friends would like and accept me. Now I understand why I've done that, and I have a better understanding of God's unconditional love and acceptance of me."

A woman who had been depressed for years said, "I have had so much anger inside, but I thought I was normal. God has used *The Search for Significance* to help me see how much of my life I've lived in bitterness and in blaming myself and others."

The lies explored in *The Search for Significance* seem to be the trigger for many people, though in most cases (including mine), seeing the extent to which we operate by these deceptions takes months, and even years. For example, when we first begin to study our belief systems, some of us will easily recognize our problems with rejection and failure, but we may not see that we also have problems with blame or shame. Months later, we may discover that these latter two deceptions have as much power in our lives as our fears of rejection and failure. As the years pass, we will likely see more situations in which we need to deal with all of these false beliefs.

The scalpel cuts more deeply as we continue to grow; however, many of us will fail to find lasting benefits from this process if we don't get into affirming relationships. Reality is just too painful to handle on our own. A person who is deeply hurt by others and who is depressed or driven needs someone to "be there" as he takes those first steps to be honest about his life. Each of the people in the previous paragraphs who were touched by the truth were able to see that truth because they were in the context of meaningful relationships. One was in a small group Bible study, another met with a friend every week, another saw a Christian counselor. God has made us relational people. Our deepest pain was probably caused by people. Fear of more pain often keeps us from pursuing new relationships. However, affirmation, love, honesty and encouragement are vital ingredients to our progress and health.

Sometimes a person needs to experience warmth and affirmation before he is open to the scalpel of truth. That scalpel should never be used apart from genuine love. The two are most powerful if the love is consistent and the scalpel of truth is used in an artful and timely manner.

• What are some specific ways you can focus on the truth about God, others and yourself?_____

_____

_____

_____

_____

_____

_____

• What current relationships are helping you develop perception, love and a sense of identity?_____

_____

_____

_____

_____

_____

_____

• Do you need to be involved in other helpful relationships? If so, how can you find these people?_____

_____

_____

_____

_____

_____

Step Three

We make a decision to turn our lives over to God through Jesus Christ.

I urge you therefore, brethen, by the mercies of God, to present your bodies a living and holy sacrifice, acceptable to God, which is your spiritual service of worship.
Rom. 12:1

The Gospel of Jesus Christ is a message of freedom, forgiveness, hope, love, joy and strength. It is the Good News, the most liberating and energizing power mankind has ever or will ever hear! Through the distorted glasses of codependency, however, this phenomenal message is often seen as oppressive, condemning and guilt-inducing. Freedom is turned to bondage, forgiveness to guilt, hope to despair, love to condemnation, joy to pessimism and divine strength to self-sufficiency. Why is it so difficult for the codependent Christian to understand and apply God's grace?

Ought's and Should's

As we have seen, codependents have a warped sense of responsibility. Since they perceive that their worth comes from their ability to perform, they are driven either to achieve as much as possible or to withdraw in hopelessness. But how does a person measure his performance so he can see if he has achieved value and worth? By doing what he *should* do. By doing what he *ought* to do and by dividing life into distinct categories: the "have-to's" and the "can't's." This black-and-white definition steals the fun and spontaneity from life and leaves a person with an overactive conscience, feeling pride if he has done well, despair if he hasn't, and a fear of failure and rejection no matter how well he has done. The codependent who is a Christian carries not only society's ought's and should's, he also adds the ought's and should's of Christianity to his already oppressive load. Instead of helping him to overcome his oppression, his wrong perspective of Christ and the Christian life oppresses him even further. Instead of grace, he experiences guilt. It is grace that ultimately produces a "want-to" motivation, though it may take a long time to develop.

A pastor lamented that he could teach for twenty-nine minutes on the love and grace of God, finishing with only one minute of application of obedience in light of that grace, and some people in the congregation would leave having heard only the last minute. The majority would completely miss the bulk of the message and the careful context of grace that couched the call to obedience. Instead, what they would hear was guilt and condemnation. This pastor was deeply saddened that these people were missing the primary motivation for obedience.

Another teacher presented a Sunday school class series on *The Search for Significance*, mentioned in step 2. Most of those in the class were encouraged and motivated by his talks and discussions, but he was chagrined that several people had just the opposite response. They somehow couldn't hear the liberating message of the material. They only heard that they had to do more and do better to be accepted by God—the exact antithesis of the material!

The codependent Christian divorces grace—the source of perspective and power—from the high moral and ethical expectations of the Bible. He then feels obliged to meet these higher expectations, having only guilt motivation and his own will to achieve them. The more he reads the Bible, the clearer these expectations and others become, increasing his sense of guilt.

There are many commands in the Scriptures that the codependent Christian misinterprets and applies in a "savior" mode to gain a sense of worth. Some of these include:

- going the second mile to help someone.
- turning the other cheek when someone hurts him.
- loving those who don't love him.
- giving cheerfully.
- denying his own desires for the sake of others.
- loving his neighbor as he loves himself.
- having a disciplined life of prayer and Bible study.
- letting no unwholesome word proceed from his mouth.

- forgiving, loving and accepting others as Christ does.
- generally speaking, the worse a person treats him, the more joyfully he serves him or her.

The codependent Christian believes that he is expected to perform these commands (and all the others) perfectly, with feelings of love, peace and joy at all times. In the Christian life, he surmises, there is absolutely no room for hurt and anger.

This denial of emotions only complicates his plight further. His hurt and anger are stuffed away with such reasoning as:

A good Christian shouldn't feel this way...so I won't.
It's so wonderful to be a Christian...(but I'm dying inside).

Sooner or later despair will catch up with him, and his thoughts will resemble these:

If I were walking with God, I wouldn't have these problems.
God has deserted me.
Nobody cares about me. I'm all alone.
Maybe I'm not really a Christian after all. Surely nobody who feels this way can be a Christian.

At the same time he will often defend God so that no one will think badly of Him. Just as the codependent denies his hurt and anger, and excuses and defends the person in his life who has hurt him, he also tries to deny the hurt and anger he perceives that God has caused. And he tries to make sure that God doesn't get any blame for his calamity. In the codependent's eyes, the Savior needs a savior.

If codependency so distorts the Christian faith that freedom becomes slavery, should the codependent throw out the Scriptures? Is codependency an excuse to disobey the Lord? No!

The Word of God, the Spirit of God and the people of God are the tools God has given us to change our behavior, but it takes perception and understanding to overcome our blindness and emerge from the eclipse of codependency. The truth of the Word of God, energized by the Spirit of God in the loving and affirming context of the people of God, enables the codependent Christian to be freed from his bondage.

When I first began to study codependency I wondered, *If codependency is such a problem, why don't the Scriptures say anything about it?* Then I realized they do! Changing warped, codependent perceptions relates directly to the dominant themes of the Bible: the character of God, the grace of God, His unconditional love and acceptance—which are not based on our performance—His declaration of our worth and value because of our identity in Christ, helping people for right reasons, etc. These transforming truths are not communicated in the language of 20th Century psychology, but in that of the ancient writers. Still, they speak powerfully to the root needs of codependents: the needs for love, acceptance, worth and value.

The following study is designed to help you develop a better understanding of Christ's character through Scripture.[1] To help you think through each passage and consider what it means, paraphrase each passage in the space provided. The goal is not to "fill in the blanks," but to reflect on what these passages are saying. This will take some time. Be thorough with this exercise and think both about the meaning of each passage and its application in your daily experience.

■ Purpose

When Adam sinned, he brought both the burden and the penalty of sin upon all mankind. As a result, man is by nature rebellious against God, separated from Him and deserving of His righteous wrath.

> Behold, the Lord's hand is not so short that it cannot save; neither is His ear so dull that it cannot hear.
> But your iniquities have made a separation between you and your God, and your sins have hidden His face from you, so that He does not hear.

Is. 59:1-2

- Paraphrase:_____

_____

> *Or do you think lightly of the riches of His kindness and forbearance and patience, not knowing that the kindness of God leads you to repentance?*
> *But because of your stubbornness and unrepentant heart you are storing up wrath for yourself in the day of wrath and revelation of the righteous judgment of God. . . .*
>
> Rom. 2:4-5

- Paraphrase:_____

_____

_____

_____

Having created man for fellowship with Him, God also created a plan whereby we can be united with Him. He sent His Son to die in our place, and through Christ's death, averted His wrath toward us. Therefore, we have fellowship with God.

> *For Christ also died for sins once for all, the just for the unjust, in order that He might bring us to God. . . .*
>
> 1 Pet. 3:18

- Paraphrase:_____

_____

> *For the grace of God has appeared, bringing salvation to all men,*
> *instructing us to deny ungodliness and worldly desires and to live sensibly, righteously and godly in the present age,*
> *looking for the blessed hope and the appearing of the glory of our great God and Savior, Christ Jesus;*
> *who gave Himself for us, that He might redeem us from every lawless deed and purify for Himself a people for His own possession, zealous for good deeds.*
>
> Titus 2:11-14

- Paraphrase:_____

_____

_____

> *And there is salvation in no one else; for there is no other name under heaven that has been given among men, by which we must be saved.*
>
> Acts 4:12

- Paraphrase:_____

_____

• From your paraphrases above, write a summary statement about the Lord's purpose:_____

_____

_____

_____

■ **Unconditional love**

Sacrificing His only Son's life on our behalf is overwhelming evidence of God's love for us.

> *By this the love of God was manifested in us, that God has sent His only begotten Son into the world so that we might live through Him.*
> *In this is love, not that we loved God, but that He loved us and sent His Son to be the propitiation for our sins.*
>
> 1 John 4:9-10

• Paraphrase:_____

_____

_____

_____

> *For God so loved the world, that He gave His only begotten Son, that whoever believes in Him should not perish, but have eternal life.*
> *For God did not send the Son into the world to judge the world, but that the world should be saved through Him.*
> *He who believes in Him is not judged; he who does not believe has been judged already, because he has not believed in the name of the only begotten Son of God.*
>
> John 3:16-18

• Paraphrase:_____

_____

_____

> *...from Jesus Christ, the faithful witness, the first-born of the dead, and the ruler of the kings of the earth. To Him who loves us, and released us from our sins by His blood,*
> *and He has made us to be a kingdom, priests to His God and Father; to Him be the glory and the dominion forever and ever. Amen.*
>
> Rev. 1:5-6

• Paraphrase:_____

_____

_____

■ From your paraphrases above, write a summary statement about God's unconditional love:_____

_____

_____

_____

■ **Complete forgiveness**

Christ's death not only averted the wrath of God from those who believe in Him, but completely paid our debt of sin so that we are completely forgiven.

> *And when you were dead in your transgressions and the uncircumcision of your flesh, He made you alive together with Him, having forgiven us all our transgressions,*
> *having canceled out the certificate of debt consisting of decrees against us and which was hostile to us; and He has taken it out of the way, having nailed it to the cross.*
>
> Col. 2:13-14

• Paraphrase:_____

_____

_____

> *For while we were still helpless, at the right time Christ died for the ungodly.*
> *For one will hardly die for a righteous man; though perhaps for the good man someone would dare even to die.*
> *But God demonstrates His own love toward us, in that while we were yet sinners, Christ died for us.*
> *Much more then, having now been justified by His blood, we shall be saved from the wrath of God through Him.*
> *For if while we were enemies, we were reconciled to God through the death of His Son, much more, having been reconciled, we shall be saved by His life.*
> *And not only this, but we also exult in God through our Lord Jesus Christ, through whom we have now received the reconciliation.*
>
> Rom. 5:6-11

• Paraphrase:_____

_____

_____

_____

Because we are forgiven by God, we can forgive others.

> *...bearing with one another, and forgiving each other, whoever has a complaint against anyone; just as the Lord forgave you, so also should you.*
>
> Col. 3:13

• Paraphrase:_____

_____

> Now one of the Pharisees was requesting Him to dine with him. And He entered the Pharisee's house, and reclined at the table.
>
> And behold, there was a woman in the city who was a sinner; and when she learned that He was reclining at the table in the Pharisee's house, she brought an alabaster vial of perfume,
>
> and standing behind Him at His feet, weeping, she began to wet His feet with her tears, and kept wiping them with the hair of her head, and kissing His feet, and anointing them with the perfume.
>
> Now when the Pharisee who had invited Him saw this, he said to himself, "If this man were a prophet He would know who and what sort of person this woman is who is touching Him, that she is a sinner."
>
> And Jesus answered and said to him, "Simon, I have something to say to you." And he replied, "Say it, Teacher."
>
> "A certain moneylender had two debtors; one owed five hundred denarii, and the other fifty.
>
> "When they were unable to repay, he graciously forgave them both. Which of them therefore will love him more?"
>
> Simon answered and said, "I suppose the one whom he forgave more." And He said to him, "You have judged correctly."
>
> And turning toward the woman, He said to Simon, "Do you see this woman? I entered your house; you gave Me no water for My feet, but she has wet My feet with her tears, and wiped them with her hair.
>
> "You gave Me no kiss; but she, since the time I came in, has not ceased to kiss My feet.
>
> "You did not anoint My head with oil, but she anointed My feet with perfume.
>
> "For this reason I say to you, her sins, which are many, have been forgiven, for she loved much; but he who is forgiven little loves little."
>
> And He said to her, "Your sins have been forgiven."
>
> Luke 7:36-48

• Paraphrase:_____

_____

_____

_____

_____

_____

_____

_____

• From your paraphrases above, write a summary statement about the Lord's complete forgiveness:

_____

_____

■ Total acceptance

Christ's payment for our sins took away the barrier between Him and us so that we are now His beloved children and His beloved friends.

> *For you have not received a spirit of slavery leading to fear again, but you have received a spirit of adoption as sons by which we cry out, "Abba! Father!"*
> *The Spirit Himself bears witness with our spirit that we are children of God,*
> *and if children, heirs also, heirs of God and fellow heirs with Christ, if indeed we suffer with Him in order that we may also be glorified with Him.*
>
> Rom. 8:15-17

- Paraphrase:_____

_____

_____

> *...in order that He might redeem those who were under the Law, that we might receive the adoption as sons.*
> *And because you are sons, God has sent forth the Spirit of His Son into your hearts, crying, "Abba! Father!"*
> *Therefore you are no longer a slave, but a son; and if a son, then an heir through God.*
>
> Gal. 4:5-7

- Paraphrase:_____

_____

_____

Because we are totally accepted by God, we can unconditionally accept others.

> *Wherefore, accept one another, just as Christ also accepted us to the glory of God.*
>
> Rom. 15:7

- Paraphrase:_____

_____

- Write a summary statement about God's total acceptance of us:_____

_____

_____

_____

■ Authority and power

Christ has infinite authority and power. In His life and death on earth, He achieved our redemption. He defeated every temptation known to man (Heb. 2:14-15; 4:15), reconciled us to God (Matt. 26:28; Rom. 5:8) and triumphed over every evil power and authority (Col. 2:15). His resurrection proves that He has authority over death and that He is alive today (Luke 24:1-49; 1 Cor. 15:3-4). His ascension sealed His victory and ours (Mark 16:19; Luke 24:50-53;

Acts 1:1-11). Scripture tells us that Jesus Christ is now seated at the right hand of God *in the heavenly places, far above all rule and authority and power and dominion, and every name that is named, not only in this age, but also in the one to come,* and that all things are in subjection to Him (Eph. 1:20-22).

Paraphrase the following passages about Christ's authority and power:

> *When He had disarmed the rulers and authorities, He made a public display of them, having triumphed over them through Him.*
>
> Col. 2:15

- Paraphrase:_____

  _____

> *And He is the image of the invisible God, the first-born of all creation.*
>
> *For by Him all things were created, both in the heavens and on earth, visible and invisible, whether thrones or dominions or rulers or authorities—all things have been created by Him and for Him.*
>
> *And He is before all things, and in Him all things hold together.*
>
> *He is also the head of the body, the church; and He is the beginning, the first-born from the dead; so that He Himself might come to have first place in everything.*
>
> *For it was the Father's good pleasure for all the fulness to dwell in Him, and through Him to reconcile all things to Himself, having made peace through the blood of His cross; through Him, I say, whether things on earth or things in heaven.*
>
> Col. 1:15-19

- Paraphrase:_____

  _____

  _____

> *. . . in Him you have been made complete, and He is the head over all rule and authority. . . .*
>
> Col. 2:10

- Paraphrase:_____

  _____

> *Therefore also God highly exalted Him, and bestowed on Him the name which is above every name,*
>
> *that at the name of Jesus every knee should bow, of those who are in heaven, and on earth, and under the earth,*
>
> *and that every tongue should confess that Jesus Christ is Lord, to the glory of God the Father.*
>
> Phil. 2:9-11

- Paraphrase:_____

  _____

  _____

  _____

• Write a summary statement about the Lord's authority and power:_____

_____

_____

_____

■ **Hope**

There is no hope of forgiveness and reconciliation to God apart from Christ.

> *...remember that you were at that time separate from Christ, excluded from the commonwealth of Israel, and strangers to the covenants of promise, having no hope and without God in the world.*
>
> Eph. 2:12

• Paraphrase:_____

_____

_____

His love, forgiveness and power give us hope for a new life.

> *Blessed be the God and Father of our Lord Jesus Christ, who according to His great mercy has caused us to be born again to a living hope through the resurrection of Jesus Christ from the dead. . . .*
>
> 1 Pet. 1:3

• Paraphrase:_____

_____

_____

> *And we know that God causes all things to work together for good to those who love God, to those who are called according to His purpose.*
>
> Rom. 8:28

• Paraphrase:_____

_____

• Write a summary statement about the hope of Christ:_____

_____

_____

_____

■ Faithfulness

Christ is always faithful to do what He has promised.

> *No temptation has overtaken you but such as is common to man; and God is faithful, who will not allow you to be tempted beyond what you are able, but with the temptation will provide the way of escape also, that you may be able to endure it.*
>
> 1 Cor. 10:13

- Paraphrase:_____

_____

_____

> *Let us hold fast the confession of our hope without wavering, for He who promised is faithful...*
>
> Heb. 10:23

- Paraphrase:_____

_____

_____

> *It is a trustworthy statement: For if we died with Him, we shall also live with Him;*
> *If we endure, we shall also reign with Him; if we deny Him, He also will deny us;*
> *If we are faithless, He remains faithful; for He cannot deny Himself.*
>
> 2 Tim. 2:11-13

- Paraphrase:_____

_____

_____

- Write a summary statement about the Lord's faithfulness:_____

_____

_____

_____

■ Wisdom

The Lord has all knowledge and all wisdom. He knows what is best for us, and He will give us wisdom to know how we can honor Him in every situation.

> *But if any of you lacks wisdom, let him ask of God, who gives to all men generously and without reproach, and it will be given to him.*
> *But let him ask in faith without any doubting, for the one who doubts is like the surf of the sea driven and tossed by the wind.*
>
> James 1:5-6

- Paraphrase:_____

_____

> *For the word of the cross is to those who are perishing foolishness, but to us who are being saved it is the power of God.*
>
> *For it is written, "I will destroy the wisdom of the wise, and the cleverness of the clever I will set aside."*
>
> *Where is the wise man? Where is the scribe? Where is the debater of this age? Has not God made foolish the wisdom of the world?*
>
> *For since in the wisdom of God the world through its wisdom did not come to know God, God was well-pleased through the foolishness of the message preached to save those who believe.*
>
> *For indeed Jews ask for signs and Greeks search for wisdom; but we preach Christ crucified, to Jews a stumbling block, and to Gentiles foolishness,*
>
> *but to those who are the called, both Jews and Greeks, Christ the power of God and the wisdom of God.*
>
> *Because the foolishness of God is wiser than men, and the weakness of God is stronger than men.*
>
> *For consider your calling, brethren, that there were not many wise according to the flesh, not many mighty, not many noble;*
>
> *but God has chosen the foolish things of the world to shame the wise, and God has chosen the weak things of the world to shame the things which are strong. . . .*
>
> 1 Cor. 1:18-27

- Paraphrase:_____

_____

_____

_____

> *"For My thoughts are not your thoughts, neither are your ways My ways," declares the Lord.*
>
> *"For as the heavens are higher than the earth, so are My ways higher than your ways, and My thoughts than your thoughts."*
>
> Is. 55:8-9

- Paraphrase:_____

_____

_____

> *Therefore be careful how you walk, not as unwise men, but as wise,*
> *making the most of your time, because the days are evil.*
> *So then do not be foolish, but understand what the will of the Lord is.*
> *And do not get drunk with wine, for that is dissipation, but be filled with the Spirit,*
> *speaking to one another in psalms and hymns and spiritual songs, singing and making melody with your heart to the Lord;*
> *always giving thanks for all things in the name of our Lord Jesus Christ to God, even the Father;*
> *and be subject to one another in the fear of Christ.*
>
> Eph. 5:15-21

- Paraphrase:_____

_____

_____

_____

- Write a summary statement about the Lord's wisdom:_____

_____

_____

_____

_____

■ Which passage in each section has been most meaningful to you? List the passage and describe why it is meaningful.

- Purpose_____

_____

_____

_____

_____

_____

- Unconditional love_____

_____

_____

_____

_____

_____

- Complete forgiveness_____

_____

_____

_____

_____

- Total acceptance_____
  _____
  _____
  _____
  _____
  _____

- Authority and power_____
  _____
  _____
  _____
  _____
  _____

- Hope_____
  _____
  _____
  _____
  _____
  _____

- Faithfulness_____
  _____
  _____
  _____
  _____
  _____

- Wisdom_____
  _____
  _____

_____

_____

_____

Trusting in Christ

Augustine observed, "Thou hast made us for Thyself, O God, and the heart of man is restless until it finds its rest in Thee." God desires to have an intimate relationship with us, and He has given us a provision for continual access to Him through His Son, Jesus Christ (John 3:16-17; Heb. 2:17).

Are you trusting in your own abilities to earn acceptance with God, or are you trusting in the death of Christ to pay for your sins and the resurrection of Christ to give you new life? Take a moment to reflect on this question: On a scale of 0-100 percent, how sure are you that you would spend eternity with God if you died today? An answer of less than 100 percent may indicate that you are trusting, at least in part, in yourself. You may be thinking, *Isn't it arrogant to say that I am 100 percent sure?* Indeed, it would be arrogance if you were trusting in yourself—your abilities, your actions and good deeds—to earn your salvation. However, if you are no longer trusting in your own efforts, but in the all-sufficient payment of Christ, then 100 percent certainty is a response of humility and thankfulness, not arrogance.

Reflect on a second question: If you were to die today and stand before God, and He were to ask you, "Why should I let you into heaven?" what would you tell Him? Would you mention your abilities, church attendance, kindness to others, Christian service, abstinence from a particular sin or some other good deed? Paul wrote to Titus:

> *But when the kindness of God our Savior and His love for mankind appeared,*
> *He saved us, not on the basis of deeds which we have done in righteousness, but according to His*
> *mercy. . . .*
>
> Titus 3:4-5

And to the Ephesians he wrote:

> *For by grace you have been saved through faith; and that not of yourselves, it is the gift of God;*
> *not c s a result of works, that no one should boast.*
>
> Eph. 2:8-9

We must give up our own efforts to achieve righteousness and instead believe that Christ's death and resurrection alone are sufficient to pay for our sin and separation from God.

In Acts 16:31, Luke wrote, *. . . Believe in the Lord Jesus, and you shall be saved. . . .* Jesus said: *I am the way, and the truth, and the life; no one comes to the Father, but through Me* (John 14:6).

We receive Jesus by invitation. Scripture says:

> *But as many received Him, to them He gave the right to become children of God, even to those*
> *who believe in His name.*
>
> John 1:12

Take some time to reflect on the two questions we examined above. Reflect on God's love, which He has expressed to you by sending His only Son to die in your place. Read Luke 22:39-46. Consider the selfless sacrifice of Jesus to carry out this divine plan. Realize that if you were the only person to walk this earth, Jesus would have done this for *you*.

If you are not 100 percent sure that you would spend eternity with God if you died today, and if you are willing to trust in Christ and accept His payment for your sins, you may use this prayer to express your faith:

Lord Jesus, I need You. I want You to be my Savior and my Lord. I accept Your death on the cross as payment for my sins, and now entrust my life to Your care. Thank You for forgiving me and for giving me a new life. Thank You for the new life that is now mine through You. Please help me grow in my understanding of Your love and power so that my life will bring glory and honor to You.   Amen.

_____	_____
(date)	(signature)

If you have placed your trust in Jesus Christ prior to reading this, consider reaffirming your faith and commitment to serve Him. You may do so by using this prayer:

Lord Jesus, I need You and thank You that I am Yours. I confess that I have sinned against You, and ask You to "create in me a clean heart, and renew a steadfast spirit within me" (Ps 51:10). I renew my commitment to serve You. Thank You for loving me and for forgiving me. Please give me Your strength and wisdom to continue growing in You so that my life can bring glory and honor to You.   Amen.

_____	_____
(date)	(signature)

It is important to understand that trusting in Christ does not guarantee an instantaneous deliverance from codependent behavior or any other problem in life. However, it does mean that you are forgiven for your rebellion against God; that you are restored to a relationship with Him that will last throughout eternity; and that you will receive His unconditional love and acceptance, as well as His strength and wisdom, as you continue to grow in recovery.

Baptism

Some people may ask, "How does baptism relate to one's conversion experience?" Water baptism is an outward demonstration of a believer's internal commitment to Christ. It enables the believer to identify himself with Christ in his culture. The act of baptism symbolizes his being dead, buried and raised with Christ. In the early church and in some countries today, this identification is a dramatic statement of being severed from the world and being bonded to the body of Christ. In our society, it is an important step of obedience as we identify ourselves publicly with Christ and His people. (For a sample of passages on Spirit or water baptism, see Acts 8:26-39; Rom. 6:1-4 and 1 Cor. 12:13.)

As a result of our trust in Christ, there are many facts and promises in God's Word that we can depend on. Facts are truths that are *already* true of us; *promises* are statements that we know will be fulfilled because of the trustworthiness of God. Here is a very short list of both:

Facts from God's Word
You are completely forgiven by God (Rom. 3:19-25; Col. 2:13-14).
You are righteous and pleasing to God (2 Cor. 5:21).
You are totally accepted by God (Col. 1:19-22).
You are deeply loved by God (1 John 4:9-10).
You are absolutely complete in Christ (2 Cor. 5:17; Col. 2:10).
The Holy Spirit dwells in you (Rom. 8:9-11).
You are God's child (Rom. 8:15-16).
You are a fellow heir with Christ (Rom. 8:17).
God works all things for good for those who love Him (Rom. 8:28).

Promises from God's Word

Christ will never leave us (Matt. 28:20; Heb. 13:5).
He will abundantly provide for our needs (Phil. 4:19).
We will be in heaven with Him (John 14:1-3).
We will reign with Him (2 Tim. 2:12).
He will strengthen us (Is. 40:29).
He will give us His peace (John 14:27).
He will accomplish His purposes (1 Thess. 5:24).
He will enable us to give generously (2 Cor. 9:6-11).
We will be persecuted (John 15:18-21).

Be honest about your feelings and thoughts. Tell them to the Lord, yourself and someone else who understands and cares about you. The deep wounds of codependency—the shame, the hurt, the anger, the unfulfilled longing to be loved—seldom heal quickly. Recovery requires lots of time and attention.

Superficial solutions sound so good. They seem to help so many people. But in the long run, quick, easy answers only prolong and exacerbate the problems of codependency. Real answers are needed that speak to the real issues of one's worth and identity. These solutions should be experienced in a long process so they will sink in deeply and profoundly.

For Additional Reflection and Application

■ What things do you feel that you have to do as a Christian to feel better about yourself?_____

_____

_____

_____

_____

■ What are some ways that the Scriptures can be misapplied to feed codependent behavior?_____

_____

_____

_____

_____

■ How does codependency affect:

• Your view of God?_____

_____

_____

_____

_____

- Your identity and worth?_____

_____

_____

_____

_____

- Your relationships with others?_____

_____

_____

_____

_____

- The standards and rules you set for yourself?_____

_____

_____

_____

_____

■ What are your dominant motivations for obedience?_____

_____

_____

_____

_____

■ What are some superficial solutions you can think of for codependency (examples: "Just pray about it," or "Spend one hour with the Lord everyday.")?

_____

_____

_____

_____

■ Why don't these superficial solutions work? _____

_____

_____

_____

_____

_____

_____

_____

Step Four

We make a searching and fearless moral inventory of ourselves.

Let us examine and probe our ways, and let us return to the Lord.
Lam. 3:40

As we learn more about how we have been affected by dysfunctional relationships, we also learn how to respond in new and more positive ways. These new responses are characterized by three essential ingredients: identify, detach and decide. First we can *identify* the behaviors, feelings, thoughts, words and actions that have become the habits of codependency. Then we can *detach* and reflect on the situation, how we can stop responding in the usual way and instead respond in a positive, healthy way. After that reflection we can *decide* on a course of action, a response based on objective reality, not a reaction based on codependent reflexes. Identify. Detach. Decide. See it. Analyze it. Choose your response.

Identify

As we learn more about our identity in Christ, and as we see the patterns of codependency in our lives, we will be able to identify many of the specific codependent things we say and do. Also, we'll be able to see some specific characteristics of codependency in others. For some, identifying codependent behavior will be fairly easy: *Oh yeah! I've done that for years!* Others will have a harder time identifying those behaviors. People like this may see a few instances, but they don't see the patterns of codependency very clearly. Still others lack objectivity to such an extent that they don't see any characteristics of their codependency at all. They just don't get the picture, and healing can't begin until the Holy Spirit begins to overcome their denial.

Identifying codependent behavior is the trigger mechanism for objective reflection and for ultimately living in freedom and godly independence. Before this realization begins, however, most of us think that our situations are normal.

What Is "Normal"?

Dysfunctional behavior destroys objectivity. As a result, codependents believe their lives are fairly normal. If we compare our lives to that of the alcoholic, drug addict, perfectionist, workaholic, bulimic, sexual abuser, or whoever in the family seems "really messed up," we think we're doing pretty well. We fail to recognize that exaggeration, guilt, loneliness, being manipulated, manipulating others and outbursts of anger are signs of relational pathology, not normalcy. But we are unable to see the devastation in our own lives (which are not "normal") because of our inability to face reality.

What is reality? Most codependents have a difficult time with it. Many of us believe that we are terrible people (though we try so hard to help), and that the other needy person in our lives is wonderful (though he or she may manipulate us through guilt, self-pity, anger and fear).

Other codependents rationalize that they are very good people with no wrong motives or hidden faults. The strength of this deception is so great that at one point, a young man I know told me that he didn't think he had ever sinned. Yet at other times in his life, this same man was overcome with guilt and morbid introspection. Fairly black-and-white, don't you think?

The truth is that our responses to life haven't been "normal." We have felt guilty even when we've tried to help. We have felt lonely when we wanted intimacy badly. We have controlled, been controlled and we have rescued people from the consequences of their choices. We haven't allowed ourselves to feel normal hurt and normal anger when these people have condemned, used and ignored us. We haven't been "normal" at all!

Reality demands that we open our eyes to the truth (the good and the bad), recognize the evil in all people (even ourselves) and realize that life is a struggle. Blindness never helps in the long run; it only diminishes our capacity for recovery from codependent behavior.

Step 4 can therefore serve as a turning point for us. We don't have to remain bound to the self-defeating behaviors that comprise codependency. We can change!

Growth and healing begin with an appraisal of our behavior. By completing step 4, we become aware of our codependent characteristics and actions. This enables us to make appropriate responses to similar situations in the future. In addition, a review of our behavior often gives us an understanding of *why* we behave in certain ways at certain times. With this understanding, we gain a new acceptance of ourselves. A positive sense of self-respect begins to emerge, and with it, a new tolerance for other people.

Finally, an objective review of the past enables us to confront our age-old enemy: denial. In the past, denial seemed to work well for us. With it, we could escape from hurtful remarks, a deteriorating self-image, frightful responsibilities and worrisome circumstances. In reality, denial is just a defense mechanism which prevents us from progressing in our lives. It locks us into self-defeating behavior.

As you move into a deeper awareness of reality, you may experience a sense of hurt, loss and grief. These feelings are normal and vital to healthy recovery. However, you may avoid an unnecessary burden by realizing that step 4 is not intended to increase your sense of guilt and shame. Instead, its purpose is to bring the hidden areas of your life into God's light so that you might experience His grace more fully (1 John 1:5-10).

Let's begin this process by examining each of the six characteristics of codependency in more detail.

A Lack of Objectivity

Why are codependents unable to see reality clearly? Why do they lack objectivity? There are basically two reasons. First, they have an impaired ability to compare reality with unreality. If the environment of their families has been steeped in deception and denial, then they, too, will probably be deceived and lack objectivity. Children believe their parents are godlike. Therefore, they conclude that however their parents treat them is how life really is. If their parents are loving, they surmise that they are lovable. If, however, their parents are manipulative, condemning or neglectful, they usually conclude that it is somehow their own fault, not their parents'. They see themselves as unlovable and unworthy of love and attention, but they still believe that their parents are always good and right. It is a convoluted, distorted and tragic perspective. Similarly, marrying or establishing any strong relationship with a person who has a compulsive disorder can slowly erode a person's objectivity. The dysfunctional person lives a lie and expects you to live it, too!

The second reason why codependents lack objectivity is that they fear reality. Solving other people's crises takes so much of the codependent's energy that the prospect of any more pain or anger is simply too much to bear. His fleeting glimpses of reality are so painful that he is afraid of being overwhelmed by it in his own life. This perception is at least partially true. Objectivity often does bring great pain and anger. At times, it can seem truly overwhelming. But reality, with its hurt and anger, is absolutely necessary for healing to occur. Crawling inside an emotional turtle shell may provide temporary relief, but it ultimately brings more long-term pain and prevents the process of healing.

A part of this fear of reality is the fear of losing one's identity. However broken and painful a codependent's self-concept may be, it is all that he has! The fear of losing that morsel of identity is very threatening. Strangely, that leaves him clinging to another dysfunctional person who brings him pain, abuse and neglect, instead of turning to reality, going through the healing process and experiencing love, freedom and strength. The term *denial*, or lack of objectivity, may sound fairly benign, but it is powerful and insidious.

Exaggerating

A codependent often exaggerates. Making people or situations a little worse than they really are (i.e., black) gives him a sense of identity, of importance. It causes others to be more concerned for him than they might be if he were more objective. Similarly, making people or situations a little better than they really are (i.e., white) makes him look better and more impressive. This is the codependent's goal in relationships: to impress people and/or to get them to feel sorry for him.

An objective person is more balanced because he sees life's good and bad at the same time. He realizes that these exist in tension with each other. A codependent, however, gives up one to embrace the other, which leads to an extreme black-or-white perspective. This exaggerated perception of life causes wide emotional swings, sometimes very quickly and sometimes when the codependent's situation hasn't changed at all!

Daydreaming

Daydreaming is a reflection of the codependent's black-or-white perspective. These daydreams reflect either the negative thoughts of a worst case scenario, or grand and glorious thoughts of the best possible scenario. A codependent can have fantasies about making millions of dollars, being praised and respected and having all the things he's ever wanted, including a sense of worth and love, especially the love of the dysfunctional person in his life. These images can be quite detailed and emotional, conjuring up all of the dreams and/or self-pity that are hidden deep in his heart. In one moment, he may feel elated. In the next instant, an ambulance may roar by, and the poor codependent may assume that his spouse or child or parent is lying critically injured and helpless. He would then be likely to assume that the reason for the accident is due to his neglect, so that his fear is compounded by intense guilt.

Many of these daydreams also include an escape from the abuse and neglect of the other needy person in the codependent's life. Often, he or she will daydream of escaping from that painful relationship to a lover who is tender, strong, wise and comforting. The deep anguish of the codependent may even be reflected in daydreams of killing the one who is hurting him or her so deeply.

Reason has virtually nothing to do with these dreams and fears. The fantasies reflect the codependent's deep hurt, desire for affirmation and fear of being hurt again.

Objectivity Inventory

■ What are some ways by which you can tell if a person perceives life in the extremes of black and white? Name the words, attitudes and actions he or she might use:

_____

_____

_____

_____

■ Which of these do you see in your own life?_____

_____

_____

_____

■ Do you tend to be more extreme (black or white) around certain people or in certain situations? If so, with whom and when?

_____

_____

_____

_____

■ Describe several of your daydreams:_____

_____

_____

_____

_____

_____

_____

• What are their common themes? _____

_____

_____

_____

_____

_____

_____

_____

A Warped Sense of Responsibility

A codependent feels like he is either a *savior* or a *Judas*: one who rescues or one who betrays, one who helps or one who fails to help. Often, these black-and-white perceptions of himself change in a heartbeat, depending on whether the other person is happy or angry with him.

A codependent in his savior mode may believe that he can do no wrong and may rescue everyone who is in need. His creed is:
- *If someone has a need, I'll meet it!*
- *If there's not a need, I'll find one and then I'll meet it!*
- *If there's a small need, I'll make it a large one. Then I'll feel even better when I meet it!*
- *Even if nobody wants help, I'll help anyway! Then when I've helped, I'll feel good about myself!*
- His family says, "We *knew* we could count on you."

A person with a savior complex thinks he is indispensable. He believes that whatever he is doing is absolutely the most important thing in the world! Nobody else's role even comes close. But in the Judas mode, the outlook is quite different. The mood is one of failure and despair. One man explained, "I feel like I *have* to rescue people, but I'm so afraid of failing that I'm paralyzed." He lives with tremendous tension and heartache. Paralyzing fear and withdrawal prevent the person with a Judas complex from rescuing actively. Therefore, he may not see himself as codependent, an erroneous analysis. He desperately wants to rescue others just like a codependent in the savior mode, but he can't. His creed is:
- *People need me, but I can't help them.*
- *Their needs are enormous, and I feel awful that I can't help.*
- *Every time I try to help, I mess up.*
- *No matter what I do, it's wrong.*
- *If I try, I fail. If I don't try, I fail. I am a miserable failure.*
- He believes his family would say, "We *thought* we could count on you, but I guess we can't."

How does a person with a savior complex nosedive into a Judas complex? There are three basic ways:

1. He tries to help, but he fails.
2. He tries to help, but he isn't appreciated.
3. He doesn't even try because he's sure he will fail.

In any of these situations, his response is usually withdrawal, guilt, loneliness, anger, self-condemnation and hopelessness.

The following charts of the savior and Judas complexities correspond roughly to the aforementioned black-and-white extremes the codependent demonstrates due to his lack of objectivity. The difference is that these charts describe the codependent's extremes in his self-concept, either as a rescuer or a betrayer.

Chronic Savior Pattern

A person who is either very skilled at pleasing people (or who is very young and hasn't experienced enough crushing blows of failure) may be in a chronic savior pattern and know of only a few times when he has felt like a Judas. Often, someone in this condition sees himself as a very healthy and successful person, not as the person he really is.

Savior
(I can help you.)

Judas
(I'll let you down.)

Mixed Savior/Judas Pattern

A person who has experienced more criticism gradually loses confidence in himself. His chart may look like this:

Savior
(I can help you.)

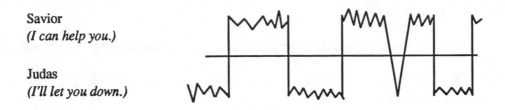

Judas
(I'll let you down.)

Chronic Judas Pattern

Through any number of painful circumstances and through manipulative, condemning people, a person's self-concept may erode to a point where it is characterized almost completely by guilt, despair, anger, loneliness and hopelessness. This may happen in childhood or much later. His life will be characterized by a chronic Judas pattern:

Savior
(I can help you.)

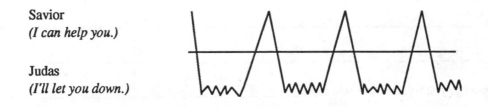

Judas
(I'll let you down.)

The savior and Judas complexities are flip sides of the same coin: the need for a sense of worth and the need to be loved and accepted. The savior feels that he is accomplishing that goal. The Judas fears that he can't.

Results of a Warped Sense of Responsibility

Trying to rescue people or failing to rescue them results in personal and relational maladies. For example:

Codependents prevent others from developing responsibility. By constantly solving, fixing, helping and rescuing, codependents deprive others of the opportunity to develop their own sense of responsibility. That keeps them dependent on the codependent, and the cycle continues.

Codependents need to let others do things for themselves!

Codependents neglect themselves. By focusing on others' needs, codependents fail to see their own needs. They derive their self-worth from the opinions of others, using all of their resources to please them. They need their own identity, their own opinions, their own time, their own friends and their own feelings.

Do things for yourself!

Codependents resent being saviors. Codependents rescue others to feel good about themselves, but this feeling often dissipates rather quickly. They rescue; then they get angry that someone has taken advantage of them; then they feel sorry for themselves. This cycle of rescue-anger-self-pity, or rescue-persecutor-victim is the insight of Stephen B. Karpman and is called the Karpman Drama Triangle.[1]

Codependents threaten, but continue rescuing. When he feels anger and self-pity, a codependent will threaten to stop helping someone, especially another codependent or someone else with a compulsive disorder. He says, "That's the limit! That's as far as I go! You have to change your behavior!" But when these threats are consistently followed by more fixing and solving and rescuing, they become meaningless and the one threatened learns he can continue to do as he pleases. He knows he always will be rescued.

Codependents lack objectivity about serving and helping others. Because so much of their lives is spent in helping others, codependents often see themselves as humble (or abused) servants. But there is a great difference between helping people because you want to, and feeling that you have to help others to prevent a loss of value and worth. One is loving service, the other is codependency.

Codependents take themselves too seriously. Several years ago a co-worker told me, "Pat, you take yourself too seriously. Lighten up!"

Fine, I thought. *I'll just give up trying to have a sense of self-worth by accomplishing enough to win the respect and approval of other people. That will help!*

He was right, of course. I was much too serious (and probably still am), but telling me not to take myself seriously doesn't solve the problem. Nor is codependent behavior the solution. It is part of the problem.

Responsibility Inventory

■ Define what it means to "rescue" someone: _____

_____

_____

_____

■ What are some ways you try to rescue others? _____

_____

_____

_____

_____

_____

■ When do you feel like a savior? How do you act? _____

_____

_____

_____

_____

■ When do you feel like a Judas? How do you act? _____

_____

_____

_____

_____

_____

■ How do you feel when you say no?_____

_____

_____

_____

■ Identify and describe the results of a warped sense of responsibility in your life as you answer the following questions.

• How do you prevent others from developing responsibility? What are the results of your actions?_____

_____

_____

_____

_____

_____

• How do you neglect yourself? Name some results of this behavior:_____

_____

_____

_____

_____

• Are you a resentful savior? If so, how does this affect you and others?_____

_____

_____

_____

_____

• Do you ever threaten to stop rescuing, only to continue doing so? Name some results of your actions:

_____

_____

_____

_____

_____

• Do you seem to lack objectivity about serving and helping others? Describe how this affects you and those you "help" or "serve":

_____

_____

_____

_____

_____

• If you take yourself too seriously, what are some results of this behavior?_____

_____

_____

_____

_____

■ How would your life be different if you weren't compelled to help, fix and rescue? How would your self-concept, your time, your values and your relationships be affected?

_____

_____

_____

_____

_____

Controlled/Controlling

Without the secure moorings of love, acceptance and significance, the codependent feels responsible for everything, but confident in nothing. He tries to find his security by pleasing people, by being right and by doing right things in the right way. His actions are thus like those of a puppet, dancing on the strings of praise and condemnation, easily controlled by the desires of others. Paradoxically, he wants to be in absolute control of his own life so that he won't fail, and he wants to control the behavior of others so that they will add to, not subtract from, his ability to perform well and please people.

Codependents Are Easily Controlled

Like everyone else, the codependent needs love and respect, but having been deprived of these precious commodities, he determines to do whatever it takes to win the approval and value he craves. His means to that end is to make people happy. His chief fear is that people will be unhappy with him. Those around him quickly learn where his buttons are and how to push them. Skillful use of praise and condemnation manipulate the codependent as artfully as a marionette manipulates a puppet.

The codependent is pressured to do more and to be more for the other person. He hears statements like:

"95 on an exam isn't good enough."

"I wish you'd get that promotion. I'd be so proud of you!"

"Why do you drive that piece of junk?"

"I'm proud of you for doing so well. I can't wait to tell my friends!"

"You are so wonderful to help me. I wish your sister were as kind as you are."

"You wouldn't be stupid enough to vote for somebody like that, would you?"

"I wish you had come; I really needed you."

"My goodness, what an unusual hair style; I'm sure it will look better when it grows out."

The one who is controlling you probably believes that he is doing you a great favor. He justifies his control over you with statements such as:

"I'm only saying this for your own good...because I love you."

"I know what's best for you. In fact, I know you better than you know yourself."

"I'm your father. If I can't say this to you, who can?"

"If it weren't for me, there's no telling what a mess you'd make of your life!"

These and a myriad of other statements range from severe to delicate manipulation. Each one may, taken alone, sound harmless. But in the context of codependency, where one feels worthless and desperate for love and affirmation, it constitutes an attack designed to change behavior through praise or condemnation. And it works!

Guilt is a primary motivator which usually results in a "have-to" mentality. There is no freedom to fail because the perceived risks of losing love and/or respect are too great. Consequently, the codependent is driven. He is obsessive-compulsive. He has to do the right thing, make the clever remark, wear the right clothes, look the right way and, in short, be perfect. (That's not asking too much, is it?) In addition to being driven, he is usually compliant. He will do anything for anybody at any time with a smile—at least for a while.

Comparison also motivates the codependent. He is compared to other members of the family, co-workers, relatives and anybody else that might urge him to do more. A friend told me what her mother tells her every month or so: "My friends' children are always doing nice things for them. They buy them clothes, take them on vacations, and buy them jewelry and nice furniture. Their children are there whenever they are needed." That's not all: "I guess I'll just have to take care of myself." Was that a neutral statement of fact, a statement of independence? No way! She used comparison to manipulate her daughter! Manipulation is not benign. It is evil, seductive and destructive.

To an objective bystander, the control an abusive person exercises in his family is almost unbelievable. The rest of the family, however, is not objective. No matter how much abuse and neglect they endure, their overwhelming thirst for the abuser's acceptance keeps them coming back for more.

Many of us have such little self-confidence that we seldom have our own ideas and desires. We only respond—or react—to the ideas and desires of others. We are like a ball in a pinball machine, being forced in one direction, then another, always doing what the outside force demands, never able to determine its own course. We learn to react to the slightest hint of praise or condemnation. In fact, we don't even wait for a hint. We anticipate what others might want from us and act accordingly. We become like puppets on autopilot!

Although the codependent eventually tires of this game, he lacks the objectivity to stop playing. He becomes angry as he realizes that he is being pressured to perform and that he is giving in to that pressure repeatedly. As a result he hates himself for his foolishness and he hates the other dependent person for manipulating him. But because this is the only game he knows, he keeps playing. His desperate need for approval keeps him on the seemingly endless treadmill of need-manipulation-anger. He may become openly hostile, or more likely, passive-aggressive, refusing to be honest and also refusing to respond. Although he may appear to be passive, his real goal is to hurt the one who has been controlling him.

Any independence demonstrated by the codependent is often tolerated and even encouraged to a certain extent; beyond that point it is strictly taboo. Past that point the other needy person may explode in anger and say, "How could you be so selfish!" or he may take a much more subtle approach: "We need to talk." What he really means is, *We need to talk so I can convince you to go back to being dependent on me, submissive to me and easily manipulated by me. There should be no limits on what you will do for me. After all, pleasing me is your way of gaining self-worth.*

One woman told me about her relationship with her alcoholic husband. She stated emphatically, "I'm independent now. I don't tell him *anything*!" Her description of their relationship was not one of her growing sense of self-worth; she simply was so hurt that she was withdrawing from him. Her identity and sense of self-confidence weren't any better. She was still "dancing on his strings," doing what he wanted her to do. She just didn't talk to him as much as she used to, but that wasn't really progress.

Controlling Ourselves

As codependents, we define ourselves by what we do, how we look and how well we accomplish tasks in life. We don't perceive failure as an option. We have to be right. We have to be in control of our lives. This is because the rest of our lives are so chaotic (with a dependent parent or spouse) that we have a strong need to find an area of our lives that can be controlled.

As is usually the case with codependents, there are two extremes: being obsessive-compulsive to gain control of life, or giving up and withdrawing. Some codependents *have* to have order in their lives. Things are in boxes—neatly labeled, of course. The home is tidy, clothes are immaculate, makeup is worn perfectly, every hair is in place, the car is clean (the tank, filled), work is done on time and with excellence. Schedules are meticulously drawn up to aid maximum efficiency and minimize distractions. At best, their sense of satisfaction for doing a job well is short-lived. It has to be done again tomorrow, and next week, and next month and. . . .

The obsessive-compulsive wants the people in his life to be in control, too. His spouse, children, co-workers—everybody—needs to contribute to his compelling need for a well-ordered life. Young children often cause the obsessive-compulsive a lot of problems precisely because they are so uncontrollable. When they cry, an obsessive-compulsive can interpret the crying to mean, *There's something wrong. Things are out of control. And it's your fault, Mother* (or *Father*)! Their crying or spilling something—any disruptive behavior—can be a threat to the stability and significance of the obsessive-compulsive because it communicates to him that things are out of control.

The obsessive-compulsive also controls his or her emotions. Not too much crying (maybe none at all), and not too much laughter either. Anger is expressly forbidden. It means you are *really* out of control.

The obsessive-compulsive's relationship with God is highly controlled, too. It is often rigid and ritualistic, with good activities but little spontaneity and warmth.

Of course no one can be in complete control of his lifestyle, schedule, work, relationships and emotions all of the time, so obsessive-compulsives are forced to choose which areas they will concentrate on (and get their self-worth from) and which areas to let slide (and say they don't care about).

For some the crushing weight of being right and neat and in complete control at all times is simply too much. They become immobilized by the perception that the job of controlling life is too massive a task. They appear to be very irresponsible when, in fact, they are obsessive-compulsives who have broken under the strain of striving for perfection. They've given up, but still have no feeling of freedom or relief. Active obsessive-compulsives feel guilty and hopeless, believing that they are terrible failures. One looks very successful. The other doesn't. In reality, both are hurting.

Controlling Others

How we relate to others is usually a mirror of our relationship with the other needy person in our lives. We may hate the way we have been treated, but modeling is a powerful teacher which shapes our patterns of behavior, including how we treat others.

We manipulate others by using the same techniques of praise and condemnation that have been used on us. We use our wit and humor to impress people. Remember, codependents usually have excellent minds and develop strong communication skills to win acceptance. We use sarcasm to cut people to ribbons. ("Just kidding!") Of course we also use praise, anger and withdrawal to get people to do what we want them to do. These techniques worked on us; they'll work on others most of the time, too.

In our attempt to control people, we usually fall into two extremes again. On the one hand, we may try to "mother" people (in the negative sense of the word), and shape their opinions and habits by constant attention in both praise and criticism. We don't let them out of our sight for long. Or, on the same end of the scale, we may become like dictators, barking orders and exercising our real or perceived authority in their lives. On the other end of the continuum is withdrawal. A person may become so tired of trying to control others, or may feel so inadequate and worthless, that he believes no one will do what he wants them to do. His poor self-concept overcomes his desire to manipulate and he gives up.

The paradox for the codependent is that while he is trying to control others, he is still being controlled by them. He wants them to perform and appreciate him, but he still gets his self-worth from their approval. One man tried to get his wife, who was addicted to prescription drugs, to pull her act together. Her behavior might cost him a promotion. But she still had him on a string. She could be happy when she wanted, or angry or sad when she chose. That way she could get him to do almost anything for her. The rabbit was chasing the dog.

We need to take our controls off of other people. We need to let them make their own decisions and live with the consequences. We need to get our self-worth from something other than their approval of us. We need to cut the strings.

Control Inventory

■ Describe three situations in which you felt pressured to perform. Who pressured you? How did he/she pressure you? What would you have lost if you hadn't performed? How did you respond? (Use an additional sheet of paper if necessary.)

_____

_____

_____

_____

_____

_____

_____

_____

_____

_____

■ How do you feel when you are manipulated and give in?_____

_____

_____

■ How do you feel when you are manipulated and don't give in?_____

_____

_____

■ Do you try to control your schedule, your lifestyle, your emotions, etc.? If so, how? What are the results?

_____

_____

_____

_____

_____

_____

_____

■ Describe some ways that people try to control others:_____

_____

_____

_____

_____

■ How did (does) your family try to control you? In what ways is this like or unlike how you try to control others?

_____

_____

_____

_____

_____

_____

■ What are some situations in which you become passive and indecisive because you are afraid to fail?

_____

_____

_____

_____

_____

■ In what situations do you feel that you have to be right and that people have to agree with you? _____

_____

_____

_____

_____

Hurt and Anger

Anger is a God-given emotional response that we all experience on occasion. Surrendered to God and used wisely, with control, it can have a positive result. Unaided and unimpeded, anger can have tragic consequences.

Anger can be a response to unmet expectations, irritation or frustration when things don't go our way or a demonstration of hostility when someone has a different opinion. Anger also can be a defensive response to a hurtful attack or to a real or perceived threat to one's self-esteem or well-being.

Like anything else, it is okay to feel angry. What we do with it is something else. Many of us use our anger destructively rather than constructively.

Destructive anger can be expressed outwardly or inwardly; either way, it can result in depression, suspicion and a low sense of self-worth. Examples of destructive anger are verbal abuse (screaming, criticism, fault-finding), physical abuse, teasing, sarcasm, and murder. Silence, neglect, and withdrawal can also be destructive expressions of anger.

The apostle Paul wrote: *Be angry, and yet do not sin; do not let the sun go down on your anger, and do not give the devil an opportunity* (Eph. 4:26-27).

Destructive anger can have catastrophic effects on our recovery. Expressed outwardly, it can alienate us from others and drive a wedge between God and us. Without these sources of strength, affirmation and acceptance, the codependent is likely to return to his compulsive habits of rescuing, caretaking or controlling. Anger turned inward is also dangerous. The codependent has a low tolerance for the burdening effects of repressed anger. If his anger is not dealt with constructively, he may begin to feel victimized and blame others again. He also may experience an increasing sense of guilt and shame, resulting in a loss of self-worth and failure to assume responsibility for his own well-being.

Hurt and anger go hand-in-glove. Hurt is the result of not being loved, not being valued. It comes from feeling abandoned, used and condemned. Anger is our reaction toward the source of the hurt.

These painful emotions are not only products of the codependent's past, they are a part of his reality every day. The need to have a sense of worth leads him to try to rescue the one who has hurt him. Inevitably, he gets hurt again and again, and sooner or later, he gets angry.

The pain and anger within a codependent's soul are deep and black. Even a glimpse of them can seem overwhelming. Elaborate defense mechanisms are thus erected to block pain and to control anger. These defensive "layers" include a denial of reality, pleasing people, being in control, keeping people at a distance, being numb to feelings, displacing anger, excusing the offender(s) and many other variations. Some of us use different defenses for different circumstances, but most of us have developed several layers to ensure our protection.

By enabling us to block out pain and control our anger to some degree, defense mechanisms bring short-term gain. But they yield long-term losses by preventing us from beginning the healing process. We need to peel away these layers of defense mechanisms to expose our pain and anger so that we can deal with these issues.

Again, objectivity is an important step toward healing. We'll gain more insight about ourselves by examining some common ways that codependents respond to their hurt and anger:

Destructive Anger

• *Numbness - I don't want to feel this way, so I won't.* This is a personal philosophy for some of us. Our pain is too great, so we block it out. Our anger is too frightening, so we act like it's not there. We are forced to live life at the surface emotionally because what's underneath is simply too much to bear. We have superficial emotions and superficial relationships.

One young lady described her parents. They divorced when she was seven years old. Her father remarried and moved away. Her mother went to work to support her brother and her. Her father sent her gifts for a couple of years after he left, but he later faded from her life. Her mother was frazzled and frantic as an abandoned, working, single parent.

"How do you think your parents' divorce has affected you?" I asked.

"Oh, not much at all."

"Do you miss your father?"

"No, not really."

"Do you feel especially close to your mother since she's taking care of you so well?"

"Yeah, I guess so, but we're not that close."

Because she seemed a bit detached from her situation, I asked a different question. "What makes you really happy? What do you really enjoy?"

She thought for a minute. "I can't think of anything."

"What makes you really angry? What upsets you?"

"Not much," she replied blankly. "I don't feel much of anything."

Over the next several months we talked more about her past, and she began to feel more. Some of the feelings were painful. Some were pleasant. It was a mixed bag, but she was becoming more in touch with her life and her feelings.

Sometimes we conclude that since feelings are painful, they must be wrong. Although we try to make others happy, we suppress our own feelings. But there's a problem: we can't be picky about which aspects of our emotions we suppress. We can't stifle the bad feelings and enjoy the good ones. When we repress the painful feelings, we quell the enjoyable ones, too.

Some of us hurt so deeply that we believe we are totally worthless. We think we cannot possibly be worthy of someone else's love. One man who had repressed his emotions throughout his life developed some relationships with people who really cared about him. Most of the time he was numb to their affection and affirmation, but occasionally they got through to him. How did he respond? He wept and he withdrew from them. He said sadly, "It hurts too much to be loved." Sooner or later the consistent environment of love and acceptance will chip away the defensive layers this young man has developed, and he will be able to feel the pain of his past as well as the love of the present and the future.

Another way we may try to avoid pain is by staying so busy that we don't have time to reflect. We can stay numb. The theme song for those of us with this tendency is Carly Simon's, "Haven't Got Time for the Pain." When we fill our lives with activities and superficial relationships, we don't have time to feel pain.

• *Pain Without Gain* - Some of us may wish we were numb, but we aren't. We hurt. We hurt so badly we can hardly stand it. There is a feeling of being crushed, hopelessly crushed. An intense feeling of loss with no hope of gain consumes us. We feel as though we've been broken into a million pieces and there isn't any glue to fix us. No healing; only hurt.

Because we can't go through life admitting this kind of hurt to others, we put up a facade of competence and happiness. Few people ever realize the blackness that lurks beneath the neon outside.

A woman whom most people would describe as healthy and mature came to see me. She said she had to talk to somebody; that she thought she was becoming deranged. Though she has lots of friends and is considered a successful mother, business woman and church member, she was dying inside.

She described her home life. On the surface it seemed normal enough: no violence, no divorce, no addictions. Yet she described her parents' relationship as cool and aloof, like an armed truce. Their relationship with each other mirrored their relationship with her. Though there were no outward signs of dysfunction, they were, in fact, quite dysfunctional. She had been left an emotional orphan, fending for herself, lacking the love, protection and support that every child needs. As with other codependents, she tried to win love by rescuing.

She wept, "My father never held me. He never told me that I was his special little girl or anything. I want to be loved so much, but no matter what I've done to please him, I've never felt that he loves me."

In fact, this dear woman is afraid to be loved. She is afraid that if she experiences someone's affection, it may be taken away from her, and the pain would be unbearable. She wants to be loved so badly, she needs it so desperately, but she's afraid of being hurt even worse than she hurts now. That is hurt with no hope, hurt with no healing.

Many of us live with a continued sense of impending doom. We believe that we don't deserve good things happening to us. We don't deserve people to love us. When good things do happen, we may then assume that something bad will occur to balance the good. One college student explained to me that he had really enjoyed his vacation at spring break, but that his enjoyment was tempered by the prevailing belief that something very bad would happen as soon as the break was over. That gloomy assumption stole his joy from a delightful situation.

Believing that we are inherently bad people who are unworthy of love leads to self-condemnation and ultimately, to self-hatred. Some of us think and say terrible things about ourselves. We call ourselves horrible, degrading names. If we heard someone saying those same things to another person, we would describe it as hatred and abuse. We don't call it abuse when we call ourselves these names, however, because we believe that we deserve that kind of treatment.

• *Excusing the Offender/Blaming Ourselves* - Often, where there is hurt without healing, there is hurt without anger at the offender. The anger is displaced, but the offender is excused for his offense. The desire to "believe the best" of the one who has hurt us blocks our objectivity. Instead of blaming him, we blame ourselves.

• *Displaced Anger* - Codependents often express repressed anger at people or things that have nothing to do with its cause. Their anger surfaces at odd times and in odd ways.

Don's disposal broke. The motor hummed, but the carrots stayed in one piece. Being a frugal homeowner, he went to an appliance store and bought a new disposal. When he got home, he rolled up his sleeves, got out his tools and plunged into the black hole under the sink. The first part of the operation went without a hitch. The old disposal came off easily. But when he tried to put the new one on, Don found that the intake and outlet holes were in different places than on his old one. This called for some creative plumbing!

The tube from the dishwasher to the disposal wasn't quite long enough, but if the disposal could be pushed over just a little, then clamped...there! So what if it slanted to the right a little, the rubber seal at the top would keep it from leaking. But with it leaning that way, the pipe that went out of the bottom on the left wasn't long enough. If the clamp could be put on really tight it would work. Wrench, please. A tug on the pipe to pull it as close as possible, then tighten the clamp...one more turn to make it really tight and...crunch! The pipe split!

Don took his wrench and beat the stuffing out of the pipe! (It wasn't split anymore; it was pulverized!) After a few expletives, he threw his wrench into the tool box and stomped off to buy more pipe.

Now why did Don get mad at that pipe? Did it call him dirty names? Did it say ugly things about his wife, or push his little girl down on the playground? It was simple physics. The pipe is a *thing*. It had no personal vendetta against Don. Why was he so mad?

When Don was growing up, his father had never been very handy around the house. He always felt like a failure when he tried to do anything mechanical. When Don tried to work on things, his father would often stand nearby and say, "You'll mess it up. You're gonna break it. You can't do it." Hearing that once would be painful, but hearing it often and in every kind of context hurt him deeply. It made Don angry with his father, but he never said anything to him about how he felt. Don wasn't angry at the pipe. He was angry with his father. His anger at the pipe was displaced anger.

• *Outbursts of Anger* - Codependents may not only get angry at the wrong thing or person, they may also become disproportionately angry. Their suppressed anger may explode like a tube of toothpaste that is squeezed until it pops and toothpaste squirts in all directions.

• *Using Self-Pity and Anger to Manipulate Others* - Hurt and anger are powerful emotions. They affect us deeply and can be used by us as powerful forces of manipulation to get others to care about us and dance to our tune.

Ken was a deeply troubled young man who was abandoned by his mother and neglected by his father during his childhood. Hurt by his parents' neglect, his seething anger often boiled over. To win the affection (i.e., pity) of others, especially that of sensitive and caring women, Ken often would describe his horrible childhood in detail. His story of occasional abuse, abandonment and heartache won the hearts of many. He also won their admiration by describing how he now had a grip on life, despite the cards stacked against him.

When his uncontrolled, violent outbursts of anger threatened to shatter the heroic image he was portraying to others, he would say sadly, "You just don't understand. If you had parents like mine, you wouldn't be nearly as mature and stable as I am." Self-pity usually restored his place of esteem.

But anger was also a means of manipulation for Ken. People became afraid of him early in their relationships with him. A raised eyebrow or a raised tone of voice meant that you were treading on thin ice, and you'd better agree with him—or else! Both violence and the threat of violence were intimidating. Ken got what he wanted: self-pity, respect (or was it only fear?) and acquiescence.

The codependent is the product of manipulation, neglect and abuse, but he can use these powerful forces on others as well. Not all are so blatant as Ken. Most are more subtle but just as effective in eliciting the responses of pity and fear (poor counterfeits of love and respect) that they really want and need.

• *Memories* - When a person begins to get in touch with the pain of his past, he will often remember events that have long been buried in his mind and heart. The hurt and anger that these memories evoke are painful, and some people may interpret this pain as going backward. But it is progress.

Constructive Anger

In recovery, we begin to discover ways we can channel anger into positive action. Because we are releasing our grip on denial, we can more often admit feelings of anger, first to ourselves and then to God.

The biblical King David offers a good illustration of handling negative emotions like anger positively. After his anointing as king and before his induction as ruler over Israel, David was continually assaulted by his outraged, half-crazed father-in-law Saul, who was then ruler over Israel and who wanted to kill David. Under constant attack, David had every reason to be defensive and angry. Yet David was able both to honor Saul and to gain victory over his negative emotions because he had learned to express those emotions to God (see 1 Sam. 26:1-25). Psalms 42 and 58 are two of many examples of this:

> *I say to God my Rock, "Why have you forgotten me?*
> *Why must I go about mourning, oppressed by the enemy?"*
>
> Ps. 42:9-10, NIV

> *Break the teeth in their mouths, O God; tear out, O Lord, the fangs of the lions!*
> *Let them vanish like water that flows away; when they draw the bow, let their arrows be blunted.*
> *Like a slug melting away as it moves along, like a stillborn child, may they not see the sun.*
> *Before your pots can feel the heat of the thorns—whether they be green or dry—the wicked will*
> *be swept away.*
>
> Ps. 58:6-9, NIV

David used his anger constructively; it drove him to his knees. Once we can admit that we are angry, we can ask God for His direction in our response. We can call our sponsor or a friend who can add objectivity to our situation. Then, if necessary, we can confront the offender with an attitude of love.

Constructive anger can give us the momentum we need to detach from a manipulative person or a harmful situation. It can give us the incentive to confront someone in love; it can motivate us to stop acting compulsively.

As we progress in recovery, we gradually learn that anger is a gift from God, intended to compel us to provide loving correction and to confront the evils which threaten His purposes. We can only begin to do this as He intends by seeking His direction before we make our response.

Hurt and Anger Inventory

■ Why is there so much hurt and anger in a codependent's life?_____

_____

_____

_____

_____

■ What are some reasons why we try to obstruct pain and control anger?_____

_____

_____

_____

_____

■ Do you see any of the following in your life? If so, describe in detail…

• Numbness:_____

_____

_____

_____

_____

• Pain without gain:_____

_____

_____

_____

• Excusing the offender/blaming yourself:_____

_____

_____

_____

_____

_____

- Displaced anger:_____

_____

_____

_____

_____

- Outbursts of anger:_____

_____

_____

_____

_____

- Using self-pity and anger to manipulate others:_____

_____

_____

_____

_____

- Constructive anger:_____

_____

_____

_____

_____

■ Are you afraid to face hurt and anger in your life? Why or why not?_____

_____

_____

_____

_____

_____

■ In what ways do you avoid responsibility for mistakes by blaming others instead of admitting your errors? Why do you think you do this?

_____

_____

_____

_____

_____

■ Who or what can help you to be honest and express your pain in a safe environment?_____

_____

_____

_____

_____

Guilt

Codependents often feel guilty. They feel guilty for what they've done and haven't done. They feel guilty for what they've said, haven't said, felt and haven't felt. They feel guilty for just about everything. Often such guilt produces feelings of worthlessness and shame.

The codependent gets his worth—his identity—from what he does for other people. He rescues, he helps, he enables, but no matter how much he does for others, it's never enough. That's the trap of living in a dysfunctional family. He rescues, but he is rejected. Lacking objectivity he concludes: *It's my fault. If I were a better person, they would love me.* So he spends his life trying to be good enough to earn the love and acceptance he so desperately wants, but fears he will never have. And he's haunted by the shame that he hasn't, or can't, measure up.

The guilt and shame that I'm referring to are not the kind that promote an objective judgment of our offense. If you have been caught going 85 mph on the highway, and the judge pronounces, "Guilty as charged," that is objective guilt. In that sense all mankind stands before God as guilty and in need of the forgiveness and acceptance of the cross. But the guilt that we are looking at here is a different kind. It lacks objectivity. It is devoid of forgiveness. It is without love and acceptance. It is the painful, gnawing perception that you are worthless, unacceptable and can never do enough to be acceptable no matter how hard you try.

There is a vast difference between these two kinds of guilt. One produces a sorrow that leads to positive, refreshing change. The other leads to a sorrow that only crushes. The apostle Paul described positive and negative guilt in his second letter to the Corinthian believers:

> *I now rejoice, not that you were made sorrowful, but that you were made sorrowful to the point of repentance; for you were made sorrowful according to the will of God, in order that you might not suffer loss in anything through us.*
>
> *For the sorrow that is according to the will of God produces a repentance without regret, leading to salvation; but the sorrow of the world produces death.*

2 Cor. 7:9-10

The realization of personal wrong coupled with a knowledge of forgiveness brings hope and change, but the realization of personal wrong without that forgiveness brings bitter pangs of condemnation and hopelessness. In dysfunctional families, personal wrongs are magnified while forgiveness, love and acceptance are withheld. Those bitter pangs of condemnation are a way of life for the codependent.

Guilt Crushes

Guilt crushes a person. It crushes his dreams, his desires and his personality. If your worth comes only from helping others, then you can't say no to anything or anyone. If you do say no, or even if you say yes and fail (or if you succeed but others don't appreciate you), then your worth is shattered. Even success and praise bring only short-term relief. There is always the nagging fear of losing that approval. To please people, you take on their dreams and desires, not your own, and lose your personality in the process.

All of us have done things that are wrong, but a codependent attaches greater weight to those wrongs than he does to forgiveness. He is deeply ashamed, feeling that at least some of those terrible things he has done cannot possibly be forgiven.

The crushing effects of guilt, shame, worthlessness, self-hatred and self-condemnation take a heavy toll. Some people escape into a shell of numbness, passivity or depression. Some develop psychosomatic illnesses. And some just plod along, day after day year after year under the oppressive weight of guilt. There are varieties of results, but one cause: the crushing nature of guilt.

Guilt Motivates

The only way to win at life, the guilt-ridden codependent surmises, is to earn the respect of others. Lacking objectivity, that's his only choice. He feels worthless, he feels unloved and he concludes that there must be something wrong with him. He then feels guilty and is thus compelled to take action which, he hopes, will make up for his shortcomings.

The hope of gaining acceptance and the threat of losing it are powerful motivators. They prompt the codependent to rescue people who take advantage of him. They motivate him to help people who don't appreciate him. Oh, he gets a little of what he craves: some appreciation and respect. He gets just enough to keep him on the hook, but not enough to really satisfy him. So he keeps running on the endless treadmill of hope, guilt and fear.

Motivation by guilt is usually associated with the desire to avoid condemnation and the desire to perform, or measure up to standards set by someone else or ourselves. We perform with a sense of urgency and desperation because we think we *have* to, not because we *want* to. Our motivation is characterized by *I have to* and *I can't* statements:

I have to accomplish this or that task today.

I have to go here.

I have to help this person in this way at this time.

I have to say yes.

I have to control my anger and hurt.

Statements like these are the creed of the obsessive-compulsive codependent. They are the painful taunts of dismal failure to the one who has given up and withdrawn into passivity. Either way, they form the warp and woof of the codependent's mental fabric.

The capacity to say no, to make our own decisions, to relax and to enjoy life are foreign to us because they don't contribute to our consuming goal in life: the acquisition of worth.

Introspection

A codependent tries to stifle pain either by putting up a wall and refusing to think about life or by thinking about himself. All day. Everyday. In this introspective mode, he analyzes his every word, action and thought. This seems paradoxical: He devotes his life to rescuing and helping others, yet he thinks about himself all the time. But remember that his reasons for rescuing and helping are to gain a sense of worth, to be loved and to gain the respect and appreciation that he so desperately wants.

There is a great difference between reflection and morbid introspection. Reflection is based on reality. It is objective, healthy and not predisposed to condemnation. Morbid introspection is quite different. An introspective person digs through his thoughts and motives and actions with twin hopes: to find the wrong in his life so he can change it, and to find right in his life so he can feel good about himself. But this incessant digging is not objective because it does not begin with a sense of value and worth. On the contrary, it begins and continues with the underlying pessimistic assumption: *There's something very wrong with me and I've got to make it right.* With that assumption, self-condemnation dominates his thinking, but since feeling hurt and anger are not permitted (they are considered "wrong"), he internalizes these painful feelings and the downward spiral continues.

In a relationship with a pathological, compulsive person, the introspective codependent tries to rescue and enable, and then feels angry because he has been used. In his blindness, however, he justifies the behavior of the other person and blames himself in vehement terms for being so selfish that he would get angry with such a "poor sick person."

This kind of self-condemning introspection is usually followed by epithets, expletives and vicious name-calling—all directed at himself. Then, a period of days or weeks of penance—feeling bad enough for long enough—is designed to pay for his sin of selfishness. The problem with this method—aside from theological reasoning—is that there usually arises another situation, similar to the one preceding it, before penance is completed for the first alleged offense. The introspective person then finds himself doing penance for several offenses at the same time, and the load becomes oppressive indeed.

Comparison

One of the prime ingredients of introspection is comparison. A person who lacks security and significance needs some means of determining where he stands. Comparison is the perfect solution! He needs to be one step further, one notch higher, one quip wittier, a bit better looking than other people.

If the codependent can't think of enough standards to compare himself to, his dysfunctional relatives will usually help him. They will compare his clothes, his hair, his job, his children, his intellect, his athletic ability...as if he needs any help!

This comparison feeds the fantasies of the introspective codependent. He imagines himself getting accolades and promotions, having beautiful things and accomplishing great feats of daring...all just a little bigger and better than someone else's.

Guilt Makes You Crazy

Deep within our minds and hearts, we sometimes ask ourselves, *What's wrong with me? Am I crazy?* Life is so hard. Even the fun things—things that we hope and dream will bring satisfaction and relief—even those things turn out to be hard. The people who are supposed to be supportive and affirming often are critical and aloof. Were they like that already, or did we somehow make them that way? Why is *everything* so hard?

A squeeze-play is at work here. On one side, pressing against you, are all the desires and hopes and dreams of asserting yourself, being creative and having a sense of worth. On the other side is guilt for being so selfish in wanting those things. In the middle, these forces squeeze out your vitality and confidence, leaving you with feelings of confusion and self-condemnation.

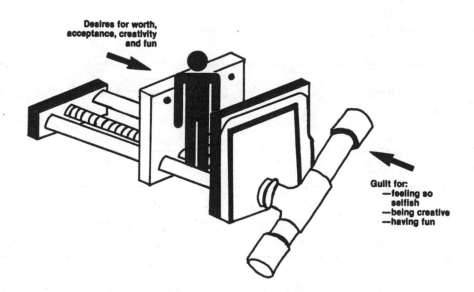

Using Guilt on Others

The law of sowing and reaping takes effect in the area of guilt just as it does in every other part of life. Like begets like, and if guilt has been used to motivate and manipulate you, you will probably use it on others. It is a strange fact that even if you detest the way you have been treated, that model is so strong that you may find yourself treating others the same way.

The same words of praise and condemnation; the same actions, tone of voice and expressions; the same aggressive, angry behavior; and the same withdrawal and passivity that are used to manipulate us are the ingredients we tend to use with others. Or, on the other end of the spectrum, instead of harshly condemning, we withdraw; instead of being passive and neglectful, we smother. A poor model will produce a poor offspring. He may be a duplicate or an opposite, but he will be out of balance either way.

Guilt is a way of life for the codependent. The nagging pain of believing, *There's something wrong with me and I've got to fix it*, is a powerful, harmful force. We need to see this for what it is: evil and destructive.

Guilt Inventory

■ Explain why codependents so often feel guilty:_____

_____

_____

_____

_____

■ What are some of the differences between the *sorrow that produces a repentance without regret* and *the sorrow that produces death?*

_____

_____

_____

_____

■ Do you see any of the following aspects of guilt in your life? If so, describe how these affect your self-concept and your relationships.

• Guilt crushes:_____

_____

_____

_____

_____

_____

• Guilt motivates:_____

_____

_____

_____

_____

_____

- Introspection:_____

_____

_____

_____

_____

_____

- Comparison:_____

_____

_____

_____

_____

_____

- Guilt makes you crazy:_____

_____

_____

_____

_____

_____

- Using guilt on others:_____

_____

_____

_____

_____

• What would your life be like if you had a strong sense of worth and were not plagued by guilt?_____

_____

_____

_____

_____

_____

_____

_____

Loneliness

Codependents spend their lives giving, helping and serving others. From the outside they may appear to be the most social people in the world, but inside they are lonely. Their attempts to please others by helping and serving are designed to win affection. Though they may occasionally see a glimpse of love and respect, it usually fades all too quickly. Then, thinking they have been abandoned by both people and God, they feel empty and companionless. They distrust authority, believing that anyone above them is against them and they build elaborate facades to hide their painful feelings of loneliness.

Abandoned by People

We feel condemned. We feel controlled. We feel confused. We feel lonely. We feel angry, but we can't say anything or we might experience even more condemnation, manipulation and loneliness. We feel hopelessly trapped.

Afraid of our emotions, we stuff them and act as if nothing is wrong. We are unwilling to say how we feel—that we are hurt and angry—because we are afraid that people will withdraw from us. We're afraid they will go away, and we'll be even more lonely. Even worse, if we don't act as if we appreciate what they say and do, they will probably get angry with us, and that risk is simply too great. We are lonely now. We don't want to feel any more so.

Although we are desperate for intimacy, we don't feel lovable, and we're afraid of losing what little warmth we already have. The combination of these factors paralyzes and confuses us. One young lady who described her loneliness, desires and fears seemed like a little girl crying, "I need help! Leave me alone!"

Abandoned by God

The unconditional love, forgiveness and acceptance of God is the message codependents need; but instead, most feel distant from Him. They feel that He, too, doesn't approve of them, and that they can't do enough to please Him no matter how hard they try.

This compounds the codependent's feelings of hopelessness, pain and loneliness because God is seen as his last hope: If He doesn't love me, who will? The codependent's view of God is almost always the same as his view of his parents. If his parents neglected him, he will feel that God doesn't care. If his parents condemned him, he will feel that God is harsh and demanding. However his parents treated him is the perception he has of God, who then is seen as part of the problem, not the solution.

Codependent Christians tend (as usual) to be one of two extremes. Their desire for intimacy with God is either squelched by a view that He is cool, distant and harsh, or they sense the love of God to an extreme depth and become "hypermystical" and feelings-oriented. As in every other area of their lives, they lack objectivity and balance, and react as extremists.

Abandoned by Authority

Codependents tend to view authority the same way they view the addicted, abusive or ill people in their lives, especially if those people are parents. They are often intensely loyal to their parents, bosses, pastors or other kinds of leaders, and in their black-or-white perception (or lack thereof), they sometimes believe that the one in authority can do no wrong. They make others omnipotent because they feel so inadequate themselves. They will put up with all kinds of mistakes until, at last, the pendulum swings and the authority figure who could do no wrong suddenly can do no right.

Beneath this is the paradox that the codependent wants to be accepted and appreciated by those who are in positions of importance and respect, so he values their opinions of him highly; in fact, too highly. He also has an innate sense that those in authority are out to get him, to use him and to manipulate him. Depending on which end of these extremes the pendulum has swung, he sees that authority as either black or white, either for or against him.

On the black side, he feels misunderstood, abused and abandoned. Even the slightest disagreement is interpreted as, *They just don't understand me! They don't care about me at all!*

Facades

People often develop facades in childhood as a survival technique. Looking calm, cheerful or tough enables them to shield their feelings. Although these facades protect them for a while, they are detrimental in the long run because they prevent the development of honest and genuine relationships.

Codependents desperately want to be understood and to feel close to others, but we're afraid. We're afraid to take the risks of involving ourselves in relationships because we might be rejected. Then we would hurt even more. To avoid this risk, to avoid more pain, we protect ourselves by appearing to be happy and well adjusted even when we are dying inside. We erect facades.

Hiding behind these facades, we don't say what we mean and we don't mean what we say. To put it bluntly, we lie a lot. We say yes, when we want to say no. We say we are just fine, when we are feeling just a step or two away from suicide. We say we want to go somewhere because we think going there will make someone else happy enough to like us, when in fact we don't want to go there at all. We get so wrapped up in other people's desires and making other people happy that we get numb and confused, and don't even know what we want! We are so busy making other people feel good that we don't even know what we feel!

We exaggerate. We make good things a little bit better so people will be a little more impressed with us, and we make bad things a little worse so people will feel sorry for us. It usually works, but it's lying.

We offer to help with a friendly smile even when we're so angry with that person we could spit nails. If our countenance slips and someone asks, "Is anything wrong?" we give an excuse that is usually partially true, but which keeps others at arms-length: "Oh, I have a headache today," or "Yeah, I'm just not having a good day, but I'm all right."

We become masterful at selling ourselves. We are enthusiastic about our jobs, our families, how well we're doing, our new hairstyles and clothes. We find something that's good and milk it for all it's worth so that people will believe we are really doing well. But in reflective moments, we realize that what we've said is a lie, that our facade is a lie— but we can't let them know the truth! As a result, we often feel dirty, guilty and alone.

Our motto becomes: *The truth hurts, so avoid it. If people knew me, they'd reject me.* So we develop elaborate and usually unconscious facades to avoid the truth and to keep people from knowing how much we hurt and how angry we really are. These facades may protect us from the risks of intimacy, but they leave us lonely. When we lock others out, we lock ourselves in.

Loneliness Inventory

■ Why does a person who devotes himself to rescuing and serving often feel lonely?_____

_____

_____

_____

■ How does a lonely person think and feel about himself?_____

_____

_____

_____

■ How does he think and feel about others?_____

_____

_____

_____

■ What are some reasons why many of us feel that taking the risk of self-disclosure and intimacy is too great?

_____

_____

_____

_____

■ In what ways do you feel:

• Abandoned by God?_____

_____

_____

_____

_____

• Abandoned by authority?_____

_____

_____

_____

_____

■ What facades do you use to keep people away? What are the results of using these?_____

_____

_____

_____

_____

The Need to Detach

When we finally observe the damage that has occurred in our lives as a result of codependency, we may be shocked by its extensiveness. It takes time and attention for healing to transpire. We need to identify that damage, reflect on the best course of action and take steps toward healing: identify, detach and decide. Let's examine some of the elements involved in healthy detachment.

Codependents are trained to react, not respond. We instinctively rescue, withdraw or attack. We feel the compassion of a rescuer while also feeling anger, hurt and self-pity. This instinct is deeply ingrained in us, but it needs to be changed. We need to detach, to separate ourselves from that codependent reaction system and take time to think, feel and reflect.

Jill invited her mother for a visit. She cleaned the house, planned the week and got her guest room in perfect shape. Soon after her mother arrived, however, she started making some "subtle" hints to Jill. "So, I see you still have those curtains." "It is hard to get dishes like that really clean, isn't it?" "Is that the same dress I gave you seven years ago?" "Oh, I'll just have to give you my recipe for this sometime!"

Jill's feelings of guilt and shame mounted with each comment. Then she realized what was happening. She had been learning about her codependency and this was a classic example. Jill went to her bedroom and wrote down how she felt and how she had responded to her mother. She realized that she didn't have to agree with her mother's insinuations about her house, her cooking, her clothes or herself. She spent some time reflecting on the contrast between her codependent identity (I'm a bad person, etc.) and her identity in Christ (unconditionally loved, forgiven, accepted, secure, etc.), and went back into the living room with a new sense of confidence. During the next several days of her mother's visit, Jill had to detach quite a few times to gain a proper perspective of her identity. Sometimes she didn't do this quickly enough, but overall, Jill began to develop a habit of detaching.

Detachment requires time, objectivity, and distance (emotionally, physically or both). Circumstances vary so widely that there cannot be a formula for detaching, but there is a question that can help you: *What do I need* (time, space, objectivity) *so that I can reflect on this situation?*

Sometimes we can identify, detach and decide in a heartbeat. This is especially true when we've had ample practice in this process. Many times, however, we need to remove ourselves from the offending person or situation to be more objective. The pressure of close proximity is simply too strong. Go to another room, take a drive in the country (under the speed limit!), go away for a weekend. Do whatever you need to do so that you can feel and think. A distraction may help you gain a sense of calm before you reflect. Read a book or magazine, watch a television show, take a walk. Do whatever helps you.

Some psychologists use detach to describe the act of isolating oneself from others in a negative, harmful way. In contrast, codependent literature uses the word to describe a positive healthy action: stepping back to obtain objectivity about a person or situation. Therefore, detachment is not the same as withdrawal, though it may appear to be at first. Withdrawal is a defensive reaction to block pain and avoid reality. Detachment has the opposite goal: to become objective, deal with reality, feel real emotions and determine the best course of action.

The Scriptures have a lot to say about reflecting on reality and truth so that we can respond wisely instead of reacting codependently. We are instructed to take time to acquire this wisdom:

> *Acquire wisdom! Acquire understanding! Do not forget, nor turn away from the words of my mouth.*
> *Do not forsake her, and she will guard you; love her, and she will watch over you.*
> *The beginning of wisdom is: Acquire wisdom; and with all your acquiring, get understanding.*
> Prov. 4:5-7

As was mentioned in step 2, a friend can sometimes be instrumental in helping us feel pain and be objective.

> *By wisdom a house is built, and by understanding it is established;*
> *And by knowledge the rooms are filled with all precious and pleasant riches.*
> *A wise man is strong, and a man of knowledge increases power. For by wise guidance you will wage war, and in abundance of counselors there is victory.*
> Prov. 24:3-6

We also can learn how to respond to people who condemn, neglect and manipulate us:

> *Do not answer a fool according to his folly, lest you also be like him.*
> *Answer a fool as his folly deserves, lest he be wise in his own eyes.*
> Prov. 26:4-5

This is just a sampling of the rich instructions offered in the Scriptures about detaching and reflecting.

Aids for Detaching

As you learn to detach so that you can be honest about your feelings and objective about your circumstances, you will see a sharpening contrast between codependent and healthy thoughts, feelings and actions. Perhaps it would be helpful to list some questions to ask yourself when you detach. These are some suggestions:

- *Why did he (she) say (do) that to me?*
- *What did he (she) mean?*
- *How do I feel about it?*
- *How would a healthy person feel?*
- *Is he (she) controlling me? Condemning me? Neglecting me?*
- *Why do I feel guilty? Driven? Afraid? Lonely?*
- *Am I rescuing?*
- *Am I acting as a savior? A Judas?*

Also, it might be helpful to develop some statements that trigger certain thinking patterns in your mind. This may seem "hokey," but getting a handle on objectivity is very difficult for codependents. Use whatever helps you! These statements may help you think and feel:

- *I'm not responsible for making him (her) happy.*
- *I'm not responsible for fixing the problem.*
- *He (she) needs to be responsible for himself (herself).*
- *I can respond calmly.*
- *I can say no.*
- *I can say yes.*
- *I can make my own decisions.*
- *I feel angry...lonely...guilty...driven...afraid.*
- *I am loved, forgiven and accepted by God through Jesus Christ.*

Soon we will be able to anticipate our need to detach, and we can practice "prevenient detachment." Prevenient means "to come before, to anticipate." Prevenient detachment means to think through the situation before it happens. Learn how to think, reflect, ask questions and be prepared for situations before they occur. Someone might think that considering a situation before it occurs is harmful introspection and vain imagining, but there is a tremendous difference between prevenient detachment and vain thoughts. Vain thoughts are based on codependent, black-or-white hopes and fears. They are not objective. Prevenient detachment is based on objectivity and truth, not unrealistic hopes and fears. One results in more blindness, more unreality and more codependent behavior. The other results in preparation, objective reality and productive steps of progress.

It is a binary trap to assume that there are only two options: either continue reacting in the same way that you have before, or stop reacting that way. It's true that you can stop, but there usually are many other options to choose from. Take some time to list some of the many possibilities. If you can anticipate awkward situations, contemplate your possible responses. To prod your thinking, ask questions such as:

- *What are realistic expectations? How does he/she usually respond to me?*
- *What do I want from this conversation (visit, encounter, etc.)?*
- *What if I do this:_____ ?*
- *What if I do that:_____ ?*
- *How can I respond if this or that happens?*

Some Perspectives on Detaching

Charting a new course for a specific situation or for a lifetime can be awkward and frightening. There are so many changes, so many emotions and seemingly, so little time. These are some perspectives on the process of detaching:

• *Detaching in love or anger* - It is best to detach calmly and with a loving attitude, but that isn't always possible. It may seem harsh or selfish to put such a premium on detachment, but being controlled by someone and pleasing him above all else is not a good thing. It is idolatry. If you have the choice either to detach in anger or in love, by all means do it in love. But by all means, detach. Melody Beattie wrote:

> *I think it is better to do everything in an attitude of love. However, for a variety of reasons, we can't always do that. If you can't detach in love, it's my opinion that it is better to detach in anger rather than to stay attached. If we are detached, we are in a better position to work on (or through) our resentful emotions. If we're attached, we probably won't do anything other than stay upset.* [2]

Anger can actually be used constructively in the process of detaching. It is a strong motivation to develop your independence and identity. Constructive anger can be seen in such thoughts as: *I refuse to be manipulated again*, or *I'm not going to take this anymore. I'm going to detach so I can develop my own identity and make my own decisions.*

• *Detaching perfectly* - Some of us are such obsessive–compulsive perfectionists that we think we have to do everything perfectly when we detach! One woman told me that she was afraid to detach because she "might not do it just right, and what would my father say if I made a mistake?" After a few minutes, she realized that this perfectionism and fear were the very reasons she needed to detach!

If we believe that we have to say and do everything perfectly when we detach, then we are still carrying an oppressive weight of responsibility. Be realistic. Detaching requires a major change in thoughts, feelings and emotions. Changes like these are not computerized. We are not robots. We are people, and people need time, practice and patience to change deeply ingrained habits.

• *Determining how a "normal" person would respond* - Drawing a comparison between our codependent reactions and the healthy responses of a "normal" person is very instructive. Some of us may recoil at this thought because our perception is that codependent people are giving and loving; "normal" people are selfish and prideful. That perception demonstrates a continued lack of objectivity about codependency. It still sees the virtue in rescuing without seeing its hidden selfishness and idolatry.

It is true that "normal" people, like all of us, are sinners who are prone to selfishness and pride, but for our purposes we are using normal to mean simply non-codependent and independent. A healthy, independent person may seem terribly selfish because he isn't controlled by the whims of others, but we don't need to label him as a terrible, awful, no good, very bad person because he makes his own decisions.

• *Expecting conflict* - When you stop playing a codependent role in your family, don't expect everybody to applaud you for your growth and development! They have lived their lives by having you rescue them as they controlled you. As they realize that you are no longer controllable, they may step up the pressure. They may use stronger manipulation: more guilt, more condemnation and more withdrawal. They may be accusing: "You are so selfish!"

When you stop playing your codependent role in the family, expect conflict; expect to be isolated from the family. As the family reforms its boundaries, family members may leave you on the outside. The fear of this isolation is the motivation that often compels codependents to continue to be used, neglected and controlled. It takes both objectivity and courage to take these bold and necessary steps.

• *Experiencing freedom, confusion and pain* - In our era of advanced technology, change can come with the push of a button. But people aren't machines. We don't make major changes quickly and effortlessly. The process of identifying, detaching and deciding produces a hodge-podge of conflicting emotions and thoughts. Like being cut free from an ocean liner that is going in the wrong direction, we have a new sense of freedom and independence. But with that freedom comes the pain of realizing how codependency has damaged your life and the confusion of not being confident and secure in your new direction.

Don't despair if you feel awkward and afraid as you learn to detach. These feelings are simply a part of the reality of change. Accept them for now. They will gradually abate as your confidence grows. You will increasingly enjoy your independence and freedom.

• *Examining the option of divorce* - For some, the pain and bitterness of their marriage makes divorce seem to be a viable, attractive form of detachment. Some counselors recommend divorce as a way to ease the pain and escape from a seemingly incorrigible relationship. This may not be the answer. A temporary separation may be in order to allow the partners to detach, get good counseling and develop biblical convictions about marriage. Too often, a hurting codependent leaves one spouse only to find another to control and rescue, and the codependent cycle continues.

This is a sticky, emotion-charged issue. The scope of this workbook doesn't include an adequate treatment of divorce, separation and remarriage. You may want to read *Jesus and Divorce*, by Bill Heth and Gordon Wenham, or *Love Must Be Tough*, by James Dobson. Before you make any major decisions about divorce, consult a competent, qualified Christian counselor or pastor.

• *Deciding if you are detached* - It would be ludicrous to say that you haven't detached until you are perfectly calm and loving in your attitudes. With detachment often comes a range of emotions which are often quite confusing in the early stages. Nonetheless, you can tell that you are detaching if you have removed yourself from situations to feel and think, if there is a growing objectivity about the contrast between codependent reactions and healthy responses, and if you are experiencing a growing sense of independence.

When you can identify your codependent feelings and behaviors, and then think clearly and objectively about them, you are detaching. Recognize your guilt, fear, rescuing and controlling tendencies, and realize that these are the pathology of codependency. Don't dabble with them. Replace them aggressively with objectivity and godly choices. Then you will be detaching.

• *Becoming attached to the Lord* - Detaching involves change: changing our perceptions, our values, our relationships, our views of ourselves and our views of others. Gradually, we become less dependent on the approval of others and grow to be more dependent on the Lord. Our relationship with Him will deepen as we realize that He is all we have longed for. He is loving and kind, strong and wise. He is not condemning, aloof and manipulative. He can be trusted.

• *Gaining the affirmation and objectivity of a consistent friend* - Detaching is difficult. It is almost impossible to do alone. Look for at least one friend to help you be objective, to encourage you and to model a healthy lifestyle for you. A true friend won't change the way he or she feels and acts toward you as you go through this difficult process. He or she will encourage you.

• *Developing habits of detaching* - Don't be too discouraged if your first attempts at detaching are painful and awkward. Drastic change takes time, patience, practice and courage. The more you try to detach, the more confident you will become and eventually, it will become a very constructive habit for you.

My friend, Jim Walter, showed me some statements that describe both the process and the product of detachment. These statements are about "letting go":

"LET GO"

to "let go" does not mean to stop caring;
it means I can't do it for someone else

to "let go" is not to cut myself off;
it's the realization that I can't control another

to "let go" is not to enable,
but to allow learning from natural consequences

to "let go" is to admit powerlessness—which means the outcome
is not in my hands

to "let go" is not to try to change or blame another;
it's to make the most of myself

to "let go" is not to "care for," but to "care about"
to "let go" is not to judge, but to allow another to be a human being

to "let go" is not to be in the middle, arranging all the outcomes, but to allow others to affect their own destinies

to "let go" is not to be protective; it's to permit another to face reality

to "let go" is not to deny, but to accept

to "let go" is not to nag, scold or argue, but instead to search out my own shortcomings and correct them

to "let go" is not to adjust everything to my desires, but to take each day as it comes, and cherish myself in it

to "let go" is not to criticize and regulate anybody, but to try to become what I dream I can be

to "let go" is not to regret the past, but to grow and live for the future

to "let go" is to fear less and love more

Detachment Inventory

■ What does it mean to detach? Why is it important to detach?_____

_____

_____

_____

_____

_____

■ What are some similarities and differences between withdrawing and detaching?_____

_____

_____

_____

_____

■ Describe some of your usual codependent responses in regard to the following:_____

• Feelings:_____

_____

_____

_____

• Thoughts:_____

_____

_____

_____

• Actions:_____

_____

_____

_____

_____

■ Make a list of questions that will help you feel and think clearly as you detach:_____

_____

_____

_____

_____

_____

_____

_____

■ Make a list of statements that will remind you of your independence and identity:_____

_____

_____

_____

_____

_____

_____

■ Think of three recent situations in which you exhibited codependent reactions. How could you have detached in each situation? What difference might it have made had you detached? Be as specific as possible as you describe your feelings, thoughts, statements and actions.

• SITUATION:_____

_____

_____

_____

- Codependent response:_____

_____

_____

_____

- Feelings:_____

_____

_____

- Thoughts and words:_____

_____

_____

- Actions:_____

_____

_____

- How detaching might have affected the situation:_____

_____

_____

- SITUATION:_____

_____

_____

_____

- Codependent response:_____

_____

_____

- Feelings:_____

_____

_____

- Thoughts and words:_____

_____

_____

- Actions:_____

_____

_____

- How detaching might have affected the situation:_____

_____

_____

- SITUATION:_____

_____

_____

_____

- Codependent response:_____

_____

_____

- Feelings:_____

_____

_____

- Thoughts and words:_____

_____

_____

- Actions:_____

_____

_____

- How detaching might have affected the situation:_____

_____

_____

- SITUATION:_____

_____

_____

_____

- Codependent response:_____

_____

_____

- Feelings:_____

_____

_____

- Thoughts and words:_____

_____

_____

- Actions:_____

_____

_____

- How detaching might have affected the situation:_____

_____

_____

■ Which "Perspective on Detaching" stood out to you? Why?_____

_____

_____

_____

■ How has your codependency affected and complicated the following areas of your life? (Use additional paper if necessary.)

• Relationships with your family:_____

_____

_____

_____

_____

• Relationships with neighbors:_____

_____

_____

_____

_____

• Relationships with co-workers:_____

_____

_____

_____

_____

• Relationship with God:_____

_____

_____

_____

_____

- Job:_____

_____

_____

_____

_____

- Finances:_____

_____

_____

_____

_____

_____

- Legal matters:_____

_____

_____

_____

_____

_____

- Health:_____

_____

_____

_____

_____

_____

- Sex:_____

_____

_____

_____

_____

_____

- Enjoyment:_____

_____

_____

_____

_____

- Fears:_____

_____

_____

_____

_____

Step Five

We admit to God, to ourselves and to another person
the exact nature of our wrongs.

Therefore, confess your sins to one another, and pray for one another,
so that you may be healed.

James 5:16a

Many of us are understandably a little squeamish about admitting our wrongs to another person. We reason, *Isn't it enough that I tell God?* I don't believe so. There are many things that we think and do before God (in private) that we would never dream of saying or doing before others (in public). There is something about our human nature which prevents us from taking action until we have confessed our struggles to another person.

By revealing ourselves to another human being, we may feel like we have everything to lose and nothing to gain. What will we lose?

- *We will lose our sense of isolation.* By confiding in another person, we are brought to a true kinship with God and man for perhaps the first time. Because the fifth step is intended to be a *dialogue*, and not a *monologue*, we will discover that we are not alone in our sinful deeds and desires. Our sense of aloneness will then begin to dissipate.
- *We will lose our unwillingness to forgive.* When we are accepted and forgiven, we realize that we can forgive others.
- *We will lose our inflated pride.* As we see and, perhaps for the first time, truly accept who we are, we will begin to gain humility, an all-important aspect of our recovery. Humility is a clear recognition of what and who we really are, followed by a greater understanding of who God is and how He relates to us.
- *We will lose our sense of denial.* Complete honesty with another person tears away any denial we still may be holding onto and confirms that we have been honest with God and with ourselves.

Confession

As Christians, it is important to understand that our confession does not make us forgiven. We are forgiven because Christ died to pay for our sins. Confession is a means for us to *experience* our forgiveness, not obtain it.

Confession should be done with an attitude of *repentance*. Repentance is not a matter of feeling sorry for ourselves because we've been caught. It is turning away from sin and turning instead to God.

Let's look at what happened to one of God's mightiest men when he turned to God under the weight of unconfessed sin.

David: Man After God's Heart

David, the shepherd, psalmist and King of Israel, was called by God "a man after My own heart." But, like all of us, David was a sinner. He committed adultery and then to cover that sin, committed murder! (See 2 Samuel 11.) What made David a man after God's heart was his attitude. He was not only remorseful about his sin, but confessed it and then repented of it. Let's look at the process of David's reconciliation to God in Psalm 32:

■ Verses 1-2: *How blessed is he whose transgression is forgiven, whose sin is covered! How blessed is the man to whom the Lord does not impute iniquity, and in whose spirit there is no deceit!*

- What word does David use to describe the one whose sin is forgiven?_____

- What does that mean?_____

■ Verses 3-4: *When I kept silent about my sin, my body wasted away through my groaning all day long. For day and night Thy hand was heavy upon me; my vitality was drained away as with the fever heat of summer.*

• What happened to David's body when he kept silent about his sin?_____

_____

• Have you seen these effects in your own life? If so, explain:_____

_____

_____

_____

■ Verse 5: *I acknowledged my sin to Thee, and my iniquity I did not hide; I said, "I will confess my transgressions to the Lord"; and Thou didst forgive the guilt of my sin.*

• What did David do about his sin?_____

• What was God's response?_____

■ Verses 6-7: *Therefore, let everyone who is godly pray to Thee in a time when Thou mayest be found; surely in a flood of great waters they shall not reach him. Thou art my hiding place; Thou dost preserve me from trouble; Thou dost surround me with songs of deliverance.*

• What does David encourage us to do about our circumstances?_____

_____

• What benefits of knowing God does David describe in the above passage?_____

_____

_____

_____

The latter part of this passage is God's response to David.

■ Verses 8-11: *I will instruct you and teach you in the way which you should go; I will counsel you with My eye upon you. Do not be as the horse or as the mule which have no understanding, whose trappings include bit and bridle to hold them in check, otherwise they will not come near to you. Many are the sorrows of the wicked; but he who trusts in the Lord, lovingkindness shall surround him. Be glad in the Lord and rejoice you righteous ones, and shout for joy all you who are upright in heart.*

• Understanding the righteous to be those who trust in God and the wicked to be those who refuse to trust in Him, what does God say will surround...

• the righteous?_____

• the wicked?_____

• Whom does God warn all of us not to be like and why?_____

_____

_____

• What does God promise to do for us when we are reconciled to Him?_____

_____

_____

_____

• What heart attitudes does God promise we will have when we are responsive to Him?_____

_____

_____

_____

Dealing with Sin: The Holy Spirit

Before we make confession, we need to know something about the Holy Spirit's work of showing us our sins. As believers, we have received the Spirit of Christ within us. This exercise will help you understand the ministry of the Holy Spirit as He convicts us of sin and guides us into truth. You also will gain insights into confession of sin.

■ Read John 14:16-17. Why do you need a Helper?_____

_____

_____

■ What do the following passages say about the role of the Holy Spirit in teaching truth to you?

• John 14:26_____

_____

• John 16:13_____

_____

• 1 Cor. 2:11-13_____

_____

■ Read 2 Tim. 3:16-17. How does the Holy Spirit use Scripture in our lives?_____

_____

■ Another role of the Holy Spirit is to convict the world concerning sin, righteousness and judgment (John 16:8-11).

• What does it mean to be *convicted*?_____

• What is the purpose of the Holy Spirit's conviction?_____

_____

_____

■ Read 1 John 1:9.

• What is *confession*?_____

_____

• Does confession make you forgiven?_____

_____

The Lord Jesus realized that once He left the world, His followers would need help. The Holy Spirit, our helper and teacher, was sent to dwell within believers and to be our source of wisdom and strength. The Holy Spirit helps us to live in a way that honors Christ by convicting us of our ungodliness. Conviction allows us to deal with sin in our lives so that we can continue to experience God's love, power and wisdom.

You may be preparing to confess your sins to God for the first time ever. If you need some help, you might use the following as a guide:

Dear Father,
The Holy Spirit has shown me that I sinned when I (name sins of thoughts and actions as specifically as possible). *Thank You that I am completely forgiven and that You choose not to remember my sins. I realize that You have declared me to be deeply loved, completely forgiven, fully pleasing, totally accepted, and a new creature—complete in Christ.   Amen.*

There are some additional insights on confession which we will benefit from as we move forward in our walk with God:

■ *All sin is against God.*
In Ps. 51:4, we find another account of David as he confessed his sin of adultery and murder before God:

Against Thee, Thee only, I have sinned, and done what is evil in Thy sight, so that Thou art justified when Thou dost speak, and blameless when Thou dost judge.

Although others had been affected by his sin, David recognized that its commission was primarily against God. In confronting David, Nathan the prophet asked, "Why have you despised the word of the Lord by doing evil in His sight?" (2 Sam. 12:9). Notice that the focus is on God, not David or others.

From this, we realize that when we have the truth of God's Word to guide us and still choose to sin, God says we are despising Him. Perhaps if before choosing to sin we would say to God, "I despise You and Your Word," we would be more aware of how sin grieves our heavenly Father.

■ *Confession recognizes the full scope of sin.*

Correct confession requires us to recognize that not only is a specific act sinful, but that the ungodly thoughts and false beliefs which generated our ungodliness are sinful as well. The excuses we might use to justify our sins are part of the ungodly thoughts that cause us to act in an ungodly manner. When dealing with sin, we must deal with the root of our actions.

■ *Confession involves accepting your forgiveness in Christ.*

All too often, Christians construct a penance cycle that they believe they must put themselves through before they can feel forgiven. Once convicted of a sin, they might plead with God for forgiveness, and then feel depressed for a couple of days just to show that they are really sorry and deserve to be forgiven.

The truth is that Jesus Christ died on the cross for our sins and has declared us justified by that deed. God not only forgives, He also forgets. Hebrews 10:17 says, *...their sins and their lawless deeds I will remember no more.*

We cannot earn forgiveness by punishing ourselves. Confession is simply an application of the forgiveness we already have in Christ. Accepting our forgiveness allows us to move on in our fellowship with the Lord and serve Him joyfully.

■ *True confession involves repentance.*

Repentance means turning away from sin and turning instead to God. When we truly repent, we have a change of attitude about sin. In fact, because repentance involves recognizing the gravity of our sin, it should grieve us as much as it does God.

■ *True confession may involve restitution.*

In confession, it may be necessary to right a wrong. You may need to go to a specific person you have wronged and ask for his or her forgiveness, return something that you stole, or fix or replace something that you damaged. Step 5 is preparation for our restitution in steps 8 and 9.

Finally, as we come before God to confess our sins, it should be with the knowledge (or reminder) that our Savior and Lord, Jesus Christ, was tempted in all areas of life just as we are. There is no temptation experienced by man that Jesus hasn't also experienced. The writer of Hebrews tells us:

> *Therefore, He had to be made like His brethren in all things, that He might become a merciful and faithful high priest in things pertaining to God, to make propitiation for the sins of the people.*
> *For since He Himself was tempted in that which He has suffered, He is able to come to the aid of those who are tempted.*
>
> Heb. 2:17-18

> *For we do not have a high priest who cannot sympathize with our weaknesses, but one who has been tempted in all things as we are, yet without sin.*
> *Let us therefore draw near with confidence to the throne of grace, that we may receive mercy and may find grace to help in time of need.*
>
> Heb. 4:15-16

• What confidence do these passages give *you* as you prepare to draw near to His throne?_____

_____

_____

_____

Choosing a Good Listener

With a better understanding of what it means to confess our wrongs to God, we are ready to analyze the best way to complete the fifth step. We begin by determining who will be the best person for us to talk with. Choosing a good listener, choosing the *right* listener is imperative for a good fifth step. In fact, this choice should be made only after prayerful consideration.

The following may be of help to you in your selection process. We urge you to pray for this person with these guidelines in mind:

■ *Choose someone who has been growing for several years or who is very familiar with both the fifth step and the issues of codependency.* A person who is familiar with this step, with recovery or with dependency issues will understand its importance for you and your recovery.

■ *Choose someone who can keep a confidence.* The information you are preparing to disclose is very personal. The person you select to talk with should be completely trustworthy in this respect.

■ *Choose an objective listener.* This is not yet the time (it may never be) to talk openly with those who are emotionally involved with us, and who may find what we have to say more than they can bear. Be considerate in this respect. Sharing is a responsibility.

■ *Choose someone who may be willing to share personal examples from his or her life with you.* The person you talk with should be a good listener, but it is often through an exchange that you will find the acceptance you especially need right now.

• List some people who might be good listeners for you:

_____   _____

_____   _____

_____   _____

_____   _____

• How will you choose the person best for you to talk with?_____

_____

_____

_____

• When will you talk to him or her?_____

_____

Telling a Story

Once we have found a good listener, we are ready to get on with the telling. We have found that this works best as a story, the story of our lives.

Perhaps the best way to begin is by taking some notes, starting from the very beginning and including those persons, circumstances and events that have affected you most along the way. You will, of course, want to refer back to your fourth step to interject other significant things you have done—positive and negative—over the years.

When you do finally sit down with the person you've chosen—your sponsor, pastor, counselor, physician or trusted friend—you may want to read from your notes or refer back to them as an outline. This is up to you. The point is to get it ALL out: everything that is significant about your life that has never been said.

As you write your story, here are some final words of caution: It has been our experience that some people who took the fifth step were disappointed because they experienced no immediate feelings of gratification afterward. A successful fifth step is not determined by feelings, but by disclosing the significant events in your life which need to be shared with another human being. We urge you to think on this *before* you take this step so that you can be realistic in your expectations.

Finally, it should be remembered that this step is for *you*. Regardless of whom we choose to share ourselves with, it is imperative to realize that our purpose in taking this step is NOT to please the listener, but to gain healing for ourselves.

Story Outline

■ What was your life like when you were a child? (Describe your relationships with your parents, brothers and sisters):

_____

_____

_____

_____

_____

_____

_____

_____

_____

_____

_____

_____

_____

_____

_____

_____

_____

_____

_____

_____

_____

■ Describe how your home life has affected you:

_____

_____

_____

_____

_____

_____

_____

_____

_____

_____

_____

_____

_____

_____

_____

_____

_____

_____

_____

■ How has rescuing and controlling others given you a sense of self-esteem and power?

_____

_____

_____

_____

_____

_____

_____

_____

_____

_____

_____

_____

_____

_____

_____

_____

_____

_____

_____

_____

_____

■ Go back through the questions in step four, and explain in detail how codependency has affected...

• your self-esteem:

_____

_____

_____

_____

_____

_____

_____

_____

_____

_____

_____

_____

_____

_____

_____

_____

_____

_____

- your relationships with your family:

_____

_____

_____

_____

_____

_____

_____

_____

_____

_____

_____

_____

_____

_____

_____

_____

_____

_____

_____

_____

_____

• your relationships with your friends:

_____

_____

_____

_____

_____

_____

_____

_____

_____

_____

_____

_____

_____

_____

_____

_____

_____

_____

_____

_____

• your job:

_____

_____

_____

_____

_____

_____

_____

_____

_____

_____

_____

_____

_____

_____

_____

_____

_____

_____

_____

_____

- your values:

_____

_____

_____

_____

_____

_____

_____

_____

_____

_____

_____

_____

_____

_____

_____

_____

_____

_____

_____

_____

_____

Step Six

*We commit ourselves to obey God, desiring that He remove
patterns of sin from our lives.*

*Humble yourselves, therefore, under the mighty hand of God, that He may exalt
you at the proper time, casting all your anxiety upon Him, because He cares for you.*
1 Pet. 5:6-7

The idea of obeying the Lord can be frightening for a codependent. Through the lenses of over-responsibility, perfectionism, repressed emotions and guilt motivation, the beauty of an intimate relationship with Christ is distorted. Instead of gaining a sense of belonging, trust and affirmation, the codependent perceives the Christian message as one of more demands, more condemnation and more guilt. Consequently, he feels driven and lonely.

Before we look at a picture of lordship, let's take a glance at some of the perspectives many codependent believers share about Christ and the Christian life:

God is mean. Many of us do not believe that God has our best interests at heart. We think He only wants to use us. We may "serve" Him with many activities, but that service is done out of fear that He will punish us if we don't do exactly what He wants.

The Lord demands too much of me. Overly-responsible codependents fear that they can't measure up to the extremely high expectations of the Christian life. We are motivated by the double-edged sword of fear that we can't meet those expectations and guilt that we have failed. We may give lip service to grace and forgiveness, but experience few of these freedoms and positive motivations.

I'm already trying as hard as I can; what more can I do? Similarly, the codependent feels anger as well as guilt at what he perceives is the demanding nature of God. Often, however, he channels his anger toward a person, church or organization because he doesn't feel like he can be angry with God.

I don't want to lose control of my life. Living his life by controlling every detail, activity and emotion, the codependent believer finds it extremely difficult to turn over that control to another person—even the Lord.

God will make me weird. Codependents are already lonely. They already feel strange and distant from others. The stories of those who take a stand for Christ and suffer ridicule do not entice many to sign up!

I can gain worth by serving God. As a flip side to these perspectives, some codependents see Christian service as a means of gaining security and worth. Instead of backing away from a "radical" Christian commitment, they plunge headlong into Christian activities in the hope of gaining recognition from others. Often, these people experience the same feelings of fear and guilt, but their thirst for approval drives them to take the risks of performing for acceptance.

If God loves me, He won't ask me to do anything hard. Codependents often read the Scriptures selectively, picking out passages that soothe, but overlooking passages that seem to feed their guilt motivation. As a reaction to the fear and guilt they have felt in their lives, some codependent believers focus entirely on one aspect of the character of God—His love—and can't see the balance of good motivations in the Scriptures.

The cumulative weight of some or all of these misguided perceptions is very destructive for believers who are in the grip of codependency. We make inaccurate conclusions about God (that He is demanding, harsh or aloof) and about ourselves (that we can never measure up, or that we can gain a sense of worth by serving Him).

A Biblical Picture of Lordship

The Scriptures, however, present a very different picture of the lordship of Christ. One of the most helpful metaphors is of believers being bond-servants to God. Writers of the New Testament often used this idea to describe their relationship with Christ. Paul, James and Peter each described himself as a "*bond-servant* of Jesus Christ" (Rom. 1:1; Phil. 1:1; Titus 1:1; James 1:1 and 2 Pet. 1:1). What does the term mean? And how can it help us to get a better picture of our relationship with the Lord?

Moses described it in Exodus 21:

> *Now these are the ordinances which you are to set before them. If you buy a Hebrew slave, he shall serve for six years; but on the seventh he shall go out as a free man without payment... But if the slave plainly says, " I love my master, my wife and my children; I will not go out as a free man," then his master shall bring him to God, then he shall bring him to the door or the doorpost. And his master shall pierce his ear with an awl; and he shall serve him permanently.*
>
> Ex. 21:1-2; 5-6

Becoming a bond-servant was based on two issues: the master's character and the slave's new identity. When it was time for the slave to be freed (verse two), the slave had a choice. If his master had been harsh, he could go free, but if he had experienced the love, protection and provision of his master, he could choose to remain with him in a new relationship. The master would put a hole in the slave's ear, signifying to everyone that the slave had freely chosen to remain in the care of the master. At that point, the slave became a bond-servant. His identity changed. His relationship with the master changed. His motivations changed. Instead of being *forced* to serve, he had *chosen* to serve. The love of the master compelled him to remain and to serve with joy, love and respect. There existed "want-to," not "have-to" motivations based on the character of the master.

These twin motivations of love and respect are too often foreign to codependents. We may use these words, but we usually mean guilt and fear instead. As usual, we lean toward one of two extremes in our response to God (or our perception of Him). We tend to respond either in fear without love, or love without respect. This chart demonstrates these extremes as well as the balanced biblical motivations:

Fear without Love	Love and Respect (Biblical Fear)	Love without Respect
Condemnation, guilt, loneliness, withdrawal, or drivenness.	The love of God and the awesome character of God motivate us to know, love, obey, and serve Him.	It doesn't matter what we do; God still loves us, so we can do whatever we want to do.

As we have seen, the typical codependent responses to distortions about God result in fear, withdrawal, guilt or drivenness to achieve a sense of worth or some combination of these. The biblical picture of being a bond-servant, however, is based on a sense of belonging, a sense of being loved, and responding to the Master in affection and obedience because His character elicits both love and respect.

Idolatry: A Major Roadblock

Codependent Christians have a major roadblock that hinders their experience of the love and power of God. Many times in these pages we have seen how codependents try to get their sense of worth from rescuing, controlling and serving others. We value the approval, the affection and the respect of people because we have believed that their affirmation will give us the security and worth that we long for. We are guilty of the same sin that the Pharisees were. Jesus reproved them, ...*for they loved the approval of men rather than the approval of God* (John 12:43). I don't mean to be too harsh, but we need to call this what it is: *idolatry.*

Any time a person tries to get his security and value from someone or something other than the Lord, it is idolatry. When we attempt to control other people or to secure power and approval by serving, we are putting ourselves in God's place. The surrender of manipulative control and the acceptance of God's grace are central to the Christian faith,[1] but as we have seen, the codependent usually tries to control his own life and the lives of others. He doesn't want to give up control; he wants more control. Almost as a truism of codependency, codependents serve to control, gain power and approval. Therefore, that service is idolatrous.

"Wait a minute!" someone might say. "What about Jesus? The Bible says that He came to serve. Was He codependent? Was His service idolatrous?"

Yes, Jesus did, in fact, serve. He served more than anyone ever has or ever will, but He definitely was not codependent. He offered His help, but He let people make their own decisions. He let them walk away, and at one point all of the multitude, except for the twelve disciples, abandoned Him. He spoke the truth and let people respond however they chose. In the garden of Gethsemane, He was completely objective about His ordeal of suffering. He didn't repress His emotions. Even when He was abandoned by the twelve, he continued to do the Father's will.

There are two dominant motivations to serve: one is to gain a sense of worth. That is idolatry. The other motivation is entirely different. It is serving out of appreciation for God's grace and your worth in Him. The first motivation results in fear, guilt, withdrawal and drivenness. The second results in love, trust and joyful obedience.

■ Are you afraid of Christ's becoming the Master of your life? If so, why? How do you normally respond to Him?

_____

_____

_____

_____

_____

■ How would responding to the Lord as His *bond-servant* change your relationship with God and your service for Him?

_____

_____

_____

_____

■ Describe ways that rescuing and controlling are idolatrous:_____

_____

_____

_____

_____

■ Describe ways that you either withdraw from others in fear or are driven to serve them to prove your worth:

_____

_____

_____

_____

_____

■ What are some ways an idolater can be transformed into a bond-servant? Be specific:_____

_____

_____

_____

_____

_____

■ Picture in your mind the process of the transformation mentioned in the preceding question. As you visualize that process, describe what you see:

_____

_____

_____

_____

Motivations for Obedience

God's love and acceptance of us is based on His grace, His unmerited favor, not on our ability to impress Him through our good deeds. If we are accepted on the basis of His grace and not our deeds, why *should* we obey God? According to scriptural principles, there are at least six proper motivations for obedience:

Christ's Love

When we experience love, we usually respond by seeking to express our love in return. Our obedience to God is an expression of our love for Him (John 14:15, 21), which comes from an understanding of what Christ has accomplished for us on the cross (2 Cor. 5:14-15). We love because He first loved us and clearly demonstrated His love for us at the cross (1 John 4:16-19). This great motivating factor is missing in many of our lives because we don't really believe that God loves us unconditionally. We expect His love to be conditional, based on our ability to earn it.

Our experience of God's love is based on our perception. If we believe that He is demanding or aloof, we will not experience His love and tenderness. Instead, we will either be afraid of Him or angry with Him. Faulty perceptions of God often prompt us to rebel against Him.

Our image of God is the foundation for all of our motivations. As we grow in our understanding of His unconditional love and acceptance, we will increasingly want our lives to bring honor to the One who loves us so much.

■ Does the love of Christ compel you to obey Him? Why or why not?_____

_____

_____

_____

Sin Is Destructive

Satan has effectively blinded man to the painful, damaging consequences of sin. The effects of sin are all around us, yet many continue to indulge in the pleasure-seeking and rampant self-centeredness that cause so much anguish and pain. Satan contradicted God in the Garden when he said, "You surely shall not die!" (Gen. 3:4). Sin is pleasant, but only for a season. Sooner or later, it will result in some form of destruction.

Sin is destructive in many ways. Emotionally, we can experience guilt and shame as well as the fears of failure and punishment. Mentally, we may experience painful flashbacks and expend enormous amounts of time and energy thinking about our sins and rationalizing our guilt. Physically, we may suffer psychosomatic disorders or a number of illnesses, some of which may result from our codependency. Relationally, we can alienate ourselves from others. Spiritually, we grieve the Holy Spirit, lose our testimony, and break our fellowship with God. The painful and destructive effects of sin are so profound that why we don't have an aversion to it is a mystery!

■ Read the first chapter of Jonah. List the results of Jonah's choice of disobedience to God:_____

_____

_____

■ In what ways have you seen specific effects of a particular sin in your life?_____

_____

_____

_____

■ How can viewing sin as destructive be a motivation for being obedient to God?_____

_____

_____

_____

Satan is a master of deception and subtlety. He whispers promising suggestions to us. When these thoughts first enter the mind, they hint only at the possibility of forthcoming pleasure, not devastating consequences. While God does allow us to be tempted—something we have no control over—He has given us His Word and His Spirit so that we can resist Satan and live in obedience to Him.

■ Read James 4:7-8 and 1 John 4:4. What comforts do you receive from these passages? _____

_____

_____

■ What are some ways you can resist Satan's attacks of temptation in the future?_____

_____

_____

The Father's Discipline

Another purpose of the Holy Spirit is to convict us of sin. Conviction is a form of God's discipline, which serves as proof that we have become sons of God (Heb. 12:5-11). It warns us that we are making choices without regard to either God's truth or sin's consequences. If we choose to be unresponsive to the Holy Spirit, our heavenly Father will discipline us in love. Many people do not understand the difference between discipline and punishment. The following chart shows their profound contrasts:

	PUNISHMENT	DISCIPLINE
SOURCE:	God's Wrath	God's Love
PURPOSE:	To Avenge a Wrong	To Correct a Wrong
RELATIONAL RESULT:	Alienation	Reconciliation
PERSONAL RESULT:	Guilt	A Righteous Lifestyle
DIRECTED TOWARD:	Non-Believers	His Children

Jesus bore all the punishment we deserved on the cross; therefore, we no longer need to fear punishment from God for our sins. We should seek to do what is right so that our Father will not have to correct us through discipline, but when we are disciplined, we can remember that God is correcting us in love. His discipline leads us to righteous performance, which is a reflection of the righteousness of Christ.

• Do you sometimes confuse God's correction with punishment? If so, why?_____

_____

_____

_____

• How can understanding God's discipline be a motivation for you to obey Him?_____

_____

_____

_____

God's Commands for Us Are Good

God's commands are given for two good purposes: to protect us from the destructiveness of sin and to direct us in a life of joy and fruitfulness. We have a wrong perspective if we only view God's commands as restrictions in our lives. Instead, we must realize that His commands are guidelines, given so that we might enjoy life to the fullest. In addition,

God's commands are holy, right and good. Therefore, since they have value in themselves, we should choose to obey God and follow His commands.

Avoid trying to keep God's commands by legalism and self-effort. That leads only to bitterness, condemnation and rigidity. The Holy Spirit will give you power, joy and creativity as you trust Him to fulfill the commands of God's Word through you.

■ Read Rom. 7:12 and 1 John 5:3. How are God's commands described?_____

_____

_____

■ Read Deut. 5:29; 6:24. What are some results of obeying God's commands?_____

_____

_____

■ How can viewing God's commands as good motivate you to obey them?_____

_____

_____

_____

Our Obedience Will Be Rewarded

Our self-worth is not based on our performance and obedience; however, what we do (or don't do) has tremendous implications on the quality of our lives and our impact on others for Christ's sake. Disobedience results in spiritual poverty; a short-circuiting of intimate fellowship with the One who loves us so much that He died for us; confusion, guilt and frustration; and an absence of spiritual power and desire to see people won to Christ and become disciples. On the other hand, responding to the love, grace and power of Christ enables us to experience His love, joy and strength as we minister to others, endure difficulties and live for Him who has ...*called us out of darkness into His marvelous light* (1 Pet. 2:9). We are completely loved, forgiven and accepted apart from our performance, but how we live is very important!

■ Read 1 Cor. 3:11-15; 2 Cor. 5:10; 1 John 4:17 and Rev. 20:11-15. According to these passages, unbelievers will be judged and condemned at the Great White Throne of Judgment for rejecting Christ. Though believers will be spared from this condemnation, we will stand before the Judgment Seat of Christ to have our deeds tested. Deeds done for the Lord will be honored, but deeds done for ourselves will be destroyed by fire. The Greek word to describe this judgment seat is the same word used to describe the platform on which an athlete stands to receive his wreath of victory for winning an event. The Judgment Seat is for the reward of good deeds, not for the punishment of sin.

The following chart demonstrates some of the differences between the Judgment Seat of Christ and the Great White Throne Judgment:

	JUDGMENT SEAT OF CHRIST (1 Cor. 3:11-15)	GREAT WHITE THRONE OF JUDGMENT (Rev. 20:11)
WHO WILL APPEAR:	Christians	Non-Christians
WHAT WILL BE JUDGED:	Deeds	Deeds
PERSONAL RESULT:	Reward	Condemnation
ULTIMATE RESULT:	Used to honor Christ	Cast out of God's presence into the lake of fire

■ Read 1 Cor. 9:24-27 and 2 Tim. 2:3-7; 4:7-8. How does receiving a reward become a motivation for obedience?

_____

_____

_____

Christ Is Worthy

Our most noble motivation for serving Christ is simply that He is worthy of our love and obedience. The apostle John recorded his vision of the Lord and his response to His glory:

> After these things I looked, and behold, a door standing open in heaven, and the first voice which I had heard, like the sound of a trumpet speaking with me, said, "Come up here, and I will show you what must take place after these things."
>
> Immediately I was in the Spirit; and behold, a throne was standing in heaven, and One sitting on the throne.
>
> And He who was sitting was like a jasper stone and a sardius in appearance; and there was a rainbow around the throne, like an emerald in appearance.
>
> And around the throne were twenty-four thrones; and upon the thrones I saw twenty-four elders sitting, clothed in white garments, and golden crowns on their heads. . . .
>
> And when the living creatures give glory and honor and thanks to Him who sits on the throne, to Him who lives forever and ever,
>
> the twenty-four elders will fall down before Him who sits on the throne, and will worship Him who lives forever and ever, and will cast their crowns before the throne, saying,
>
> "Worthy art Thou, our Lord and our God, to receive glory and honor and power; for Thou didst create all things, and because of Thy will they existed, and were created."
>
> Rev. 4:1-4, 9-11

Each time we choose to obey, we express the righteousness we have in Christ. Our performance, then, becomes a reflection of who we are in Him, and we draw on His power and wisdom so that we can honor Him.

■ Read 1 Cor. 3:16-17 and 1 Pet. 2:9. How are you described?_____

_____

_____

_____

■ What purposes for our lives do these passages suggest?_____

_____

_____

_____

■ How much are you motivated by each of these six reasons to obey God? Reflect on these motivations and rate ea on a scale of zero (no motivation to you at all) to ten (a persistent, conscious, compelling motivation):

_____ The love of Christ motivates us to obey Him.
_____ Sin is destructive.
_____ The Father will discipline us if we continue in a habit of sin.
_____ His commands for us are good.
_____ We will receive rewards for obedience.
_____ Christ is worthy of our obedience.

■ Do any of these seem "purer" or "higher" to you? If so, which ones? Why?_____

_____

_____

_____

_____

■ Which of these do you need to concentrate on? What can you do to develop this motivation further?

_____

_____

_____

_____

Improper Motivations for Obedience

Jesus repeatedly emphasized that His concern is not only what we do, but why we do it. The Pharisees obeyed many rules and regulations, but their hearts were far from the Lord. Motives are important! The following represent some poor motivations for obeying God and their possible results:

Someone May Find Out

Many people obey God because they are afraid of what others will think of them if they don't obey. Allen went on church visitation because he feared what his Sunday school class would think if he didn't. Barbara was married, but wanted to go out with a man at work. She didn't because of what others might think.

There are problems with determining behavior solely on the opinions of others. First, there are times when no one is watching. If the motive to refrain from sin is missing, we may indulge in it. A second problem is that our desire to disobey may eventually exceed the peer pressure to obey. Finally, once someone has found out we've sinned, we may no longer have a reason to obey.

■ Is the "fear of someone finding out" a motivation for you to obey God? If it is, identify the specific sin you are trying to avoid; then go back over the six reasons to obey Him. Which of these proper motives seems to encourage you most in regard to your specific sin?

_____

_____

God Will Be Angry with Me

Some people obey God because they think He will get angry with them if they don't. We've already discussed the difference in God's discipline and punishment, but to reiterate, God disciplines us in love, not anger. His response to our sin is grief, not condemnation (Eph. 4:30).

Hank was afraid that God would "zap" him if he did anything wrong, so he performed for God. He lived each day in fear of God's anger. Predictably, his relationship with the Lord was cold and mechanical.

God doesn't want us to live in fear of His anger, but in response to His love. This produces joyful obedience instead of fear.

■ If you knew that God's response to your sin was grief instead of anger, would that affect your motivation to obey Him? Why or why not?

_____

_____

_____

_____

I Couldn't Approve of Myself if I Didn't Obey

Some people obey God in an attempt to live up to certain standards they've set for themselves. Sadly, the idea of yielding their lives to a loving Lord is often far from their minds. They are only trying to live up to their own standards, and if they don't meet those standards, they feel ashamed. These people are primarily concerned with do's and don'ts. Instead of an intimate relationship with God, they see the Christian life as a ritual, with the key emphasis on rules. If these people succeed in keeping the rules, they often become prideful. They may also tend to compare themselves with others, hoping to be accepted on the basis of being a little bit better than someone else.

Phillip was raised in a strict church family. He was taught that cursing is a terrible sin. All of Phillip's friends cursed, but he never did. He secretly thought that he was better than his friends. The issue with Phillip was never what God wanted or God's love for him. Instead, it was his own compulsion to live up to his standards. Phillip needed to base his behavior on God and His Word, not on his own standards.

God gave us His commands out of love for us. We are protected and freed to enjoy life more fully as we obey Him.

■ What things are you not doing because you couldn't stand yourself if you did them? What are you doing to obey God with the motivation to meet your own standards?

_____

_____

I'll Obey to Be Blessed

God doesn't swap marbles. If our sole motive to obey is to be blessed, we are simply attempting to manipulate God. The underlying assumption is: *I've been good enough...bless me*. It's true that we will reap what we sow. It's true that obedience keeps us within God's plan for us. But our decision to obey should never be based solely on God's rewarding us.

Brian went to church so that God would bless his business, not because he wanted to worship God. Cheryl chose not to spread gossip about Diane because she had told God that she wouldn't tell anybody about Diane if He would get her the promotion she wanted.

Similarly, we may try to bargain with God, saying, *I'll obey You if You will "fix" me*. We reason that if we are "fixed," we will be better equipped to serve God (and we'll be freed from having to deal with a particular problem or temptation). However, God sometimes has something important to teach us through a particular weakness.

The apostle Paul entreated the Lord three times, asking Him to remove a "thorn," or difficulty, from him. The Lord responded to him: *My grace is sufficient for you, for power is perfected in weakness* (2 Cor. 12:9). Paul concluded: *Most gladly, therefore, I will rather boast about my weaknesses, that the power of Christ may dwell in me. Therefore I am well content with weaknesses, with insults, with distresses, with persecutions, with difficulties, for Christ's sake; for when I am weak, then I am strong* (2 Cor. 12:10).

■ Do you try to make deals with God? Why or why not? _____

_____

_____

_____

■ How can you apply Paul's words to overcoming codependent thinking and behavior? _____

_____

_____

_____

■ To any other situation? _____

_____

Christ has freed us from the bondage of sin so that we can respond to Him in obedience. We have discussed six biblical reasons to be involved in good works:

1. The love of Christ motivates us to obey Him.
2. Sin is destructive.
3. The Father will discipline us.
4. His commands for us are good.
5. We will receive rewards.
6. Obedience is an opportunity to honor God.

There are times when our feelings seem to get in the way of our obedience. We may want to indulge in some particular sin, or we may be afraid of failure or what someone might think of us. We may be selfish or maybe just tired. But the Lord never said pleasant emotions were a prerequisite for following Him. He said, "If anyone wishes to come after Me, let him deny himself (and the right to pleasant emotions), and take up his cross daily, and follow Me" (Luke 9:23). This doesn't mean we should deny our emotions, whether they are positive or negative. We should express them fully to the Lord, telling Him how we feel, and then act in faith on His Word. But spiritual growth, character development and Christian service should not be held hostage by our emotions. God has given each of us a will and we can choose to honor the Lord in spite of our feelings.

In different situations, we will draw upon different motivations for obedience. Sometimes we will need to be reminded of the destructiveness of sin in order to choose righteousness. At other times we will be truly overwhelmed by God's love and want to honor Him. Either way, it is our underlying motive which determines if our actions are done to honor God or to make us more acceptable to Him, to others or ourselves.

■ Are your emotions prompting you to postpone obedience in any area of your life? If yes, what area(s)?

_____

_____

_____

■ What steps of action do you need to take to obey the Lord?_____

_____

_____

_____

As you become more aware of correct motives for obedience and begin to identify improper motivations in your life, you may think, *I've never done anything purely for the Lord in my whole life!* You may feel a sense of pain and remorse for your inappropriate motives. But try not to demean yourself for your past attitudes...they are common to all of us. Instead, realize that the Lord wants you to make godly choices today so that you can enjoy the benefits of those decisions in the future. Then ask the Holy Spirit to help you develop a sense of intensity about these choices, as Paul wrote, ...*we have as our ambition...to be pleasing to Him* (2 Cor. 5:9).

Your motives won't become totally pure until you see the Lord face to face (1 John 3:2), but the more you grow in your understanding of Him and relationship with Him, the more you will desire to honor Him with your love, loyalty and obedience.

Deciding

Obedience is largely an act of one's will. It is possible for us to detach, to feel, to think and to consider our options, but then to be immobilized and not make any decisions at all. After we have reflected, we need the courage to act in positive, healthy ways. We need to *stop* rescuing and controlling, and *start* saying and doing those things that reflect independence, security, strength and health. This is extremely important, both for our own sake *and* for the sake of those we typically rescue and control.

In the remainder of this step, we will examine a process that you can use to help you take steps toward emotional and relational health. The process has four components: making independent choices, setting limits, surrendering control of others and enjoying life.

Making Independent Choices

When we detach and become objective, we are able to admit how we feel. We can be angry, sad, glad or afraid in a safe environment. And we are able to consider our options and make the best choice. Then we can act in confidence.

When we aren't sure of what to do, or when we feel pressured to react, we often use evasive language. A good friend of mine nailed me on this. Michael and I spent a lot of time together several years ago in Missouri. One day, another person asked me if I wanted to go to a party. I really didn't want to go, but to be polite (actually, to avoid offending the person and therefore avoid rejection) I said, "We'll see." Mike piped up and said, "When Pat says, 'We'll see,' he really means 'no'." Touche! Making independent choices also means making honest statements, not using evasive language or double-talk. It is saying what we mean and meaning what we say.

Setting Limits

A vital part of healthy living is recognizing our limitations and setting realistic limits in our relationships with others. My friend, Mark Baker, has a very helpful analogy about the lack of limits in a codependent's life. He says that every person is given a piece of land when he is born, but a codependent allows people to take water from the property, cut down its trees and trample its pasture. In fact, he encourages people to take advantage of his land, all in the hope of winning their approval. When his house has been burned, his crops and pastures trampled, and everything has been stolen, he finally gets angry and determines to set limits. At first, he doesn't let anyone even set foot on his property. He guards it with his rifle to be sure no one takes advantage of him again. After he has rebuilt his home, planted new crops and become established again, he will be more willing to let people on his land. Even then, he will ensure that others do not take advantage of him.

Codependent behavior has very few limits. We feel responsible for everyone and everything. We try to help everybody. We feel guilty about everything. But as our sense of identity, independence and objectivity grows, we will quickly realize that we can't continue life without limits. We need to set limits clearly and firmly, such as:

- This is what I will do. This is what I won't do.
- I will not take this kind of behavior anymore.
- I'm not responsible for his (her) happiness.
- I refuse to be manipulated.
- I'm sorry, I wish I could help you, but I can't.
- Why did you say that to me? Do you know how I feel when you say things like that?
- I don't want to talk about this.
- I want to talk about this.

Instead of anticipating the needs of others and jumping in to rescue them, you can listen patiently and wait for them to ask for your help. Then you can make a decision about whether to help or not. Often, people explain their troubles and wait for you to volunteer to help without even being asked. (That's what you've done before!) If others want help, let them ask for it; then you can make an objective decision.

"This seems so selfish!" someone might say about setting limits. "They need me! What about being a servant and going the extra mile?" Again, the question is: What is a rescuing, compulsive, codependent reaction to others' needs, and what is a healthy, independent, loving response? Inherent in this compulsive sense of being needed is the idea that *It's all up to me*, and *If I don't help him, who will?*

Can the Almighty, Omnipotent, Sovereign Lord take care of that person you are so determined to rescue? Are you so indispensable that you take the place of God? You may, indeed, be hindering that person's development of responsibility and independence by continually rescuing him. And you may also be blocking his, as well as your own dependence on God to provide and protect. It's not up to you! The Lord can take care of that person, and He can take care of you as you learn to identify, detach and objectively decide to be independent of compulsive rescuing.

Stop Controlling Others

Just as you are seeking to make your own independent decisions, give other people the freedom to make their own choices. Don't try to control them. Too often we have tried to control the attitudes and behavior of others by praise and condemnation. Since most people live for acceptance, our manipulation has often worked. Now, as you are learning to be independent and make your own decisions, you can help others to do the same.

Calmly and clearly let people know what the consequences of their decisions will be. Love them, encourage them, but let them know that their choices make a difference. Instead of yelling or withdrawing, say something like, "That hurt me a lot. If you say things like that to me, it will hurt our relationship," or, "If you continue to treat me that way, I don't want to see you," or, "Until you have proven that you are responsible, I won't trust you to do this or that."

The pattern of controlling with praise and condemnation, anger and withdrawal, and overt expressions or subtle gestures is used extensively on children. It works most of the time, but the intensity is usually raised as the child tests his limits and gets used to each level of manipulation. Calm, loving discipline is much different from codependent manipulation, allowing the child to develop much needed responsibility and learn the consequences of his own behavior. Trying to control him through praise and condemnation may prevent his ability to see situations clearly and make objective decisions. In adulthood, he will probably treat his children the same way. The cycle will then continue.

Some of the consequences of codependent living are difficult, both for us and for those in our families. Years of alcohol or drug addiction can result in the reality of financial collapse. Bitterness, manipulation and lying often result in broken relationships and estrangement. The emotional trauma of guilt, hurt, anger and loneliness are deep wounds that aren't easily mended. There are no quick and easy answers to these problems, but we can pick up the pieces, find a friend to help us and trust the Lord to give us a fresh start.

Enjoying Life

Enjoying life is the fourth component in the process of developing emotional and relational health. As we grow in our independence and objectivity, we will begin to feel free and spontaneous. Instead of being driven to please others— and often being disappointed by their response—we will begin to experience unconditional love from God and from a new set of friends. We will begin to enjoy life, really enjoy life!

Many of the things that have seemed so desperately important will fade in their importance. Love, intimacy, spontaneity, and new goals and dreams will take their places. The perverted self-denial that characterized our lives will change to healthy giving and receiving. One man told me that anytime he was offered something, even ice cream, his first response was to refuse it. "Why?" I queried. "I'm not sure," he said. "I guess I just didn't think I was worthy of receiving a gift or having fun." Now he's learning to value himself, to give freely and to receive with freedom and gratitude. He's beginning to enjoy life.

What would you enjoy? What have you withheld from yourself because you deem yourself as unworthy? What goals and dreams can replace the driven and compulsive desires of codependency? What can you do this week (today!) just for the fun of it? Go out to dinner. Buy a game. Go to a movie. Buy a canoe. (I did!) Take a vacation. Tell a joke. Laugh. Help somebody because you *want* to. Dream new dreams. Make new friends. Relax. (This may sound like prosperity theology or blatant hedonism, but it's not. The encouragement for a guilt-ridden, overly responsible person to relax and have some fun is meant to give balance and health to his life, not hedonism.)

For Additional Reflection and Application

■ Name some differences between codependent and independent choices:_____

_____

_____

_____

_____

_____

_____

_____

■ What does the Lord want you to do about your codependency? In your relationships?_____

_____

_____

_____

_____

■ Make a list of statements that will enable you to set and maintain limits. How will these help you?

_____

_____

_____

_____

_____

■ List some benefits of stating consequences instead of controlling people:_____

_____

_____

_____

_____

■ In what ways do you enjoy life? In what ways do you not enjoy life?_____

_____

_____

_____

_____

■ How can you apply the three ingredients: _identify_, _detach_ and _decide_ today?_____

_____

_____

_____

_____

■ Write several statements on a 3x5 card to help you take some practical steps to act in a strong, healthy way. Consider having one statement from each of the four components of the decision-making process in this step.
Examples:
- *Give my opinion (without vacillating) to my mother.*
- *If John asks me to lend him more money, I will say no.*
- *I am not going to tell Suzanne how to act. She needs to make her own choices.*
- *I'm going to ask Fred to tell me a joke today.*
- *I'm going out to lunch.*

_____

_____

_____

_____

    Keep this 3x5 card with you to remind you to act in a strong, independent and healthy way. Change the statements on the card whenever you want to and after a while, you will develop a habit of making independent choices, setting limits, surrendering your control of others and enjoying life more.

Step Seven

*We humbly ask God to renew our minds so that our codependent patterns can
be transformed into patterns of righteousness.*

*And do not be conformed to this world, but be transformed by the renewing of your mind, that
you may prove what the will of God is, that which is good and acceptable and perfect.*
                                                                            Rom. 12:2

One of the major difficulties in overcoming codependency is the problem of distorted thinking. Dysfunctional families have provided a fertile environment for confusion and delusion. This step is designed to help us examine our thinking process so we can see substantive, positive changes in the way we think about God, others and ourselves.

Renewing Our Minds

Although the Spirit of Christ lives within us and enables us to evaluate our experiences, our minds tend to dwell on worldly thoughts instead of on God's truth. Why?

Since the Fall, man's mind has been darkened (Eph. 4:17-19), and he has chosen to believe the lies of Satan instead of the truths of God's Word. Satan's lies are a direct result of his character:

*...He (Satan) was a murderer from the beginning, and does not stand in the truth, because there
is no truth in him. Whenever he speaks a lie, he speaks from his own nature; for he is a liar, and the
father of lies.*
                                                                            John 8:44

Satan's goal is to keep our minds unrenewed so that our lives won't be transformed. He does this by establishing fortresses of deception, destructive belief systems that are reinforced over the years by the thoughts, emotions and actions they produce.

Solomon wrote, *As* (a man) *thinks within himself, so he is* (Prov. 23:7). Our thoughts usually affect the way we feel, the way we perceive others and ourselves, and ultimately, the way we act. The way we think can determine whether we will live according to God's truth or the world's value system. Writing to the Christians in Rome, Paul explained the serious implications of how we think:

*And do not be conformed to this world, but be transformed by the renewing of your mind, that you
may prove what the will of God is, that which is good and acceptable and perfect.*
                                                                            Rom. 12:2

Although the way we think often affects the way we feel (and thus, the way we act), it is also true that feelings affect our thoughts and behavior, and that our behavior can affect our feelings and our thinking. In other words, the relationship between thinking, feeling and acting is not always unidirectional. Our thoughts, emotions and behaviors are dependent on each other; none exists in a vacuum. However, because beliefs can play a powerful role in shaping our behavior, we will use a model adapted from psychologist Albert Ellis's Rational Emotive Therapy as a starting point for further consideration of their effect on our lives. A simple explanation of this approach is:

Situations

⇩

Beliefs ⇨ **Thoughts** ⇨ **Emotions** ⇨ **Actions**

We often interpret the situations we encounter through our beliefs. Some of these interpretations are conscious reflections; most of them, however, are based on unconscious assumptions. These beliefs trigger certain thoughts, which in turn stimulate certain emotions, and from these emotions come our actions. In order for an emotion to persist, our belief system must continue to produce certain thoughts. For example, we often will not stay sad without continuing to think sad thoughts. Think of it in this way: Our minds contain deeply held beliefs and attitudes which have been learned through our environment, experiences and education. These beliefs and attitudes produce thoughts which reflect how we perceive the events in our lives. These thoughts, then, combined with past experiences, relationships and patterns of behavior, are often the source of our emotions, and our emotions then become the launching pad for our actions.

False Beliefs

If what we believe about ourselves is founded on the truth of God's Word, we are likely to have a positive sense of self-esteem. However, as we mentioned in step 2, Satan has deceived most of mankind by convincing us that:

Our Self-Worth = Performance + Others' Opinions

The four false beliefs we included there serve as a summary of the many lies Satan tells us. These beliefs are listed again below. To what extent are you affected by them? Estimate the percentage which you think indicates how much you live by each belief from zero to 100 percent:

____% *I must meet certain standards in order to feel good about myself.*

____% *I must have the approval of certain others (boss, friends, parents) to approve of myself. If I don't have their approval, I can't feel good about myself.*

____% *Those who fail are unworthy of love and deserve to be blamed or condemned.*

____% *I am what I am. I cannot change. I am hopeless. In other words, I am the sum total of all my past successes and failures, and I'll never be significantly different.*

The chart on the following two pages identifies each belief with its consequences, God's specific solution and the increasing freedom we will gain by living out His solution.

FALSE BELIEFS	CONSEQUENCES OF FALSE BELIEFS
I must meet certain standards in order to feel good about myself.	The fear of failure; perfectionism; being driven to succeed; manipulating others to achieve success; withdrawing from healthy risks
I must have the approval of certain others to feel good about myself.	The fear of rejection; attempting to please others at any cost; being overly sensitive to criticism; withdrawing from others to avoid disapproval
Those who fail (including me) are unworthy of love and deserve to be punished.	The fear of punishment; propensity to punish others; blaming self and others for personal failure; withdrawing from God and fellow believers; being driven to avoid punishment
I am what I am. I cannot change. I am hopeless.	Feelings of shame, hopelessness, apathy, inferiority; passivity; loss of creativity; isolation, withdrawing from others

GOD'S SPECIFIC SOLUTION	RESULTS OF GOD'S SOLUTION
Because of *justification*, we are completely forgiven and fully pleasing to God. We no longer have to fear failure.	Increasing freedom from the fear of failure; desire to pursue the right things: Christ and His kingdom; love for Christ
Because of *reconciliation*, we are totally accepted by God. We no longer have to fear rejection.	Increasing freedom from the fear of rejection; willingness to be open and vulnerable; able to relax around others; willingness to take criticism; desire to please God no matter what others think
Because of *propitiation* we have the capacity to experience God's love deeply. We no longer have to fear punishment or punish others.	Increasing freedom from the fear of punishment; patience and kindness toward others; being quick to forgive; deep love for Christ
Because of *regeneration*, we have been made brand new, complete in Christ. We no longer need to experience the pain of shame.	Christ-centered self-confidence; joy, courage, peace; desire to know Christ

We will now examine these false beliefs with God's solution for each one:

The Performance Trap

The false belief, *I must meet certain standards in order to feel good about myself*, results in a fear of failure. How affected are you by this belief? Take the following test to determine how strongly you fear failure.

Fear of Failure Test

Read the following statements. Look at the top of the test and choose the term which best describes your response. Put the number above that term in the blank beside each statement.

1	2	3	4	5	6	7
Always	Very Often	Often	Sometimes	Seldom	Very Seldom	Never

____ 1. Because of fear, I often avoid participating in certain activities.

____ 2. When I sense I might experience failure in some important area, I become nervous and anxious.

____ 3. I worry.

____ 4. I have unexplained anxiety.

____ 5. I am a perfectionist.

____ 6. I am compelled to justify my mistakes.

____ 7. There are certain areas in which I feel I must succeed.

____ 8. I become depressed when I fail.

____ 9. I become angry with people who interfere with my attempts to succeed, and as a result, make me appear incompetent.

____ 10. I am self-critical.

_____ Total (Add up the numbers you have placed in the blanks.)

Interpretation of Score

If your score is...

57-70

God has apparently given you a very strong appreciation for His love and unconditional acceptance. You seem to be free of the fear of failure that plagues most people. (Some people who score this high are either greatly deceived, or have become callous to their emotions as a way to suppress pain.)

47-56

The fear of failure controls your responses rarely or only in certain situations. Again, the only major exceptions are those who are not honest with themselves.

37-46

When you experience emotional problems, they may relate to a sense of failure or some form of criticism. Upon reflection, you will probably relate many of your previous decisions to this fear. Many of your future decisions will also be affected by the fear of failure unless you take direct action to overcome it.

27-36

The fear of failure forms a general backdrop to your life. There are probably few days that you are not affected in some way by this fear. Unfortunately, this robs you of the joy and peace your salvation is meant to bring.

0-26

Experiences of failure dominate your memory and have probably resulted in a great deal of depression. These problems will remain until some definitive action is taken. In other words, this condition will not simply disappear; time alone cannot heal your pain. You need to experience deep healing in your self-concept, in your relationship with God and in your relationships with others.

Effects of the Fear of Failure

In the following exercise, we will examine the effects of the fear of failure, which stems from the false belief, *I must meet certain standards in order to feel good about myself.*

■ List two recent situations in which your performance did not measure up to the standard you had set for yourself. Identify the standard you felt you needed to meet. Then try to remember what thoughts and emotions accompanied each occasion, and the actions you took that reflected those thoughts and feelings:

Example

- Situation: *I failed to make a sale.*

- Standards: *I must meet my quota to feel good about myself.*

- Thoughts: *I'm a failure. I'll never make my quota. I'll never get promoted. I'll probably be fired any day now.*

- Emotions: Fear, anger, depression

- Actions: *I avoided my boss for three days. I yelled at my wife and kids, taking out my anger on them.*

- SITUATION: _____

  _____

- Standards: _____

  _____

- Thoughts: _____

  _____

- Emotions: _____

  _____

- Actions: _____

  _____

- SITUATION: _____

  _____

- Standards: _____

  _____

- Thoughts: _____

  _____

- Emotions: _____

  _____

- Actions: _____

  _____

■ Do you see any patterns reflected in your emotions and actions? If so, what are they?_____

  _____

  _____

■ Why do people use performance as a measurement of personal worth?_____

  _____

■ Do you have to be successful in order to feel good about yourself?_____

- What would you have to be or do to feel like you are a success?_____

  _____

  _____

- In what area(s) would you *never* allow yourself to fail? _____

  _____

■ Through what roles or activities (including Christian service) are you trying to gain a greater sense of self-worth?

  _____

  _____

  _____

■ Does performing these activities make you more pleasing to God?_____

■ How has your desire to meet certain standards affected your compulsive tendencies?_____

  _____

  _____

■ How does your desire to meet your performance standards affect your relationships with others?_____

_____

_____

_____

■ How do you feel toward those who hinder your ability to meet your standards?_____

_____

_____

_____

■ What do you do to avoid failure?_____

_____

_____

_____

■ How do you think your life would be different if you did not experience the fear of failure?_____

_____

_____

_____

The fear of failure is like stacking marbles—a very difficult task, but not any more difficult than trying to win the performance game. When we evaluate ourselves by our performance, we're ultimately going to lose no matter how successful we are at the moment.

If we believe that our self-worth is based on our success, we will try to avoid failure at all costs. Most of us have become experts at avoiding failure. We attempt only those things in which we are confident of success. We avoid those activities where the risk of failure is too great. We spend time around those who are not a threat to us. We avoid people who, either by their greater success or by their disapproval of us, make us feel like failures. We have trained ourselves very well!

Another consequence of having to meet certain standards in order to feel good about ourselves is a rules-dominated life. Many of us know people who have a set of rules for everything, and who always place their attention on their performance. However, the focus of the Gospel is on relationships, not regulations. Christ's exercise of His lordship in our lives is dependent on our attending to His moment-by-moment instruction. Focusing only on rules will relegate our lives to the prison of self-examination.

On the other hand, we may be feeling very good about ourselves because we are winning the performance game. We may be so talented that we are reaching virtually every goal we have set for ourselves. We can't afford to mistake this pride for positive self-worth. We must realize that God is able to bring about whatever circumstances are necessary to cause us to stop trusting in ourselves. God intends to bring us to Himself through prayer and the study of His Word so that we can know, love and serve Him. Sometimes He will allow us to fail miserably so that we will look to Him instead of to ourselves for our security and significance. Before becoming upset that God would allow you to experience failure, remember that any life less than God intended is a second-class existence. He loves you too much to let you continue to obtain your self-esteem from the empty promise of success.

God's Answer: Justification

As a result of Christ's death on the cross, our sins are forgiven and God has imputed Christ's righteousness to us. We have been *justified* by Christ. Therefore, we are fully pleasing to God.

■ Read Rom. 3:19-28; 4:4-5; 5:1-11. What does it mean to be *justified*?_____

_____

_____

■ Read 2 Cor. 5:21; Col. 1:22; 3:12 and Heb. 10:14. Are you as righteous, holy and blameless as Christ? Why or why not?

_____

_____

■ Read Rom. 3:9-23; 5:6-10 and Eph. 2:1-3. Why did you need to be justified and have Christ's righteousness attributed to you? Describe God's view of you before your justification:

_____

_____

_____

■ How was your justification accomplished?

• Rom. 3:24; Titus 3:7 _____

_____

• Rom. 3:28; Gal. 2:16 _____

_____

• Rom. 5:1; Gal. 3:24 _____

_____

• Rom. 5:9; Heb. 9:22 _____

_____

■ What are the results of justification?

• Rom. 4:7-8 _____

_____

• Rom. 5:1 _____

_____

• Rom. 5:9 _____

_____

• Rom. 8:1, 33-34 _____

_____

• 2 Cor. 5:14-15 _____

_____

• 2 Cor. 5:21 _____

_____

• Titus 3:7: _____

_____

■ Read Rom. 4:6-8 and Heb. 10:17. Are you remembering sins that God has forgotten? If so, why?

_____

_____

• Does remembering sin help you in any way? If so, how?_____

_____

_____

■ How does being justified and having Christ's righteousness lead you to the conclusion: *I am completely forgiven by God, and am fully pleasing to Him*?

_____

_____

■ If your good works won't make you more pleasing to God, why should you be involved in good works? (See Rom. 6:12-13; 1 Cor. 6:18-20; Col. 3:23-24 and Titus 2:11-14.)

_____

_____

■ Read 1 Cor. 3:11-15. What will determine whether or not a deed will honor God? (See also Rom. 14:23 and 1 Cor. 10:31.)

_____

_____

■ Review the situations you described on pages 142-143. Using one of the occasions you listed, chart how your behavior would have been different if you had believed the truth that *you are completely forgiven by God, and are fully pleasing to Him*, rather than the false belief, *I must meet certain standards in order to feel good about myself.*

• SITUATION: _____

_____

• Belief: *I am completely forgiven and fully pleasing to God.*

• Thoughts:_____

_____

• Emotions:_____

_____

• Actions:_____

_____

■ Memorize Rom. 5:1.

If we base our self-worth on our ability to meet standards, we will try to compensate, either by avoiding risks or by trying to succeed no matter what the cost. Either way, failure looms as a constant enemy. But God has a solution for the fear of failure! He has given us a secure self-worth totally apart from our ability to perform. We have been justified, placed in right standing before God through Christ's death on the cross, which paid for our sins. But God didn't stop with forgiving us; He also granted us the very righteousness of Christ!

Visualize two ledgers: on one is a list of all your sins; on the other, a list of the righteousness of Christ. Now exchange your ledger for Christ's. This exemplifies justification—transferring our sin to Christ and His righteousness to us. In 2 Cor. 5:21, Paul wrote: *He made Him* (Christ) *who knew no sin to be sin on our behalf, that we might become the righteousness of God in Him.*

Justification carries no guilt with it, and has no memory of past transgressions. Christ paid for all our sins at the cross—past, present and future. Hebrews 10:17 says, *And their sins and their lawless deeds I will remember no more.* We are completely forgiven by God! In the same act of love through which God forgave our sin, He also provided for our righteousness: the worthiness to stand in His presence.

By imputing righteousness to us, God attributes Christ's worth to us. The moment we accept Christ, God no longer sees us as condemned sinners. Instead, we are forgiven, we receive Christ's righteousness and God sees us as creatures who are fully pleasing to Him.

God intended that Adam and his descendants be righteous people, fully experiencing His love and eternal purposes. But sin short-circuited that relationship. God's perfect payment for sin has since satisfied His righteous wrath, enabling us again to have that status of righteousness and to delight in knowing and honoring the Lord.

God desires for those of us who have been redeemed to experience the realities of His redemption. We are forgiven and righteous because of Christ's sacrifice; therefore, we are pleasing to God in spite of our failures. This reality can replace our fear of failure with peace, hope and joy. Failure need not be a millstone around our necks. Neither success nor failure is the proper basis of our self-worth. Christ alone is the source of our forgiveness, freedom, joy and purpose.

Approval Addict

Living by the false belief, *I must be approved by certain others to feel good about myself*, causes us to fear rejection continually, and to conform virtually all of our attitudes and actions to the expectations of others. How are you affected by this belief? Take the following test to determine how strongly you fear rejection.

Fear of Rejection Test

Read the following statements. Look at the top of the test and choose the term which best describes your response. Put the number above that term in the blank beside each statement.

1	2	3	4	5	6	7
Always	Very Often	Often	Sometimes	Seldom	Very Seldom	Never

____ 1. I avoid certain people.

____ 2. When I sense that someone might reject me, I become nervous and anxious.

____ 3. I am uncomfortable around those who are different from me.

____ 4. It bothers me when someone is unfriendly to me.

____ 5. I am basically shy and unsocial.

____ 6. I am critical of others.

____ 7. I find myself trying to impress others.

____ 8. I become depressed when someone criticizes me.

____ 9. I always try to determine what people think of me.

____ 10. I don't understand people and what motivates them.

_____ Total (Add up the numbers you have placed in the blanks.)

Interpretation of Score

If your score is...

57-70

God has apparently given you a very strong appreciation for His love and unconditional acceptance. You seem to be free of the fear of rejection that plagues most people. (Some people who score this high are either greatly deceived, or have become callous to their emotions as a way to suppress pain.)

47-56

The fear of rejection controls your responses rarely or only in certain situations. Again, the only major exceptions are those who are not honest with themselves.

37-46

When you experience emotional problems, they may relate to a sense of rejection. Upon reflection, you will probably relate many of your previous decisions to this fear. Many of your future decisions will also be affected by the fear of rejection unless you take direct action to overcome it.

27-36

The fear of rejection forms a general backdrop to your life. There are probably few days that you are not in some way affected by this fear. Unfortunately, this robs you of the joy and peace your salvation is meant to bring.

0-26

Experiences of rejection dominate your memory and have probably resulted in a great deal of depression. These problems will persist until some definitive action is taken. In other words, this condition will not simply disappear; time alone cannot heal your pain. You need to experience deep healing in your self-concept, in your relationship with God and in your relationships with others.

Effects of the Fear of Rejection

The following exercise is designed to help you understand the fear of rejection and the resulting false belief, *I must be approved by certain others to feel good about myself.*

■ Are you adversely affected by anyone's disrespect or disapproval? If so, list those individuals or groups:

_____

_____

_____

_____

■ To see how others' expectations can affect you, select one of the people in the first question and answer the following:

• _____would be more pleased with me if I would:

   a) _____

   b) _____

   c) _____

• _____is proud of me when I:

   a) _____

   b) _____

   c) _____

• How does_____attempt to get me to change by what he or she says and does?

   a) _____

   b) _____

   c) _____

- Things I do or say to get_____to approve of me include:

  a)   _____

  b)   _____

  c)   _____

  (Use a separate sheet of paper for each of the people or groups you listed on page 149.)

- ■ List several specific instances when others (friends, boss, parents) have withheld approval, or have used criticism, silence or sarcasm to manipulate you into doing what they wanted you to do. What did they say or do? Did they succeed? Why or why not?

  - _____

    _____

    _____

  - _____

    _____

    _____

    _____

  - _____

    _____

    _____

  - _____

    _____

    _____

■ What belief is rooted in the fear of disapproval?_____

■ How has the fear of rejection influenced your moral standards (drinking, drug abuse, theft, lying, sexual behavior, lifestyle, etc.)? Can you recall specific instances in your life when this fear has greatly influenced your morals? If so, list them. How did the fear of rejection affect your behavior?

_____

_____

_____

_____

■ If you run from rejection, who is really in control of your life?_____

■ How have you used disapproval, silence, sarcasm or criticism to get others to do what you wanted them to do?

_____

_____

_____

■ How did you use alcohol or drugs to get others to do what you wanted them to do?_____

_____

_____

_____

■ Sometimes, rather than praising others because we genuinely appreciate them, we use praise as a form of manipulation. Our motive is to influence them to do something we want them to do.

• How do you feel when people praise you only to manipulate you?_____

_____

_____

• Have you used praise to manipulate others? If so, why, and how have you used it?_____

_____

_____

_____

• How could manipulating others by praising them be considered a form of rejection?_____

_____

_____

For whatever reason and to whatever degree we have experienced rejection, our fear of going through that pain again can affect us profoundly. We learn how to deal with physical injury early in life, but because emotional pain is sometimes perceived as a sign of weakness, and because we have not learned how to respond appropriately to this pain, we avoid it. If we are hurt, we may attempt to deny our pain by ignoring it. We may drive ourselves to accomplish tasks which we think others will approve of. Some of us can't say no for this reason. Or, we may become passive, withdrawing from others and avoiding those decisions and activities which others might criticize, or which can't guarantee success for us. Our goal in these instances is usually to avoid the pain of rejection by not doing anything which might be objectionable, but this also prevents us from enjoying the pleasures of healthy relationships and achievements.

Other behaviors related to the fear of rejection include:

1. being easily manipulated
2. being hypersensitive to criticism
3. defensiveness
4. hostility toward others who disagree with us
5. superficial relationships
6. exaggerating or minimizing the truth to impress people
7. shyness
8. passivity
9. nervous breakdown

Evaluating our self-worth by what we and others think of our performance leads us to believe that any time our performance is unacceptable, we are unacceptable as well. To some extent, virtually all of us have internalized the following sentence into our belief system, and hold to it with amazing tenacity: *I must have acceptance, respect and approval in order to have self-worth.* This is the basic false belief behind all peer pressure.

Rejection can be communicated in a number of ways. We can easily see how criticism, sarcasm and silence convey this message, but it may not be quite so obvious that praise can also serve as a form of manipulation and is, therefore, a form of rejection. We must ask ourselves what we are trying to accomplish when we praise someone. What is our goal? If we desire to help the person, to build him or her up, and to instill encouragement through appreciation, then praise is a godly form of communication. If, however, our desire is to get someone else to assist in accomplishing our goals, to contribute to our program or to help us look good in front of others, then praise is a subtle but powerful form of rejection. Unfortunately, many people—including us—fall prey to this manipulative praise because we so desperately want to be appreciated, and will often do whatever it takes to get it from others.

If you realize that you manipulate others through praise, confess it as sin and choose to seek their good instead of your goal. Be willing to ask, *What am I trying to accomplish?* in your interaction with others, and strive to communicate genuine, heartfelt appreciation because Christ has given them worth by sacrificing His life for them.

There are four basic levels of acceptance and rejection. Understanding these will help you understand the nature of your relationships with other people, concerning both how you are treated and how you treat them. These levels center around the question: *What does one have to do to be accepted?* These levels are:

1. *Total Rejection*: "No matter what you do, it's not good enough." Example: relationships characterized by deep bitterness or hurt.
2. *Highly Conditional Acceptance*: "You must meet certain requirements to be accepted." Examples: most jobs, relationships with demanding people.
3. *Mildly Conditional Acceptance*: "I will be more happy with you if you do these things." Examples: most marriages, most parent-child relationships, most friendships.
4. *Unconditional Acceptance*: "I love you and accept you no matter what you do. There is nothing you can do that can make me stop loving you." (This does not mean that we can do as we please or that we are to ignore unacceptable behavior in others. Unconditional acceptance may include loving confrontation, correction, and in some cases, discipline. The focus here is on the individual rather than his or her behavior.) Examples: God, and typically, relationships in which one person's needs are not dependent on the other's.

■ Make a list of the major relationships in your life: family members, friends, people in your school, office, church, etc. How does each of these people tend to treat you? How do you tend to treat each of them? How should you respond to each of them? How can you put fewer demands and conditions on your acceptance of them?

_____

_____

_____

_____

_____

_____

_____

_____

_____

_____

God's Answer: Reconciliation

God's answer to the pain of rejection is reconciliation. Christ died for our sins and restored us to a proper relationship with God. We are both acceptable to Him and accepted by Him. We are not rejected! We are His.

■ Define *reconcile*. (Use a dictionary if necessary). _____

_____

• Who caused the alienation in your relationship with God (Is. 53:6; 59:2; Rom. 3:9-12)?_____

_____

■ Read Eph. 2:1-3 and 2 Thess. 1:8-9. How severe was the barrier between you and Holy God?_____

_____

■ Read Col. 1:21-22. Compare your former state to your present condition in Christ:_____

_____

_____

■ Read Rom. 5:8-11. Who initiated restoring your relationship with God?_____

• How did God reconcile you to Himself?_____

_____

• What is your response to God? (What does it mean to *exult*?)_____

_____

_____

■ What is wrong with the statement, *Thank You, Lord, for accepting me even though I am so unacceptable?*

_____

_____

• Are you currently acceptable?_____

• To what degree are you acceptable?_____

• To whom are you acceptable?_____

• Why are you acceptable?_____

■ If you are completely and fully accepted by the perfect Creator of the universe, why is it still so painful to be rejected by other people?

_____

_____

■ Read John 17:19-26 and 20:17 to see the extent of your reconciliation to God.

• Whom does the Father love more: Jesus Christ or you?_____

• How does Christ refer to you in John 20:17?_____

• How do these verses make you feel?_____

_____

■ Can you think of two recent situations in which you felt rejected, or in which someone disapproved of something you said or did? If so, list them. Describe your response. How would your response have been different if you had believed the truth of your total acceptance in Christ?

• SITUATION:_____

_____

• Your Response:_____

_____

• How Believing the Truth Would Have Changed Your Response:_____

_____

_____

• SITUATION:_____

_____

• Your Response:_____

_____

• How Believing the Truth Would Have Changed Your Response:_____

_____

_____

■ Memorize Col. 1:21-22.

When God chose to redeem us so that we could relate to Him and rule with Him, He did not go part way. He did not make us partially righteous, nor has He allowed for our righteousness to be marred by poor performance. The blood of Christ is sufficient to pay for all sin. Because of His blood, we are holy and righteous before God, even in the midst of sin. This does not minimize the inherent destructiveness of sin, but it glorifies the indescribable sacrifice of Christ.

There is no biblical tenet more neglected in its practical application than the doctrine of reconciliation. The Colossians reference to this doctrine reveals its application to us:

> *And although you were formerly alienated and hostile in your mind, engaged in evil deeds,*
> *yet He has now reconciled you in His fleshly body through death, in order to present you before*
> *Him holy and blameless and beyond reproach. . . .*
>
> Col. 1:21-22

Relish those last words. God sees us as *holy and blameless and beyond reproach* at this very moment. This is not merely a reference to our future standing; it describes our present status as well. We are totally accepted by God.

God received us into a loving, intimate, personal relationship the moment we placed our faith in Christ. We are united with God in an eternal and inseparable bond (Rom. 8:38-39). We are born of God in an indissoluble union as fellow heirs with Christ. Recognizing that no sin can make a Christian unacceptable to God is God-honoring faith in a blood-sealed warrant with the Holy Spirit, *who is given as a pledge of our inheritance, with a view to the redemption of God's own possession*... (Eph. 1:14).

Since our relationship with God was bought entirely by the blood of Christ, no amount of good works can make us more acceptable to Him. Titus 3:5 says: *He saved us, not on the basis of deeds which we have done in righteousness, but according to His mercy*. . . . Because Christ has reconciled us to God, we can experience the incredible truth, *We are totally accepted by and acceptable to God.*

What should we do when we have failed or when someone disapproves of us? A practical way of summarizing the truth we've examined is: *It would be nice if _____ (my boss liked me, I could fix the refrigerator, my complexion were clear, James had picked me up on time, or...), but I'm still deeply loved, completely forgiven, fully pleasing, totally accepted and complete in Christ.*

This statement doesn't mean that we won't feel pain or anger. We need to be honest about our feelings. A statement like the one above is simply a quick way to gain God's perspective on whatever we are experiencing. It is not magic, but it enables us to reflect on the implications of biblical truth. We can apply this truth in every difficult situation, whether it involves someone's disapproval, our own failure to accomplish something or the failure of another person. Memorize the truth in the above statement and begin to apply it in your situations and relationships.

The Blame Game

This false belief, *Those who fail (including me) are unworthy of love and deserve to be punished,* is at the root of our fear of punishment and our propensity to punish others. How deeply are you affected by this lie? Take the test below to determine how much it influences your life.

Fear of Punishment/Punishing Others Test

Read the following statements. Look at the top of the test and choose the term which best describes your response. Put the number above that term in the blank beside each statement.

1	2	3	4	5	6	7
Always	Very Often	Often	Sometimes	Seldom	Very Seldom	Never

_____ 1. I fear what God might do to me.

_____ 2. After I fail, I worry about God's response.

_____ 3. When I see someone in a difficult situation, I wonder what he or she did to deserve it.

_____ 4. When something goes wrong, I have a tendency to think that God must be punishing me.

_____ 5. I am very hard on myself when I fail.

_____ 6. I find myself wanting to blame others when they fail.

_____ 7. I get angry with God when someone who is immoral or dishonest prospers.

_____ 8. I am compelled to tell others when I see them doing wrong.

_____ 9. I tend to focus on the faults and failures of others.

_____ 10. God seems harsh to me.

_____ Total (Add up the numbers you have placed in the blanks.)

Interpretation of Score

If your score is...

57-70

God apparently has given you a very strong appreciation for His unconditional love and acceptance. You seem to be free of the fear of punishment that plagues most people. (Some people who score this high are either greatly deceived, or have become callous to their emotions as a way to suppress pain.)

47-56

The fear of punishment and the compulsion to punish others control your responses rarely or only in certain situations. Again, the only exceptions are those who are not honest with themselves.

37-46

When you experience emotional problems, they may tend to relate to a fear of punishment or to an inner urge to punish others. Upon reflection, you will probably relate many of your previous decisions to this fear. Many of your future decisions will also be affected by the fear of punishment and/or the compulsion to punish others unless you take direct action to overcome this tendency.

27-36

The fear of punishment forms a general backdrop to your life. There are probably few days that you are not affected in some way by the fear of punishment and the propensity to blame others. Unfortunately, this robs you of the joy and peace your salvation is meant to bring.

0-26

Experiences of punishment dominate your memory, and you probably have experienced a great deal of depression. These problems will remain until some definitive plan is followed. In other words, this condition will not simply disappear; time alone cannot heal your pain. You need to experience deep healing in your self-concept, in your relationship with God, and in your relationships with others.

Effects of the Fear of Punishment and Propensity to Punish Others

This exercise will help you understand the fear of punishment and the false belief, *Those who fail are unworthy of love and deserve to be blamed and condemned.*

■ Do you really deserve to feel good about yourself? Why or why not?_____

_____

■ Describe three recent incidents in your life in which you feared being blamed or punished. What prompted this fear?

1. _____

_____

_____

2. _____

_____

_____

3. _____

_____

_____

■ Do you spend much time thinking about your weaknesses and failures? If so, why? (List as many reasons as you can.)

_____

_____

_____

• What are the three most negative terms you use to describe yourself? What derogatory names do you call yourself?

_____

■ Does condemning yourself help you to be a better person? Why or why not?_____

_____

_____

■ Think of a close friend or family member with whom you've had a conflict.

  • What did you say or do to inflict emotional pain? _____

_____

_____

_____

  • What are some reasons you said or did those things? _____

_____

_____

_____

■ After sinning, do you ever believe you have to feel badly about yourself before you can feel good about yourself? If so, list some of the situations in which you've done this:

_____

_____

_____

_____

■ Do you want to go to the Father after you've sinned? Why or why not? _____

_____

■ If something goes wrong, do you assume the Lord is punishing you? _____

■ Does God punish His children? _____

    The proof of blame's effectiveness is that we use it so often. We often believe that we deserve to be blamed for any significant shortcoming, and think self-inflicted punishment will clear us of guilt and enable us to feel good about ourselves again. Why?

    We have been conditioned to accept personal blame or condemnation every time our performance is unsatisfactory. After reading this, some people immediately recognize this automatic response in their lives, but others do not. You may think that you are not affected by this false belief at all—but you probably are. Do you generally have an urge to find out who is at fault when something fails? Do you look for excuses when you fail?

    Rather than evaluating our problems objectively, most of us tend to defend ourselves. Counterattack triggers counterattack. The more we criticize other people, the more defensive they usually get, and the less likely they are to admit their errors (especially to us). Criticism can lead to a counterattack from both sides, and pretty soon it's like a volleyball game, with each person intensifying the pace while returning blame to the other person's side.

    However, it is sometimes even more destructive for people to accept blame without defending themselves. Tom was becoming an emotional zombie under his wife's incessant condemnation, but instead of fighting back, he kept thinking, *Yes, Suzanne's right. I am an incompetent fool.* He was like the worn-out punching bag of a heavyweight fighter.

Both self-inflicted punishment and the compulsion to punish others result from the false belief: *Those who fail are unworthy of love and deserve to be blamed and condemned.*

God's Answer: Propitiation

At the cross, God poured out His wrath against sin. This exercise will help you see that God's wrath has been satisfied; therefore, we have no need to fear punishment.

■ Define *propitiation*. (Use a dictionary if necessary)._____

_____

_____

■ We each have had an incalculable number of sinful (disobedient, self-centered) thoughts and actions. How many sins can a Holy God overlook?

_____

■ Read Ezek. 7:8-9; Rom. 2:4-5 and Eph. 2:1-3. Does God's wrath have a specific object? If so, what is it?

_____

■ Read Gen. 19:1-26; Jer. 4:4; Ezek. 5:11-17; 23:22-30 and 2 Thess. 1:6-10. List some characteristics of God's wrath from these passages:

_____

_____

_____

_____

_____

■ Read 1 John 4:9-10.

• Are you loved by the Father?_____

• How do you know you are loved?_____

• Do you feel loved?_____

■ Consider what it would be like to experience the wrath of Almighty God, and then read Is. 53:4-10. Place your name in the place of appropriate pronouns ("Surely He took up_____'s infirmities.") The wrath that you deserved has been poured out on Christ.

• In what ways can you express gratitude to Christ for what He has done for you?_____

_____

_____

_____

_____

■ The more we understand God's love and forgiveness, the more we will be willing and able to forgive others. If we think about it, the things that others do to us are all trivial in comparison to our sin of rebellion against God that He has graciously forgiven. This is why Paul encouraged the Ephesian Christians to forgive each other *just as God in Christ also has forgiven you* (Eph. 4:32), completely and willingly.

• Are there any sins (or even personality differences) in others that you have difficulty forgiving? If so, list them and confess to God your lack of forgiveness:

_____

_____

_____

_____

_____

_____

• How do these compare to your sins that deserved God's wrath, but received the payment of Christ's substitutionary death?

_____

_____

■ Memorize 1 John 4:9-10.

God's plan for us is centered in the cross. To understand His plan, we must first understand the meaning of propitiation.

Prior to our spiritual birth, even our good deeds were despicable to God (Is. 64:6). If we are honest about our performance, we must admit that we have sinned thousands of times, even after having accepted Christ. The problem with our sinfulness is that God is absolutely holy, pure and perfect. There is absolutely nothing unholy in Him. *God is light, and in Him there is no darkness at all* (1 John 1:5). Therefore, since God is holy, He cannot overlook or compromise with sin. It took one sin to separate Adam from God. For God to condone even *one* sin would instantly defile His holiness, which He indicates by His righteous condemnation of sin (Rom. 6:23).

The Father did not escape witnessing His Son's mistreatment: the mocking, the scourging and the cross. He could have spoken and ended the whole ordeal, yet He kept silent. Confronted with the suffering of His Son, He chose to let it continue so that we could be saved. What an expression of love! Its depth is unsearchable.

Try to recall an experience in which you felt loved by someone else. That person cared about you and wanted to be with you. You didn't have to perform; just being you was enough. The thought of that person selecting you to love was intoxicating. All other facets of life seemed to diminish. He or she loved you, and that love was soothing to you and satisfied many of your inner longings.

If the love of a person can make us feel this way, consider how much greater joy the heavenly Father's love can bring. We can't truly appreciate the Father's love unless we realize that it supersedes any experience of being loved by another man or woman.

God loves you, and He enjoys revealing His love to you. He enjoys being loved by you, but He knows you can love Him only if you are experiencing His love for you. Propitiation means that His wrath has been removed and that you are deeply loved!

Many of us have a distorted concept of the heavenly Father. We believe that God is thrilled when we accept Christ and are born into His family. But many of us also believe that He is proud of us for only as long as we perform well, and that the better our performance, the happier He is with us.

In reality, God loves us, and not a moment goes by that He isn't thinking loving thoughts about us (Ps. 40:5). We are His children, and we are individually special to Him because of Christ! Propitiation, then, means that Jesus Christ has satisfied the Father's righteous condemnation of sin by His death. The Scriptures give only one reason to explain this incredible fact: God loves you!

Shame

When we base our self-worth on past failures, dissatisfaction with personal appearance or bad habits, we often develop a fourth false belief: *I am what I am. I cannot change. I am hopeless.* This lie binds people to the hopeless pessimism associated with poor self-esteem. Take the following test to establish how strongly you experience shame.

Shame Test

Read the statements below. Look at the top of the test and choose the term which best describes your response. Put the number above that term in the blank beside each statement.

1	2	3	4	5	6	7
Always	Very Often	Often	Sometimes	Seldom	Very Seldom	Never

_____ 1. I often think about past failures or experiences of rejection.

_____ 2. There are certain things about my past which I cannot recall without experiencing strong, painful emotions (i.e., guilt, shame, anger, fear, etc.).

_____ 3. I seem to make the same mistakes over and over again.

_____ 4. There are certain aspects of my character I want to change, but I don't believe I can ever successfully do so.

_____ 5. I feel inferior.

_____ 6. There are aspects of my appearance that I cannot accept.

_____ 7. I am generally disgusted with myself.

_____ 8. I feel that certain experiences have basically ruined my life.

_____ 9. I perceive of myself as an immoral person.

_____10. I feel I have lost the opportunity to experience a complete and wonderful life.

_____ Total (Add up the numbers you have placed in the blanks.)

Interpretation of Score

If your score is...

57-70

God has apparently given you a very strong appreciation for His love and unconditional acceptance. You seem to be free of the shame that plagues most people. (Some people who score this high are either greatly deceived, or have become callous to their emotions as a way to suppress pain.)

47-56

Shame controls your responses rarely or only in certain situations. Again, the exceptions are those who are not honest with themselves.

36-46

When you experience emotional problems, they may relate to a sense of shame. Upon reflection, you will probably relate many of your previous decisions to a poor sense of self-worth. Many of your future decisions will also be affected by low self-esteem unless you take direct action to overcome it.

27-36

Shame forms a generally negative backdrop to your life. There are probably few days in which you are not affected in some way by shame. Unfortunately, this robs you of the joy and peace your salvation was meant to bring.

0-26

Experiences of shame dominate your memory and have probably resulted in a great deal of depression. These problems will remain until some definitive action is taken. In other words, this condition will not simply disappear one day; time alone cannot heal your pain. You must deal with its root issue.

Effects of Shame

This exercise examines the shame that can arise from a negative evaluation of our past performance and/or our physical appearance. Shame leads to the false belief: *I am what I am. I cannot change. I am hopeless.*

■ Define *shame*:_____

_____

■ When do you experience shame?_____

_____

_____

■ In what ways does shame make an impact on our sense of self-worth? How does shame lock us into a low opinion of ourselves?

_____

_____

■ Is there anything you can't keep from doing? When you've tried to stop but then do it again, how do you feel about yourself?

_____

■ List aspects of your appearance or past performance which prevent you from viewing yourself as a fully pleasing and totally accepted person.

• Appearance:_____

_____

_____

_____

_____

_____

- Past Performance:_____

_____

_____

_____

_____

■ When people with a poor self-concept succeed at something, one would think that they would be encouraged and have a more positive outlook. Often, however, pessimistic people explain or minimize their success and continue in their hopelessness.

- Do you do this when you succeed?_____

- If so, what do you tell yourself and others?_____

_____

_____

- Why do you say those things?_____

_____

_____

■ What sources of input reinforce this low view of yourself?_____

_____

_____

■ Read Ps. 139:13-16. What was God's involvement in the formation of your physical appearance and personality?

_____

_____

■ If you have a poor self-concept, what do you think it will take to overcome it and experience the joy and power of your new life in Christ?

_____

_____

■ How do you think other people would describe you?_____

_____

_____

• What are their expectations of you?_____

_____

_____

• How have their expectations affected your self-esteem?_____

_____

_____

    Shame often results from instances of neglect or abuse, and is then reinforced by failures in our performance or "flaws" in our appearance. Even when others don't know of our failure, we assume their opinion of us is poor and adopt what we think their opinion might be.

    If we base our self-worth on our performance long enough, our past behavior will eventually become the sole basis of our worth. We will see ourselves with certain character qualities and flaws because that's the way we have always been. We then have unconsciously incorporated Satan's lie into our belief system: *I must always be what I have been and live with whatever self-worth I have, because that's just me.* Interestingly, we claim only our *poor* behavior as *That's just me.* We never hear anyone saying, "That's just me. I'm so wonderful, honest and bright."

    We may think that humility is self-depreciation, but true humility is an accurate appraisal of our worth in Christ: We deserved God's righteous condemnation, yet we are recipients of His unconditional love, grace and righteousness through Christ. We are deeply loved, completely forgiven, fully pleasing, totally accepted and complete in Him. Thankfulness, generosity, kindness and self-confidence constitute true humility!

    Another aspect of a poor self-concept relates to personal appearance. Most of us have some aspect of our appearance that we wish we could change, but much about our appearance can't really be altered. We may not only base our self-worth on our appearance, but may tend to base our acceptance of others on their appearance, even the color of their skin. We may never be any more cruel than when we accept or reject others based on their appearance.

    Are you angry with God for the way He made you? Do you compare and rank your appearance with that of others? If you do, you will suffer at some point in your life because there will always be someone prettier, stronger, cuter or more handsome. Even if you are spectacularly beautiful or strikingly handsome, you will suffer because you will be afraid of losing your good looks, the basis of your self-worth.

    If we insist on valuing our worth by our appearance and performance, sooner or later God will graciously allow us to see the futility of that struggle. God created our need for a sense of significance. However, He knows we will never come to Him until we find the importance of people's opinions to be empty and hopeless. At that point, we can turn to Him and find comfort and encouragement in the truths of His Word.

God's Answer: Regeneration

This exercise will help you see yourself as a new creature in Christ, with new potential and new capacities. The truth that you have been made new in Christ will enable you to develop a strong, positive self-esteem in spite of "flaws" in your appearance or past failures.

■ Do you really think that you can view yourself any differently than you always have? If not, why?

_____

_____

■ Read 2 Cor. 5:17.

• Define *regeneration*:_____

_____

• What does your having been made *a new creature* mean to you?_____

_____

_____

_____

■ How was your regeneration accomplished?

• John 1:12-13_____

• John 3:16_____

• Titus 3:5_____

• 1 Pet. 1:3_____

• 1 Pet. 1:23_____

■ Read Eph. 4:22-24 and Col. 3:9-10. What process do you need to complete in order to experience your new self?

_____

_____

_____

■ On the following page, list characteristics of your old and new self based on the passages given there.

CHARACTERISTICS OF MY NEW SELF	CHARACTERISTICS OF MY OLD SELF
Gal. 5:19-21_____	Rom. 8:16-17_____
_____	_____
_____	_____
_____	2 Cor. 5:21_____
_____	_____
Eph. 4:17-22_____	_____
_____	Gal. 5:22-23_____
_____	_____
_____	_____
_____	Eph. 4:23-32_____
Col. 3:5-9_____	_____
_____	_____
_____	Col. 2:10_____
Titus 3:3_____	_____
_____	_____
_____	Col. 3:10-15_____
	_____
	_____
	1 Pet. 1:16_____
	_____
	_____

■ Read Rom. 6:12-23 and 1 Cor. 6:9-11. How does the truth of regeneration free you from evaluating yourself by your past performance?

_____

_____

■ Read 1 Sam. 16:6-7 and Ps. 139:13-16. How does the truth of regeneration free you from the shame of flaws in your physical appearance?

_____

_____

■ How could understanding your newness in Christ affect your personal fitness or grooming habits?_____

_____

_____

■ How can knowing that you have a new life in Christ affect the way you think, feel and act?_____

_____

_____

■ Do you use past failures, your appearance or some other "flaw" as an excuse for not living for Christ? If so, what is your excuse? How valid is it?

_____

_____

■ Memorize 2 Cor. 5:17.

Regeneration is the renewing work of the Holy Spirit by which a person literally becomes a new creation. Our regeneration occurred at the instant of our conversion to Christ. At that moment, we were given more than a change of direction; we received the impartation of new life.

The part of us that the Holy Spirit regenerated is our spirit. The Holy Spirit has energized our inner spirit with new life. Jesus called it a new birth in John 3:3, 5-6, saying, "That which is born of the flesh is flesh, and that which is born of the Spirit is spirit" (John 3:6). Regeneration is the Spirit-wrought renewal of our human spirit, a transforming resuscitation so that *the spirit is alive* within us (Rom. 8:10).

The Holy Spirit has been joined to our human spirit, forming a new spiritual entity. A new birth has produced a new being. *Therefore, if any man is in Christ, he is a new creature; the old things passed away; behold, new things have come* (2 Cor. 5:17). Study these words carefully. Ephesians 4:24 says that our new self *has* (already) *been created in righteousness and holiness of the truth*, but we must yet *put on* this new self in order to progressively produce godly thoughts and actions—as the acorn produces an oak tree!

What is the basis of your self-worth? Are you living by scriptural truths or by false beliefs? False beliefs are all a part of Satan's insidious plan. By now, you may see deception as a part of his scheme to steal, and kill and destroy mankind.

In order to prevent him from victimizing us with lies, it will be helpful not only to recognize and reject them, but to replace them with the truth of God's Word.

The following exercises provide some steps we can take to reject Satan's lies and replace them with a stronghold of truth in our minds.

■ Making a Truth Card

• A simple 3x5 card can be a key factor in helping you base your self-worth on the liberating truths of the Scriptures. On the front, write out both the following truths and their corresponding verses from Scripture. On the back of the card, write out the four false beliefs.

I am deeply loved by God (1 John 4:9-10).
I am completely forgiven, and am fully pleasing to God (Rom. 5:1).
I am totally accepted by God (Col. 1:21-22).
I am a new creation—complete in Christ (2 Cor. 5:17).

Carry this card with you continuously. Each time you are about to do a routine activity, like having something to drink, look at the front side and slowly meditate on each phrase. Thank the Lord for making you into a person who has these qualities. By doing this for the next twenty-eight days, you will develop a habit of remembering that you are deeply loved, completely forgiven, fully pleasing, totally accepted and complete in Christ.

If you have not already done so, memorize the supporting verses listed on the card over the next four days. Look in your Bible for other verses that support these truths and commit them to memory. Doing this will establish God's Word as the basis for these truths (Col. 3:16). Also memorize the false beliefs. The more familiar you are with these lies, the more you will be able to recognize them in your thoughts. Then, as you recognize them, you can more readily replace them with the truths of God's Word.

■ Exposing Ungodly Thoughts

Our thoughts reveal what we really believe, yet it is difficult for most of us to be objective in our thinking simply because we haven't trained ourselves to be. We usually let any and every thought run its course in our minds without analyzing its worth. Is it a God-honoring thought, or is it a *speculation*, or a *lofty thing raised up against the knowledge of God?* (2 Cor. 10:5).

As we grow in our knowledge of God's Word, we will increasingly be able to identify thoughts that reflect Satan's deceptions. Then, we can reject those lies and replace them with scriptural truth, just as our Lord did when He was tempted by Satan in the wilderness (Matt. 4:1-11). One way of identifying deceptive thoughts is to state what is true and see what comes to mind. Hopefully, our thoughts will increasingly reflect our thankfulness to God for who He is and what He has done for us, but sometimes we will respond by contradicting the truth.

For example, you might respond to the truth that you are fully pleasing to God by thinking, *No, I'm not! I mess up all the time, and to be fully pleasing, I'd have to be perfect!* When we see it written out, we more easily recognize that response as a lie. However, we seldom write down our thoughts and analyze their validity.

As a first step in this analysis, write down your thoughts in response to the four truths we've examined. (Again, they will probably be mixed: some positive, thankful and godly, and some contradictory to the truth.)

• *I am deeply loved by God:*_____

_____

_____

- *I am completely forgiven and fully pleasing to God:* _____

_____

_____

- *I am totally accepted by God:* _____

_____

_____

- *I am complete in Christ:* _____

_____

_____

Thoughts that contradict these truths are lies. Reject them and replace them with passages of Scripture to reinforce the truth in your mind. Here are some passages to reflect on:

Propitiation: Matt. 18:21-35; Luke 7:36-50; Rom. 3:25; 8:1-8; Col. 3:12-14; Heb. 2:17.
Justification: Rom. 3:19-24; 4:4-5; 5:1-11; Titus 2:11-14; 3:4-7.
Reconciliation: John 15:14-16; Rom. 5:8-10; Eph. 2:11-18.
Regeneration: 2 Cor. 5:17; Gal. 5:16-24; Eph. 2:4-5; 4:22-24; Col. 3:5-17.

As we become increasingly aware of the battle within us between the Spirit and the flesh, as we identify false beliefs that prompt sinful behavior and then renew our minds with the truth of God's Word, we can confidently ask God to remove our sinful patterns of behavior, and begin to live in His resurrection power. It is true that we will never be sinless until we reign with Him in His kingdom, but as we grow in Him, we will sin less.

■ How will understanding and experiencing these truths (in the context of honest, affirming relationships) affect each characteristic of codependency in your life?

- A lack of objectivity: _____

_____

_____

_____

- A warped sense of responsibility (savior and Judas): _____

_____

_____

_____

- Controlled/controlling:_____

_____

_____

_____

- Hurt and anger:_____

_____

_____

_____

- Guilt:_____

_____

_____

_____

- Loneliness:_____

_____

_____

_____

Bargaining

When a person gets a glimpse of the effects of codependency in his life, he will often respond by trying to bargain with himself, his family and God. Christy learned about dysfunctional families from a close friend, and quickly saw those painful effects in her own life. At the end of the conversation, she was desperate for an answer. She blurted out, "Then how can I get my father to love me?" Her friend explained, "That's the wrong question, Christy. It's not up to you to get your father to love you. He is responsible for that. It's up to you to be independent and secure in the Lord, whether your father ever loves you or not."

Bargaining takes many shapes and forms, but its goal is to get other people to change by offering some change in ourselves. *I'll be a better husband to her. I'll spend more time with him. I won't nag him anymore, then he'll love me the way I want to be loved. I'll keep the house clean. I'll get a job. I'll be more affectionate.* We can come up with all kinds of "deals" to get people to love us, but bargaining is still not totally objective. The responsibility still remains on us alone, and we are still believing the best about the other person.

Believing the best of others is usually good and right. It is usually a virtue. But when a person has proven by months and years of irresponsible, manipulative behavior that he is pathological, then believing the best is not a virtue. It is naive and foolish. It is the haven of denial.

Bargaining is an expression of hope; hope that the other person will change and give us the love and worth that we need. But it is a false hope. The hard truth, the reality of objective observation, leads us to a painful but honest conclusion: We need to give up. We need to abandon the vain hope that the other person will change and give us what we need. Giving up doesn't sound very spiritual. It doesn't sound very godly, but it is. Giving up is a reflection of reality. It is an act of abandoning the idol of pleasing others and being accepted and loved by them as the way to win self-worth. Actually, it is an act of worship to the Lord.

The Awkwardness of Change

Many of us will experience wide swings in feelings and behavior during these early stages of growth and acceptance. As the cap is taken off of our emotions for perhaps the first time, we may feel more hurt, anger and fear than we ever thought possible. We may become afraid of the intensity of our emotions and put the cap back on until we have more courage to experiment again with these feelings. We may also feel more joy and freedom and love than ever before. We may cry for the first time in years. We may feel loved and comforted for the first time ever. We may ask hundreds of questions, or we may become more introspective than we've been before.

These wide swings in mood and behavior are understandable. Don't try to clamp them; instead, realize that sudden surges of emotion are perfectly understandable for someone who has repressed them for years. It will take time to work through your feelings. Be patient with yourself.

- What are some reasons we try to bargain?_____

_____

_____

_____

_____

_____

- Why is it so difficult to stop bargaining?_____

_____

_____

_____

_____

- How can you tell if you have stopped bargaining?_____

_____

_____

_____

_____

Step Eight

We make a list of all persons who have hurt us and choose to forgive them; we also make a list of all persons we have harmed and become willing to make amends to them all.

And just as you want people to treat you, treat them in the same way.
Luke 6:31

True Forgiveness

Typically, a person will apply the truth of God's love, forgiveness and acceptance only as deeply as he has experienced the reality of pain in his life. If he is only superficially objective, then he will experience only superficial love, comfort and forgiveness (though he may think that this level is all there is). As he gains a deeper sense of reality, he will also be able to experience a deeper sense of comfort, a heightened feeling of love and a greater sense of forgiveness. Our ability to forgive others is often an indicator of the depth of our experience of reality.

Cindy asked if she could talk to me about her father. She said, "When you talked about forgiveness tonight, I was confused. I've forgiven my father for all he did to me. I've worked through all of that, but I still hate him. I know I've forgiven him. What's wrong with me?"

When I asked her a few questions about her father, I learned that he had neglected her. His only contact with her seemed to have been characterized by verbal abuse. Cindy had been hurt deeply by him.

"Cindy," I told her, "we often forgive in stages. Your forgiveness of your father only will be as deep as your experience of the pain he has caused you. That may seem like a lot of pain to you, but that's why you're confused about forgiveness."

I explained to Cindy that two things are necessary for a person to be able to forgive others genuinely. The first is an experience of whatever pain is generated by the offense. Others' wrongs toward us hurt! If we repress those hurt feelings, it confuses our efforts to be forgiving: We will think that we have forgiven, but will still harbor resentment toward the source of our pain. If instead we are open and honest about our pain, we will know exactly why we are extending forgiveness.

David modeled this honesty about his hurt and anger in the Psalms. Christ didn't deny His feelings either. He experienced anger with those who rejected Him, fear at the imminent crucifixion and hurt that his followers abandoned Him.

It may take a lot of time for us to uncover our repressed emotions. Our forgiveness of others may follow the progress of our objectivity about their offenses.

A second necessity for genuine forgiveness is a deep appreciation of the forgiveness we have through Jesus Christ. Our forgiveness of others reflects the depth of the grasp we have on our own forgiveness. The more we realize that we have been completely forgiven for our bitterness, pride, malice and neglect of others, the more able—and motivated—we will be to forgive those who have hurt us. Paul encouraged the Ephesian Christians:

> *And be kind to one another, tender-hearted, forgiving each other, just as God in Christ also has forgiven you.*

Eph. 4:32

Those of us who have been hurt deeply do need to forgive those who have hurt us. Forgiveness is often the foundation for further growth, but that forgiveness is based on an honest appraisal of the depth of pain caused by the offense and a deep experience of the forgiveness of Christ.

- How much have you felt the hurt caused by those who have harmed you? Explain:_____

_____

_____

_____

_____

- How much are you experiencing Christ's forgiveness of you? Explain:_____

_____

_____

_____

_____

Relating to the "Other Person": Lordship or Love

One of the most pressing issues for the person emerging from the darkness of codependency is: *How do I relate to the one who has hurt, neglected, used and condemned me?* Relating to "that other person" (a parent, spouse or any significant other) is where "the rubber meets the road" in our growth and freedom. Our growing objectivity and honest emotions produce a cataclysmic upheaval in our lives. Relating to that particular person is often the most difficult part of the whole process.

Some of the issues we will examine in this step have been expressed elsewhere, but at the risk of being redundant, I think it is wise to draw some of these thoughts together here. The primary issue is idolatry or independence: Are we going to continue to let a person determine our behavior and thus, be our lord, or are we going to be independent and make our own decisions, including loving him or her unconditionally?

Idolatry or Independence

Most of us have defined love erroneously in the context of codependency. We have thought of love as rescuing, worrying, feeling guilty, being compliant to manipulation and pitying that other person whom we care for. The desire to be accepted and the desire for intimacy have been so strong that we would do anything to make that person happy. We've called it love. It's not. It's idolatry. It's bondage. We have allowed a person to be our lord and to determine our thoughts, feelings, words and actions. Comments from people who are finally being objective about this bondage reveal the depth of this lordship:

One woman lamented: "I've lived to please my father all of my life. He said, 'Jump!' and I said, 'How high?' No, I didn't even ask, 'How high?' I just jumped as high as I could as often as I could. I got some praise for what I did, just enough to keep me jumping, but not enough to give me a sense of security."

Terry remembered: "My mother always could get me to do anything she wanted me to do. She rarely yelled at me, but she could get a powerful message across with the expressions on her face."

Brad talked about his daughter: "I did everything I could do to get her to stop eating. I begged, I threatened, I hid food, I sent her to classes, I screamed at her, I avoided her. I can't tell you how many nights I lay awake trying to think of ways to get her to stop. I thought she was the one who was 'hooked,' but I was an addict, too, an addict to her performance and happiness."

Dan hadn't gotten to the part of objectivity yet. He looked puzzled at the thought of independence and the idea of letting his wife live with the consequences of her actions. "She needs me. What would happen to her if I didn't help her?"

There is only One who is worthy of our ultimate affection and obedience. If we put others in His place, if we try to please others as a means of gaining love and value, then we are committing idolatry. Paul wrote to the believers in Corinth that pleasing Christ is worthy of our ambitions:

> *Therefore also we have as our ambition, whether at home or absent, to be pleasing to Him.*
> 2 Cor. 5:9

Paul also wrote to the Galatians to remind them of the difference between pleasing people and pleasing Christ:

> *For am I now seeking the favor of men, or of God? Or am I striving to please men? If I were still trying to please men, I would not be a bond-servant of Christ.*
> Gal. 1:10

Once we have trusted Christ and accepted His payment for our sins, our identity is secure in Him. We are His beloved children, recipients of His unconditional love, forgiveness and acceptance. As we experience His grace, we will become willing bond-servants and enjoy a healthy independence from the bondage of pleasing others.

It may be difficult or painful, but we need to be objective about our relationship with that "other person." Call a spade a spade. Call it idolatry. Don't try to bargain. Don't try to get that person to give you the love and acceptance he or she has never given even though you have tried so hard to get it. Turn from that idolatry by getting your significance and worth from Christ alone. Then, and only then, will you be able to respond to that person the way the Lord wants you to—in objectivity, healthy independence, forgiveness and unconditional love.

Responding in a Healthy, Realistic Way

Your relationship with that particular person you care for has probably been characterized by some combination of rescuing, outbursts of anger, displaced anger, compliance, withdrawal, guilt, hurt, loneliness, pity for him and pity for yourself. A sense of loyalty has probably contributed to your inability to see the relationship objectively. You may have thought that any negative thoughts or emotions (even though you've had many of them) are signs that there is something dreadfully wrong—with you!

Now you are growing in your objectivity. You are learning that you've repressed emotions that you didn't even know existed. This is difficult, but you're getting in touch with your feelings. Your source of security is changing. You're learning to make your own decisions. All of these are good things, but there's *that* person: your spouse, your sibling, your parent, your child, your classmate, who has hurt you deeply. What do you do? What do you say?

Remember to identify, detach and decide. Recognize how you feel and how you act when you see or think of that person. Then detach so you have the time and space necessary to think and feel. You may be able to detach calmly, but you may not. Even if you have to detach in anger, remember that not detaching is prolonging idolatry. So, detach. Ask yourself questions so you will see what is really going on. Then make your own choices about what to say and do.

Set limits. Decide what you can live with for right now. Decide on the extent of your communication and contact with that person. Determine which issues you will discuss and which ones you won't. If you decide on these ahead of time, you will be much less likely to succumb to the pressure of the moment and give in to manipulation or condemnation. The relationship has been on his or her terms for perhaps your whole life, but it can be on your terms now. (This isn't selfish. Remember, *you're* the one who is trying to live in reality, not the other person. It is perfectly good and right to insist on making your own decisions based on reality. Too often, we have believed lies, lived by deception and made our codependent decisions to rescue and feel guilty based on a world of unreality. This can end now. Base your life on what is *really* real, not on what that other person believes and says is real.)

How much do you say? Do you tell that person all about codependency and how messed up you've been because of your relationship with him? Do you describe your dark thoughts, your bitterness, hatred and fear? The principle here is: Express yourself fully to God and express yourself appropriately to the other person. As you recall, David encouraged us to: *Trust in Him at all times...Pour out your heart before Him...* (Ps. 62:8), but we are *not* to pour out our hearts to people. Only a fool delights in telling all he knows: *A fool does not delight in understanding, but only in revealing his own mind* (Prov. 18:2). The question is not: *How much can I blast him?* but, *What will help that person? How much does he need to know at this time and place?* As you consider what to do in this relationship, seek the advice of a mature, godly, knowledgeable person to give you perception and encouragement.

Don't expect to do all of this perfectly (you perfectionist, you!). Give yourself a break! *All* of this is new. Because this is such a contrast to how you have related in the past, you can expect to have all kinds of conflicting thoughts and emotions.

And don't expect the other person to say, "Well, now I completely understand. Thank you so much for saying all of this. I'll change today and never treat you the same way again." He may say he'll change, but that's what he's said a hundred times before. He may weep and try to elicit your pity. He may withdraw from you. He may say, "Let's talk about this," but he probably doesn't really want to understand your point of view. He probably wants to convince you that you are wrong (poor, misguided, confused person that you are) so that you will return to being the docile, compliant puppet you've always been.

Or he may say, "It's all your fault." The denial of personal responsibility is a common characteristic in manipulative, condemning people. Scott Peck described such people in his book, *People of the Lie*. He wrote that they do not recognize their "dark side," that propensity to evil that all of us have. They are so steeped in denial that they cannot even see how they manipulate and condemn others. They may say, "I'm sorry," but what they mean is, *I'm sorry you feel that way. I've never done anything wrong, but you have!* They want quick, superficial forgiveness so the relationship can go back to its pathological status quo.

When we detach from that "other person," it is usually awkward. Karen said, "I can't even pray for him anymore. I feel so strange. I know what I'm doing is right, but shouldn't I be able to pray for him?" She was feeling guilty and confused. A friend helped her to understand the situation more clearly. "That's okay, Karen. God can take care of him without your prayers. He wants you to concentrate on detaching and getting your security from Him for now. Later, you can start praying for him again." Your life is changing, so expect a variety of changes in your thoughts and emotions. It's all a part of the process.

Realistic expectations are vital to your relationship. He or she may change, but it is foolish to expect resolution and reconciliation very soon, if ever. Let your identity in Christ and His lordship fill your thoughts, not dreams of intimacy with "that person." He or she may never change, but you can. You can be unhooked. You can be independent, healthy and realistic.

■ In what ways is a codependent's relationship with the "other person" idolatrous?_____

_____

_____

_____

_____

■ How would you have defined or described love in the past? How about now?_____

_____

_____

_____

_____

_____

■ Describe your relationship with the person(s) who has hurt you deeply. How has he (she) treated you? How have you responded (emotions, thoughts, actions)?

_____

_____

_____

_____

_____

_____

■ What limits do you need to set in your relationship with that person?_____

_____

_____

_____

_____

_____

■ Is it selfish to have the relationship on your terms now? Why or why not?_____

_____

_____

_____

_____

■ How much should you say to him or her? How and when will you say it? How can you be well-prepared?

_____

_____

_____

_____

_____

_____

_____

_____

■ Describe the difference between excusing and forgiving that person:_____

_____

_____

_____

_____

_____

■ What do you need to know, be or do to respond to him or her in a healthy, independent, loving, realistic way?

_____

_____

_____

_____

_____

_____

■ How do you realistically expect this person to respond?_____

_____

_____

_____

Excusing vs. Forgiving

As codependents, we have been quick to excuse people for how they have hurt us. Excusing, though, is not forgiving. Forgiveness acknowledges the reality of the offense, the full weight of the wrong and the consequences of the wrong. It then chooses to not hold that offense against the person. When Christ died on the cross, His blood was the payment for our sins so we could be truly forgiven, not just excused for our sins. Our forgiveness of others can mirror the depth of that forgiveness. Paul wrote:

> *Let all bitterness and wrath and anger and clamor and slander be put away from you, along with all malice. And be kind to one another, tender-hearted, forgiving each other, just as God in Christ also has forgiven you.*

> Eph. 4:31-32

Forgiveness does not imply that you have to trust the one you have forgiven. Some of us link the two. We believe, *If I can't trust him, then I haven't really forgiven him.* That belief is not true, and it causes undue pressure and guilt. If a person has proven over the course of months or years that he is not trustworthy, then he can be forgiven, but he should not be trusted. Trusting a proven liar is foolishness, not godliness.

Similarly, understanding is not the same as forgiving. Understanding the painful background of those who have hurt us is often a helpful perception, but most codependents respond in pity, excusing harmful behavior and feeling guilty for being angry. In that case, we have understood, but we haven't forgiven.

Beth had been married to Timothy for four years. Timothy was a compulsive workaholic who spent eighty hours a week at the office and thought about work-related problems when he was at home. Beth had put up with it for a long time, even encouraging him because he was doing so well in his position. But after four years, enough was enough. At the time that Beth was becoming exasperated with Timothy's work habits and neglect of his family, the couple visited his parents at Christmas. On previous visits, Beth had noticed how Timothy's father seemed to be busy most of the time with projects around the house. He had built them a dresser when they were married and several other things as the years had gone by.

Beth now looked at her father-in-law with a more jaundiced eye. *He is a workaholic, too. That's why Timothy is the way he is! No wonder he works so hard. That's all he has ever seen in his father. And Timothy's father neglects his wife the same way Timothy neglects me.* That flash of insight helped Beth put a lot of pieces together. She felt better. She understood.

As the months went by after their visit with Timothy's parents, Beth tried to excuse Timothy's neglect and preoccupation with his work. Soon, however, she realized that excusing him wasn't the same as forgiving him. She had begun to pity Timothy instead of loving him, but his behavior was wrong. It hurt. Instead of continuing to pity and excuse him, Beth forgave Timothy and committed herself to loving him unconditionally. That meant loving him enough to confront him with the reality of his workaholism and its effects on both of them.

Timothy didn't respond very well. He was angry and defensive, but he agreed to read a book and talk to their pastor about their relationship. After a while, Timothy began to recognize his addiction to success and performance. Together, he and Beth began to experience healing and intimacy in their relationship. It started with reality, forgiveness, unconditional love and courage.

When a person first learns about codependency, there is a tendency for his view of the one who hurt him and manipulated him to flip-flop from white (he can do no wrong) to black (he can do no right). The anger generated by the realization of hurts, offenses and damage is a motivation to detach, to stop the idolatry of the relationship and to begin to establish a new, secure identity. As time goes by, however, greater objectivity will color in shades of gray where black has been before, and the codependent will be able to see the person who has hurt him more clearly. Anger will turn to grief, and grief, to acceptance and health. Then he will be able to see both the good and the bad in that person. He may continue to be blinded, manipulated and condemned. His relationship may still be void of trust and intimacy, but he will have confidence that he is living in reality with no grudges. No, it's not a fairy tale ending, but it is good and right and acceptable.

The following exercise is designed to help you extend the forgiveness God has given you to other people.

■ Read Matt. 18:21-35.

• How great was the debt of the king's servant?_____

• Was it possible for him ever to repay it?_____

■ Likewise, before you trusted Christ, how great was your debt to God for your sin? Was it possible for you ever to repay it?

_____

■ What did the servant ask for?_____

• What did the king grant him?_____

■ Why was the king's servant so harsh with his fellow servant over such a small debt?_____

_____

■ Read Luke 7:36-50 (especially verse 47) and compare it with the parable in Matt. 18:21-35. What is the foundation for being able to love and forgive others?

_____

_____

■ Read Eph. 4:32 and Col. 3:12-13.

• To what degree are we to forgive others?_____

_____

• Describe how God has forgiven you:_____

_____

■ What are some of the effects people experience when they fail to forgive, e.g., attitudes toward others, opinion of themselves, quality of relationships, etc.?

_____

_____

_____

_____

■ Do your answers to the above questions correspond to any effects of failing to forgive in your life? In your attitude toward others? Toward yourself? If so, explain:

_____

_____

_____

_____

■ Is there any particular sin for which you haven't experienced God's forgiveness? If so, what do you need in order to do so?

_____

_____

Being offended by others is a frequent experience in life. We go through periods when it seems that almost everybody is letting us down. We want freedom from being offended but the beat goes on. We are hurt by both our experience of the offense and our reliving of it. In fact, the initial pain of the wrong usually amounts to only a small fraction of the total hurt. After a while, it should become obvious to us that it is impossible to avoid being offended. However, the majority of our pain can be avoided if we will learn to deal with offenses rather than reliving them countless times. Unforgivingness is a sure way to cut the flow of God's power in our lives. In fact, there are a number of negative consequences which often result from failing to forgive others. Before we examine these, let's look at some of the reasons why we may withhold forgiveness:

Reasons for Not Forgiving

We often fail to forgive others (and ourselves) because we don't think it's possible. We forget how God has graciously forgiven all of our sins through Christ's death, and rationalize why we can't forgive. These are some of the countless excuses we make for our unwillingness to forgive others and ourselves.

■ *The offense was too great.* Grant's wife had committed adultery, and he was bitter toward her. Her infidelity was too great a sin for him to forgive. But almost two years after the incident, God began to impress Grant with the idea that he should forgive his wife *just as God in Christ also had forgiven him,* completely and willfully. When Grant finally did forgive her, his forgiveness was coupled with a commitment to rebuild his relationship with her so that she would not be compelled to repeat the incident with someone else.

Roger sat shaking with anger as he recalled his wife's rape. His anger was destroying his health and his relationship with his wife. *How could any man, who really is a man, forgive such an act?* he wondered. The transient who had raped his wife had moved on, and in his perversion, had probably forgotten the incident. He was never caught. Continuing to allow the offense to produce bitterness might ultimately do more harm to Roger and his family than the destructive act of the rape.

■ *He(she) won't accept responsibility for the offense.* How many people have offended us but won't agree that they were at fault? The offense might be something slight, such as being overlooked at a social event, or something major, such as being emotionally neglected as a child. Having others agree that they've offended us isn't necessary for us to respond properly to their offense.

■ *He(she) isn't truly sorry.* John pulled a practical joke on you which caused you to be late for class, and your professor refused to accept your paper because you didn't have it in on time. John doesn't see anything wrong with a little joke—

he's slightly sorry, but he still thinks it was hilarious. Even if John doesn't recognized the pain he's caused you, you can still extend forgiveness to him through Christ and refuse to hold the offense against him.

■ *He(she) never asked to be forgiven.* For whatever reason, the offender never got around to asking you for forgiveness. Are you going to withhold forgiveness until it's requested? Who is suffering, you or the offender? What would God have you do? (Read 1 Cor. 13:5 and Eph. 4:32.)

■ *He(she) will do it again.* Candy's husband had been out late every Friday night playing cards for three years. On some nights he didn't come home. "Me? Forgive that jerk?" Candy asked. The Lord said that the number of times we're to forgive is seventy times seven…in other words, regardless of the number of offenses. Forgiveness doesn't mean condoning or accepting unacceptable behavior. Some situations calling for forgiveness also require confrontation and/or allowing the offender to experience the consequences of his or her wrongful behavior. For Candy, failing to both forgive and confront her husband will cause her to be the bitter loser.

■ *He(she) did it again.* David had been a horrible husband to Mandy. However, after much effort, Mandy had forgiven him for his insensitivity, his greater concern for the guys on his softball team, his lack of affection for the children and his callous, domineering attitude. Then, David saw how poor his behavior had become. He began to change. His relationship with Mandy started to improve—until he stayed out late again with the guys. He had done it again! One mistake set the whole conflict back in motion.

■ *I don't like him(her).* Generally, we don't have a great deal of appreciation for those who have wronged us. In fact, every emotion within us may call for retaliation against the creep! Only when we realize that forgiveness is an act of the will, and not of the emotions, will we choose to forgive those who have hurt us.

■ *He(she) did it deliberately.* "He knew what he was doing, and he did it anyway!" George had been swindled out of ten thousand dollars by his "best friend," Hal. It had been a complex scheme which had required precise timing over a period of several months. As George sat stunned, his mind raced through those times he had been generous to Hal. He thought of how much he had loved Hal and had repeatedly trusted him. The swindle had been completely deliberate, and Hal had used him. George had been played for a sucker. Hal must be laughing at him now. Whether the offense was deliberate or not, God still wants George to forgive Hal.

■ *If I forgive the offense, I'll have to treat the offender well.* Ben excused his slander of Steve by pointing out how Steve had offended him. He felt justified in destroying Steve's reputation even though most of the things he had said about Steve were lies.

Shirley was cold to Greg, and had been for two weeks. It was her plan to punish Greg because he had offended her. She would forgive him all right—as soon as she was through punishing him.

■ *Someone has to punish him(her).* How often do we want God to be merciful to us and yet want Him to skin other people alive? When we don't see them suffer, we take it upon ourselves to be God's hand of vengeance.

Charles was their pastor, but according to Gloria, he had wasted the church's money. Gloria was in charge of the church women's group. She waited patiently for God to nail Charles, but when God didn't do what she thought He should, she just knew she was the divining rod for Charlie's back. Soon the church had taken sides—pro-Charles or anti-Charles. The result was that the church disgraced itself by splitting in hatred.

■ *Something keeps me from forgiving.* Satan actively promotes unforgivingness. When you attempt to deal with this problem honestly, you may be in for a tremendous spiritual battle, with both confusing and conflicting thoughts and emotions. Don't be surprised if you have to resist the devil at every turn in order to accomplish the task of forgiving the offender. Again, forgiveness is primarily an act of the will, not a warm feeling.

■ *I'll be a hypocrite if I forgive, because I don't feel like forgiving.* We often confuse hypocrisy with obedience. We are hypocritical only if we do something for selfish gain. For instance, a hypocrite might be a politician who comes to church in order to get its members to vote for him in the next election, but who despises the church and its people. To forgive as an act of the will in obedience to the Lord's command is true spirituality, not hypocrisy.

■ *I'll forgive, but I won't ever forget.* If we continue to harbor the memory of an offense, we are only fooling ourselves in thinking we have forgiven the offender, and we will not experience any freedom. In true forgiveness, we give up the right to remember an offense or to bring it up again during arguments. (Note: This doesn't mean that when we forgive a wrong, we'll never think of it again. But it does mean that we won't relish the memory. Choose to think about things that are true, honorable, right, pure and lovely [Phil. 4:8].)

■ *I'll forgive because I have found an excuse for the offense.* Hank had been very irresponsible during the early years of his marriage. His wife Sally had always been able to forgive him by placing the blame on his mother, who had babied Hank even after he was grown. Yet Sally was continually angered by Hank and his mother. In fact, her volatile temper was destroying her marriage.

Sally thought that she had forgiven Hank when she really had just excused him. By blaming Hank's mother for his immaturity, she had rationalized his behavior and had reduced her perception of his offensive actions like this:

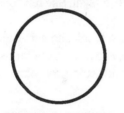

ORIGINAL OFFENSE   REDUCED OFFENSE

After reducing the offense, she then forgave it. The problem was that she did not deal with the real offense, but with a distortion of it. Therefore, the real offense remained intact in spite of her efforts at "forgiveness."

When you offend someone, or when someone offends you, do you immediately look for a "reason"? If you do, you may only be rationalizing. If you come up with an excuse for the question, *Why did I forgive him (or her)?* then you have not truly forgiven the offense. You have excused it.

Results of Not Forgiving

■ *Stress:* Living with the high level of tension brought by an unforgiving attitude in a relationship can result in a weakening of one's mental resources, emotional difficulties, physical exhaustion, and in some cases, illness.

■ *Self-Inflicted Reinjury:* Robert recalled this incident: "As I drove home, flashing into my memory was a guy I played basketball with in college. He was a great antagonist of mine, and was one of the few people I have ever met whom I truly wanted to punch out. I began to remember the unkind things he had done to me. Soon, anger started creeping up inside me, and I realized that I had never forgiven him for what he had said and done those many years ago. Each time I would think of him, I would get a knot in my stomach and I'd be preoccupied with feelings of hurt and thoughts of revenge for hours, and sometimes, days." How many times are you reinjuring yourself because past offenses haunt you?

■ *No More Love:* "I don't know if I can ever love someone again" is a frequent complaint from those offended by a lover. Our deepest hurts come from those we love. One way we deal with the pain of being offended is simply to withdraw, refusing to love anymore. We often make this unconscious decision when we have not adequately dealt with an offense. We may desperately want to love again, but feel that we are incapable of it. Refusing to experience love and feeling unable to love are both devastating conditions.

■ *Bitterness:* Emotions trace their lines on our faces. We think others don't notice what's going on inside, but our anger can be detected by even the casual observer. One person recalled seeing a neighbor go through difficulties in her marriage. Hate created such an impression on her that her face became snarled. She still has an ugly look on her face. Unforgivingness produces ugliness of all sorts.

■ *Perpetual Conflict:* A couple, both of whom had been previously married, received counseling several years ago. Having been hurt in their first marriage, they anticipated hurt from their present spouse. At the smallest offense they would each react as if their spouse were about to deliver the final blow. They were constantly on the defensive, protecting themselves from the attacks they imagined their mate would deliver. Having been offended in the past, they anticipated more hurt in the present and future, and reacted in a way that perpetuated the conflict.

■ *Walls That Keep Others Out:* Strangely, many of us refuse the love that others want to give us. We often may become anxious and threatened when personal intimacy becomes possible.

Jane hoped and prayed that her husband Frank would come to know the Lord. This, she thought, would allow him to be more loving toward her and their children. One day, Frank accepted Christ and over time, his life began to change. He became interested in Jane, and started spending time with her and the children. He was sensitive and loving. Was it a dream come true? Instead of rejoicing, Jane deeply resented Frank for not changing sooner! *If Frank is able to love us like this now, then he's always had the ability*, she thought. She felt confused and guilty about her anger.

Jane's anger was a defense mechanism to keep distance between Frank and her. The closer they might get, the more pain she might experience if he reverted to his old ways. She had never truly forgiven Frank, so the bricks of unforgivingness were stacked to form a wall that kept him from getting too close. Hiding behind a wall of unforgivingness is a lonely experience.

Summary of Reasons for Not Forgiving
1. *The offense was too great.*
2. *He(she) won't accept responsibility for the offense.*
3. *He(she) isn't truly sorry.*
4. *He(she) never asked to be forgiven.*
5. *He(she) will do it again.*
6. *He(she) did it again.*
7. *I don't like him(her).*
8. *He(she) did it deliberately.*
9. *If I forgive the offense, I'll have to treat the offender well.*
10. *Someone has to punish him(her).*
11. *Something keeps me from forgiving.*
12. *I'll be a hypocrite if I forgive, because I don't feel like forgiving.*
13. *I'll forgive, but I won't ever forget.*
14. *I have forgiven a lesser offense after excusing the real offense.*

Forgiveness Is Not Erasure
The modern idea of forgiveness is to approach an offense with a large eraser and wipe it off the books. God has never forgiven like this. He demanded full payment for each offense. This is the reason for the cross. Beside every offense on our ledger is the blood of Christ, which has paid for our sins in full.

The Christian has a unique capacity to extend forgiveness because he or she can appropriate the forgiveness of the cross. God has forgiven us fully and completely. We of all people know what it is like to experience unconditional forgiveness. As a result, we can forgive those around us. Think of it this way: *There is nothing that anyone can do to me (insult me, lie about me, annoy me, etc.) that can compare with what Christ has forgiven me for.* When we compare the offenses of others to our sin of rebellion that Christ has completely forgiven, it puts them in perspective. In Eph. 4:32, Paul writes, *And be kind to one another, tender-hearted, forgiving each other, just as God in Christ also has forgiven you.*

List ten things for which you are glad God in Christ has forgiven you. This will prime you to be willing to forgive all other offenders.

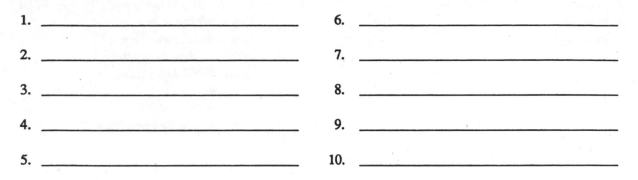

1. _____   6. _____

2. _____   7. _____

3. _____   8. _____

4. _____   9. _____

5. _____   10. _____

The exercise on the following pages will help you to recognize any lack of forgiveness in your life and extend forgiveness to others as God in Christ has forgiven you.

■ Offense: Describe in some detail an event which caused you pain.

■ Persons to Be Forgiven: List everyone who participated in the offense.

■ Reasons for Not Forgiving: Go through the summary of reasons for not forgiving. Which ones apply?

■ Act of Forgiving: Choose to forgive, remembering the complete forgiveness you have in Christ.

■ At the conclusion of the exercise, use the prayer on page 188 (or use your own) as an exercise of faith for each offense.

Example:

Offense	Persons to Be Forgiven	Reasons for Unforgiveness	Date
My brothers never had anything to do with me.	*Harry, Frank*	*The offense was too great; they didn't agree that they'd offended me; they never asked me to be forgiven; they'll do it again.*	4-28-89

Offense	Persons to Be Forgiven

Reasons for Not Forgiving	Date

Dear Lord,

I forgive _____ *for* _____ *(offense)* on the basis that God has *freely forgiven me and commanded me to forgive others. I have the capacity to do this because Christ has completely forgiven me. I do not excuse this person's offense in any way, nor do I use any excuse for not extending forgiveness. Thank You, Lord Jesus, for enabling me to forgive him (her).*

I also confess that I have sinned by using the following excuses for not forgiving:

_____

_____

_____

_____

_____

_____

_____

_____

_____

_____

_____

Seeking Forgiveness from Those We Have Harmed

Having examined the importance of forgiving others, we must now ask, *What have I done to others that merits my seeking their forgiveness?* Step 4 has prepared us for this step by enabling us to see *what* we've done wrong. Now we need to know *whom* we have wronged.

We are not yet ready to make amends with these people. Our task here is simply to list their names. In preparing this list, it may be helpful to use these guidelines and to refer back to step 4:

- Whom did I rescue instead of letting them be responsible for themselves?
- Whom did I control and manipulate through condemnation, praise, silence, etc.?
- Whose separateness did I fail to respect, imposing my own feelings, thoughts and decisions on them?
- Whom have I blamed because I was unwilling to be responsible for my own behavior?
- From whom did I cheat or steal?
- What promises and/or confidences did I break (sexual infidelity, lying, sharing something told to me as a secret) and whom did I hurt or betray?
- For whom did I cause pain by missing family obligations (birthdays, anniversaries) or other special days or commitments?
- What social responsibilities (laws, commitments) did I break or avoid, and who was harmed by this?
- What financial obligations did I avoid or wrongly create, and who was harmed or inconvenienced by my behavior?
- What have I done to harm those with whom I've worked?
- What physical damage—to either property or people—resulted from my compulsive behavior, and whom did I harm?
- To whom have I neglected to show gratitude?
- Who was victimized by my anger, resentment, blame or fear?

Persons I Have Harmed   **How I Harmed Them**

1. _____   _____
2. _____   _____
3. _____   _____
4. _____   _____
5. _____   _____
6. _____   _____
7. _____   _____
8. _____   _____
9. _____   _____
10. _____   _____
11. _____   _____
12. _____   _____
13. _____   _____
14. _____   _____
15. _____   _____
16. _____   _____
17. _____   _____
18. _____   _____
19. _____   _____
20. _____   _____
21. _____   _____
22. _____   _____
23. _____   _____
24. _____   _____
25. _____   _____
26. _____   _____
27. _____   _____
28. _____   _____
29. _____   _____
30. _____   _____

Motivations for Making Amends

There are many benefits we will receive from reconciling ourselves to others by making our amends with them. For one thing, it will release us from the control these people currently have on us. Think about those persons you have been avoiding: those you've been dodging, hoping they won't see you, or those you've been excluding from your circle of friends altogether. Have you ever considered that your guilt and fear are controls which are keeping you from the full enjoyment of life and love God desires for all who know Him?

To make amends is to be released from our relational past. It releases us from the fear of someone's finding out something about us that we don't want them to know, a fear that will haunt and control us for the rest of our lives if unconfessed. Making amends will enable us to enjoy increased fellowship with others, a key factor in our continued recovery. Finally, as we take action to forgive others and experience their forgiveness, we will be able to forgive ourselves more completely. We will better understand that while our behavior may have been shameful, we as persons are not worthless. Learning how to love and forgive ourselves is a prerequisite for genuinely loving and forgiving others.

Read the Scriptures below and answer the questions that follow:

> *Therefore, since we have so great a cloud of witnesses surrounding us, let us also lay aside every encumbrance, and the sin which so easily entangles us, and let us run with endurance the race that is set before us,*
>
> *fixing our eyes on Jesus, the author and perfector of faith, who for the joy set before Him endured the cross, despising the shame, and has sat down at the right hand of the throne of God.*
>
> Heb. 12:1-2

> *Do you not know that those who run in a race all run, but only one receives the prize? Run in such a way that you may win.*
>
> 1 Cor. 9:24

■ Understanding that a runner is more likely to win a race by facing forward throughout its duration, how will making amends enable you to be a better runner in the "race" of life?

_____

_____

_____

_____

_____

■ What do you fear most about making amends?_____

_____

_____

• Do you think this is a realistic fear? Why or why not?_____

_____

_____

_____

_____

- Are you willing to lay this encumbrance of fear aside and make amends even though it may be painful to do so?

_____

_____

■ What possible joys might result from making amends?_____

_____

_____

_____

■ To which of these do you most look forward and why?_____

_____

_____

_____

_____

_____

_____

_____

Step Nine

We make direct amends to people where possible, except when doing so will injure them or others.

If therefore you are presenting your offering at the altar, and there remember that your brother has something against you, leave your offering there before the altar, and go your way, first be reconciled to your brother, and then come and present your offering.
Matt. 5:23-24

Making amends with others does *not* mean that we revert to old patterns of rescuing and manipulation in our relationships with them. This reversal, however, is exactly what some people expect of us—and want from us.

Family members rarely applaud when a rescuer stops rescuing. They usually want him or her to continue. If he or she stops, who will take care of them? The codependent's growth and independence is a threat to the systems of behavior established in the dysfunctional family. For that reason, family members often attempt to pressure the recovering codependent into reverting to the old patterns of behavior. Such pressure may take the form of subtle passive-aggressive manipulation or outright condemnation and ridicule. "How could you be so selfish? You *never* think about us!"

This kind of manipulation has worked wonders in the past. It will work again unless we prepare ourselves for it before it happens. We can do so by reflecting on what genuine love is and by asking ourselves questions like, *How do people treat each other when they love each other? Are members of my family valuing me and respecting my separateness? How would they treat me if they genuinely loved me?* Discussing these kinds of questions with a trusted friend or group will add to our sense of objectivity. We may conclude that we never will be loved by families or others the way we want to be loved. Realizations like these may propell us from the bargaining stage.

Our relationships—and our decisions to make amends for our wrongs in those relationships—need to be based on the firm foundation of security and healthy separateness, not manipulation and guilt. Then we can make amends because we *want* to, not because we feel that someone is forcing us to do so.

When we do make amends, it should be with the understanding that we are not responsible for making others happy with us. We especially want to avoid satisfying others at the expense of losing our identities. We need to find a balance between assuming responsibility for our wrongs and avoiding responsibility for someone else's response. Remember, some people may never be satisfied with us until we've reverted to being easily manipulated, and that's no longer an option for us.

Direct Amends

In making our amends, we must be *direct*. No anonymous phone calls, letters or payments to those we have wronged. In fact, unless extreme geographical logistics prevent us from doing so, we must go in person. Once we have looked someone squarely in the eye to confess our wrongdoing, we will be able to look that person and others in the eye always. Why? Because having gained their respect, we will regain ours. If a personal interview is absolutely impossible, a phone call is our second choice. One of our objectives is to open a door for dialogue.

Being direct also means assuming complete responsibility for our wrongs. This is not an opportunity to go and point the finger at someone else, e.g., "I'm very sorry, but if you hadn't done what you did..." Nor do we want to diminish our responsibility by blaming a third party, e.g., "Well, I'll admit to using poor judgment, but if Joe hadn't told me..." Our point in making amends is not to admit how we were misled, though this may have been the case, but to confess that we had a choice in the matter and made the wrong one.

The story of the prodigal son provides a good illustration for making direct amends. The younger of two brothers had demanded his portion of his father's inheritance. After the father graciously gave the son his share of what was coming to him, the son squandered it. Out of money and in need of a job, the son one day determined that he could return to his father and gain employment from him as a hired hand (see Luke 15:11-24). Here's what he said:

I will get up and go to my father, and will say to him, "Father, I have sinned against heaven, and in your sight...."
Luke 15:18

The son was not going to send an apology by messenger, but planned to go directly to his father and confess that he had wronged both him and God.

Restitution

Making amends is more than just making apologies. Restitution means setting things back in order, righting our wrongs. So far as this is possible, restitution is our goal. We want to demonstrate not only an acknowledgment of our wrongs, but a change of heart resulting in a change of *action*. Whenever our actions demonstrate a positive change of direction, we have truly repented.

■ Define *restitution*:_____

_____

■ Read the following passage:

> *If a wicked man restores a pledge, pays back what he has taken by robbery, walks by the statutes which ensure life without committing iniquity, he will surely live; he shall not die.*
>
> Ezek. 33:15

■ What does this passage say to you about making restitution with creditors, the government, local law enforcement agencies, or in instances of theft?

_____

_____

■ Seeing that you may or may not be able to make full restitution with the above persons or agencies, what can you do to show a willingness to pay back what you owe to each party you have wronged?

_____

_____

_____

■ What do you "owe" someone you have controlled and rescued?

_____

_____

■ To whom do you need to express gratitude?

_____   _____

_____   _____

_____   _____

_____   _____

_____   _____

• What action—large or small—can accompany your words to show that you really mean what you say?

_____

_____

_____

_____

Indirect Amends

The eighth step states that we will make direct amends to others *where possible*. We are again confronted by something we cannot change: the past. The children we may have wronged may now be grown. We cannot go back and erase the poor example we might have been for them or the abuse we might have given them. Nor can we make restitution with persons who have died or who have now moved to places unknown to us.

There are, however, some positive, constructive things we can do in these instances by way of *indirect amends*: We can learn from our mistakes and apply that knowledge to present and future situations. If someone we wronged has moved or died, we can pay what debts we may owe to one of their survivors or make a charitable donation in their name; we can treat their survivors with a special act of kindness. We can do for other people's children or parents what we wish we'd done for our own, not as an act of guilt, but in love. We can pray for those whom we know are still living, but cannot locate.[1]

■ These are only a few suggestions. List any others you can think of in the spaces provided below:

_____   _____

_____   _____

_____   _____

Avoiding Injury to Others

Some situations call for making **partial restitution**. By this, we mean partial disclosure of your wrongdoing. What situations call for this kind of action? The most obvious is sexual infidelity. Telling your spouse about your sexual escapades could cause him or her severe mental and emotional anguish, and could damage your marital relationship beyond repair. In the same way, exposing the person(s) with whom you committed infidelity could be damaging to them. Causing others such pain is both needless and harmful. Our goal in making amends is not to do further damage to others, but to right our wrongs.

How can we make restitution in such instances? *First, we can repent.* If we haven't already, we can break off the adulterous relationship(s) and resolve that with God's help, we will remain faithful to our spouse for the rest of our lives (one day at a time). *We can also demonstrate renewed interest toward our spouse,* giving him or her the time and attention he or she deserves from us.

Other situations calling for partial restitution may be those which would threaten our family's well-being. This could be the loss of employment or a legal implication which would harm family members, co-workers or friends. Again, our goal is not to avoid reaping the consequences of our sins, but to demonstrate careful consideration for other people in what we do and don't expose about others and ourselves.

Without knowing your situation in detail, it would be impossible to direct you in making a decision about matters such as these. God knows your situation. Consider the matter with Him in prayer. As you seek His direction, it will be wise for you also to consult with an objective minister or Christian counselor (or perhaps, your sponsor)—someone with whom you can talk candidly and from whom you can expect a godly response.

■ List below the people or circumstances in your life which may call for making **partial amends.** Beside each instance, identify the possible damage that could result from making full disclosure:

Person or Situation	Damaging Results
_____	_____
_____	_____
_____	_____
_____	_____

■ From the above, in what ways can you demonstrate partial restitution by a change of action:

Person or Situation	Specific Action
_____	_____
_____	_____
_____	_____
_____	_____

Still other situations may call for **delayed restitution.** Of course, we never want to make amends with anyone without first considering what we will say and what actions we can change. But what we are really thinking of here are those instances in which the hurt you have caused someone else is still so recent that any present discussion might end in a broken relationship. In these cases, it may be prudent to wait to take action.

Careful, prayerful consideration, combined with wise counsel and timing are all-important in successfully completing step 9.

■ List below the people or circumstances in your life which may call for **delayed amends.** (These may include situations where you still have not resolved your own negative emotions.) Beside each instance, list the possible harm that you could cause by making amends now:

Person or Situation	Damaging Results
_____	_____
_____	_____

_____   _____

_____   _____

_____   _____

■ Name some things you can do about these situations while you are waiting for the right time to make amends:

_____   _____

_____   _____

_____   _____

Take all of these issues to your sponsor, pastor or counselor; ask him or her to pray through each one with you, and wait with an *open mind* for God's direction.

For Additional Reflection and Application

Making restitution often brings favorable results. Many are completely disarmed by our willingness to be open and honest, and by our admission of wrongdoing. These people usually respond with gracious appreciation for our desire to right our wrongs and our relationships with them. But this isn't always the case. There are those who will respond in anger, shock, indifference or disapproval. The fear of such a response—or the experience of it in any instance—should not deter us from completing our errand. We must remember that we cannot control the responses of other people. Scripture tells us that *their* response is not the issue. Romans 12:18 says, "...so far as it depends on *you*, be at peace with all men."

Action Sheet

■ Turn back to the page in step 8 where you listed all the persons you have harmed. In the spaces provided on the following two pages, rewrite those names, and beside each, list the action you plan to take, the date the action is to be completed (if any) and the result of your interview with him or her.

(Note: This exercise may take weeks or even months to complete as you prayerfully determine your best course of action; the point is to have a reminder of both those you need to make amends with and what you're going to do to demonstrate repentance toward them. This will also serve as a source of encouragement for you when you need courage to face more difficult amends.)

Person	Specific Action to Be Taken
1.	
2.	
3.	
4.	
5.	
6.	
7.	
8.	
9.	
10.	
11.	
12.	
13.	
14.	
15.	
16.	
17.	
18.	
19.	
20.	

Date for Completion   **His/Her Response**

1. _____ | _____
2. _____ | _____
3. _____ | _____
4. _____ | _____
5. _____ | _____
6. _____ | _____
7. _____ | _____
8. _____ | _____
9. _____ | _____
10. _____ | _____
11. _____ | _____
12. _____ | _____
13. _____ | _____
14. _____ | _____
15. _____ | _____
16. _____ | _____
17. _____ | _____
18. _____ | _____
19. _____ | _____
20. _____ | _____

Step Ten

We continue to take personal inventory,
and when we are wrong, promptly admit it.

Therefore let him who thinks he stands take heed lest he fall.
1 Cor. 10:12

Our codependency often diminishes our ability to recognize real instances of wrongdoing in our lives. Some of us have dulled consciences, and fail to recognize when we hurt someone or sin in some other way. Most of us, however, have overly active consciences. We are morbidly introspective, often reliving and condemning many of the things we've said and done. Our self-worth plummets, and as it does, our sense of guilt rises. We begin to perform for God in a desperate attempt to win His approval and boost our esteem. We may feel pretty good for a while...until we sin again or perceive that we've sinned again. Then we repeat the same cycle.

We examined proper motivations for obedience in step 6. Our goal in obedience is not to perform for God, but to cooperate with Him by allowing His Holy Spirit to perform through us. Galations 5:16 says, ...*walk by the Spirit, and you will not carry out the desire of the flesh.*

In order to walk by the Spirit in the light of honesty, it is imperative that we learn how to take a daily inventory. Before doing this, however, it will be helpful to understand the difference between the Holy Spirit's conviction and guilt.

Guilt vs. Conviction

Perhaps no emotion is more destructive than guilt. It causes a loss of self-respect. It causes the human spirit to wither and eats away at our personal significance. Guilt is a strong motivator, but it plays on our fears of failure and rejection; therefore, it can never ultimately build, encourage or inspire us in our desire to live for Christ.

Guilt has a restricted meaning in the New Testament. It refers only to man's condition *prior to salvation*. Only the non-Christian is actually guilty before God. He has transgressed the law of God and must face the consequences. Guilt shakes its fist and says, "You have fallen short and must pay the price. You are personally accountable."

In Rom. 8:1, Paul wrote: *There is therefore now no condemnation for those who are in Christ Jesus.* Our condemnation is removed only through Christ. He took all of our guilt upon Himself when He accepted the penalty for our sins and suffered the full punishment for all sin. Because of His substitution, we need never face guilt's consequences. We are acquitted and absolved from guilt, free from our sentence of spiritual death.

Many of us have been told that we are still guilty even after we have trusted Christ to pay for our sins. And sadly, we have heard this in churches—places that should be loudly and clearly proclaiming the forgiveness and freedom found in the cross. Perhaps some people think that if they don't use guilt motivation, we won't do anything. Guilt may motivate us for a short while, until we adjust to being properly motivated. A short period of waiting is well worth the long-term results of grace-oriented, intrinsic motivation.

The love of Christ is powerful. He is worthy of our intense zeal to obey and honor Him. The result of proper motivation is an enduring, deepening commitment to Him and His cause, rather than the prevalent results of guilt motivation: resentment and the desire to escape.

Although Christians are free from guilt, we are still subject to the *conviction* of sin. Conviction deals with our *behavior*, not our status before God. Conviction is the work of the Holy Spirit. He directs and encourages our spiritual progress by revealing our sins in contrast to the holiness and purity of Christ. Conviction is His way of showing the error of our performance in light of God's standard and truth. His motivation is love, correction and protection.

Guilt brings depression and despair; conviction leads us to the beautiful realization of God's forgiveness and enables us to experience His love and power.

Perhaps the summary on the next page will better reveal the contrasting purposes and results of guilt and conviction:

- **Basic Focus:**

    GUILT focuses on the state of being condemned: *I am unworthy.*

    CONVICTION focuses on behavior: *This act is unworthy of Christ and is destructive.*

- **Primary Concern:**

    GUILT prompts concern about our loss of self-esteem and wounded self-pride: *What will others think of me?*

    CONVICTION causes us to be concerned with the loss of our moment-by-moment communion with God: *This act is destructive to me and interferes with my walk with God.*

- **Primary Fear:**

    GUILT produces a fear of punishment: *Now I'm going to get it!*

    CONVICTION produces a fear of the destructiveness of the act itself: *This behavior is destructive to me and to others, and it robs me of what God intends for me.*

- **Agent:**

    The agent of GUILT is Satan: *...the god of this world has blinded the minds of the unbelieving, that they might not see the light of the gospel of the glory of Christ* (2 Cor. 4:4).

    The agent of CONVICTION is the Holy Spirit: *...but if by the Spirit you are putting to death the deeds of the body, you will live* (Rom. 8:13).

- **Behavioral Results:**

    GUILT leads to depression and more sin: *I am just a low-down, dirty, rotten sinner;* or to rebellion: *I don't care. I'm going to do whatever I want to do.*

    CONVICTION leads to repentance, the turning from sin to Christ: *Lord, I agree with You that my sin is wrong and destructive. What do You want me to do?*

- **Interpersonal Result:**

    The interpersonal result of GUILT is alienation, a feeling of shame that drives one away from the person who has been wronged: *I can't ever face him again.*

    The interpersonal result of CONVICTION is restoration, a desire to remedy the harm done to others: *Father, what would You have me do to right this wrong and restore the relationship with the one I have offended?*

- **Personal Result:**

    GUILT ends in depression and bitterness: *I'm just no good.*

    CONVICTION ends in comfort, the realization of forgiveness: *Thank You, Lord, that I am completely forgiven and totally accepted by You!*

- **Remedy:**

    The remedy for GUILT is to trust in Christ's substitutionary death to pay for the condemnation of sin.

    The remedy for CONVICTION is confession, agreeing with God that our sin is wrong, that Christ has forgiven us, and that our attitude and actions will change.

■ To complete the following exercise, go back to step 4 and select four incidents from your personal inventory that have caused you to feel guilty. In the spaces below, list for each your *primary concern*, your *primary fear*, the *results guilt had on your behavior* and on your *interpersonal relationships*:

- INCIDENT:_____

_____

_____

- Primary Concern:_____
  _____
  _____

- Primary Fear:_____
  _____

- Behavioral Results:_____
  _____
  _____

- Interpersonal Results:_____
  _____
  _____

- INCIDENT:_____
  _____
  _____

- Primary Concern:_____
  _____
  _____

- Primary Fear:_____
  _____

- Behavioral Results:_____
  _____
  _____

- Interpersonal Results:_____
  _____
  _____

- INCIDENT:_____

  _____

  _____

- Primary Concern:_____

  _____

  _____

- Primary Fear:_____

  _____

- Behavioral Results:_____

  _____

  _____

- Interpersonal Results:_____

  _____

  _____

- INCIDENT:_____

  _____

  _____

- Primary Concern:_____

  _____

  _____

- Primary Fear:_____

  _____

- Behavioral Results:_____

  _____

  _____

• Interpersonal Results:_____

_____

_____

Although Christians are no longer subject to condemnation, we will not be free from its destructive power until we learn to distinguish between guilt and conviction. The Holy Spirit wants us to be convinced that we are forgiven, accepted and loved—totally secure—because of Christ. The Holy Spirit is the *Paraclete*, or "one called alongside," to lift us up and encourage us. As a part of His ministry, He faithfully makes us aware of any behavior that does not reflect the characteristics of Christ. He helps us understand both our righteousness before God and the failures in our performance.

Knowing this, how can we deal with feelings of guilt? First, we need to affirm that Christ has forgiven us and has made us judicially righteous before God. Our sins do not bring condemnation, but they are harmful, and they dishonor God. We can confess our sins to God, claim the forgiveness we already have in Christ and then move on in joy and freedom to honor Him. The following prayer expresses this attitude:

Father, I affirm that I am deeply loved by You, fully pleasing to You and totally accepted in Your sight. You have made me complete and have given me the righteousness of Christ, even though my performance often falls short. Lord, I confess my sins to You. (List them. Be specific.) *I agree with You that these are wrong. Thank You for Your grace and forgiveness. Is there anything I need to return, anyone I need to repay or anyone to whom I owe an apology? Thank You.*

It is important that we affirm our righteousness in Christ as well as confess our sins. God does not need to be reminded of our right standing in Him, but we do. Therefore, we need to make this prayer a daily experience and let it pervade our thoughts and hearts. As we yield to the gentle prodding of God-given conviction, confess our sins and affirm our true relationship with Him, we will gradually be shaped and molded so that we may increasingly *honor Him who died and rose again on* [our] *behalf* (2 Cor. 5:15).

Identifying False Beliefs

One goal in taking a personal inventory is to identify the false beliefs that govern our actions, and learn how to replace them with the truth of God's Word. It is helpful to first recognize where our emotions and actions come from. Jesus said, *Out of the abundance of the heart the mouth speaketh* (Matt. 12:34, KJV). In other words, our communication (which reveals our thoughts, emotions and the intent of our actions) comes from our heart (our belief system). Because a number of the situations in our lives are interpreted by what we believe, our belief system, not the situation, is usually the key to our response! The following diagram illustrates this process:

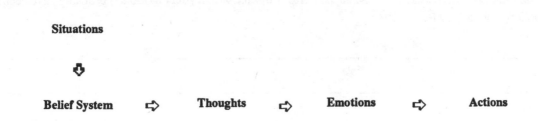

In addition to comprising our reactions to immediate events, our emotions are products of our family backgrounds, our past experiences, relationships and patterns of responses. Many of us come from homes where we were not loved and affirmed as children. We may have learned to repress painful emotions because we didn't want to believe that something was wrong with our families, our source of stability and security. Some of us have become numb, unable to feel either anger or joy, hurt or love. Some of us have developed a habit of forgetting difficult instances and their accompanying pain as a defense mechanism. There are many different ways to block pain in our efforts to gain a sense of worth, but we need to begin reversing this trend by finding someone who will encourage us to be honest about our feelings. We can then use our feelings as a gauge to determine if our response to a situation is based on the truth or a lie.

It is important to realize that feelings are neither right nor wrong. They are signals which tell us something about our environment. We need to be honest about our emotions so that they can tell us what we need to know about our perceptions. When our emotions are painful or distressing, we can ask, *Why am I responding this way? Am I believing a lie? If so, which one?*

Tracing Emotions to Root Beliefs

Let's suppose that someone (Bill) picked you up late, so you are late to work (or school, church, committee meeting). Your response is anger. You can trace that anger back to its root false belief in order to replace it with corresponding truths from the Scriptures or a characteristic of Christ presented in step 3. Here is how it would look:

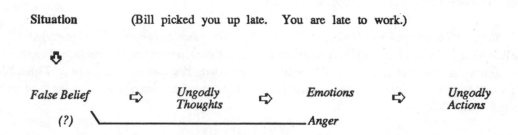

Situation   (Bill picked you up late. You are late to work.)

False Belief ⇨ *Ungodly Thoughts* ⇨ *Emotions* ⇨ *Ungodly Actions*

(?) —————————————————— *Anger*

How do you determine the false belief responsible for your anger? Ask yourself, *Why am I angry? Am I angry because...*

- *I hate to be late* (your "certain standard"), *and my lateness makes me feel badly about myself?* (**I must meet certain standards...**)
- *My boss will be displeased with me because I'm late, and her opinion of me means so much?* (**I must be approved by certain others...**)
- *Bill failed by being late to pick me up? It was his fault, that creep!* (**Those who fail are unworthy of love and deserve to be punished.**)
- *No matter what I do, something always goes wrong?* (**I am hopeless. I can't change. I'll always be this way.**)

Note that the proper response is not, *I'm not angry*, when in fact you are. Denial only compounds our problems; it is not a solution. We need to be honest with the Lord and with ourselves about our feelings.

■ If the situation in the above example had happened to you, what would your emotion(s) probably have been? Which false belief(s) could you trace it to?

_____

_____

_____

_____

_____

Red Flags

Throughout these pages, we have looked at many examples of codependent behavior. These should serve as red flags for us. *That's me; that's what I do!* or, *My wife does that to me!* or, *I respond that way to my husband.* Some of us see a few particular events, but don't see any deep-rooted patterns in our behavior. One man told me about his relationship with his condemning, manipulative father. "I've been angry with my father several times, so I guess I'm pretty objective," he surmised. He didn't see the pervasive insecurity and myriad of defense mechanisms that he had developed during his life. We need to see both the patterns of our behavior and the specific events that make up those patterns.

At the risk of being redundant, we will review some of the more common codependent feelings and behaviors. We will divide these by the savior and Judas categories for simplicity. Which of these, or variations of these, can you identify in your life? Circle the feelings, thoughts, words and actions that characterize your life to a significant degree. Is there a pattern?

Savior	Judas
Feelings: grandiose importance, superior, certain, euphoric, confident, appreciated, angry, self-righteous, jealous, possessive, easily hurt	**Feelings:** depressed, lonely, angry, helpless, confused, fear, hurt, inferior, hopeless, guilt, numbness, trapped, martyr, persecuted, lethargic, worthless, ashamed, tired
Thoughts and Words: *It's all your fault.* *You made me fail.* *I can help.* *He (she) needs me.* *Why aren't people as perceptive as I am?* *I deserve their respect and love.*	**Thoughts and Words:** *It's all my fault.* *I'm a failure.* *I can't do anything right.* *Everything I do is wrong.* *Yes,* but I mean *no.* *No,* but I mean *yes.* *I don't deserve their respect and love.*
Black or White: *People really need me.* *I am indispensable to the kingdom of God.* *People won't be helped and the Great Commission can't be fulfilled without me.*	**Black or White:** *People really need me, but I'll only let them down.* *Good Christians wouldn't think or act this way.* *God must be mad at me. He'll punish me.*
Actions: exaggerate (high), self-promotion, overcommitted, workaholism, easily manipulated, control others through praise and condemnation, rescue people without being asked, deny reality, compulsion to avoid failure, giving, helping, try to please people, defensive, overly responsible, outbursts of anger, rationalizes, trusts self and others	**Actions:** exaggerate (low), self-denigration, withdrawal, avoid people and risks, easily manipulated, control others through self-pity, deny reality, passive-agressive, afraid to fail, believes he can't please anybody, defensive irresponsible, outbursts of anger, rationalizes, doesn't trust self but may trust others

■ Take some time to identify current codependent behavior in your life. Using the savior/Judas chart on the previous page, be as specific as possible as you describe your feelings, thoughts, statements and actions.

SAVIOR

- Feelings:_____

_____

_____

_____

_____

- Thoughts and words:_____

_____

_____

_____

_____

- Actions:_____

_____

_____

_____

_____

JUDAS

- Feelings:_____

_____

_____

_____

- Thoughts and words:_____

_____

_____

_____

_____

• Actions:_____

_____

_____

_____

_____

Identifying codependent behavior may seem like a very cognitive exercise, but it usually elicits a flood of emotions as we realize how deeply we have been affected. The good news is: There is hope! The Lord can give us wisdom and strength, and a friend can give us the encouragement we need to fight our battles. The bad news is: What you see is probably only the first layer of the onion. As you deal with the hurts, fears, anger and habits there, yet another layer will be exposed. Is that discouraging to you? It probably is, but this is reality, and we need to face reality no matter how difficult it is. Remember, you are not alone. The Lord will give you the grace to endure and progress. Paul encouraged the believers in Corinth:

> *No temptation has overtaken you but such as is common to man; and God is faithful, who will not allow you to be tempted beyond what you are able, but with the temptation will provide the way of escape also, that you may be able to endure it.*
>
> 1 Cor. 10:13

The way of escape so that we may endure begins when we *identify* our codependent behavior, *detach* and reflect on reality, and finally, *decide* on the best course of action.

For the next fifteen days, develop a habit in your scheduled activities which could permanently change your life by selecting a specific time and place to complete the following daily inventory. Everything else of value in your life usually happens as a result of scheduling. You have a regular time to eat, to begin the workday and to rest. Schedule a time to *identify* daily situations that ellicit a codependent response from you. Then *detach* to reflect on the situation. Were you acting like a savior or a Judas? What were you thinking? What did you say? How did you feel? Which false belief(s) were you believing? What is God's truth? Then *decide*. What are you responsible for in this situation? What will be your plan of action and how will you implement that plan? Finally, *pray*. Thank God for the insights He has given you. Claim the truth of His Word and ask Him to provide what you need to gain victory over a similar situation in the future.

Day One

Date:_____/_____/_____

■ **Identify**

- Situation:_____

_____

_____

_____

- Codependent Response:_____

_____

_____

_____

■ **Detach**

- Were You Acting Like a savior or a Judas?_____

- Feelings:_____

_____

- Thoughts and Words:_____

_____

_____

- Actions:_____

_____

_____

■ If you were following Satan's lie(s), identify which from the chart on page 39 in step 2, and describe how you applied it to this situation:

_____

_____

_____

■ From page 39, what is God's truth and how does it apply to your situation?_____

_____

_____

_____

■ **Decide**

- What are you responsible for in this situation?_____

_____

_____

_____

- What are you not responsible for?_____

_____

_____

_____

- What would have been a healthy response to this situation?_____

_____

_____

_____

- What is your plan of action?_____

_____

_____

_____

■ **Pray.** Thank God for the insights He has given you. Claim the truth of His Word and ask Him to provide what you need to gain victory over a similar situation in the future.

Day Two

Date:_____/_____/_____

■ **Identify**

• Situation:_____

_____

_____

_____

• Codependent Response:_____

_____

_____

_____

■ **Detach**

• Were You Acting Like a savior or a Judas?_____

• Feelings:_____

_____

• Thoughts and Words:_____

_____

_____

• Actions:_____

_____

_____

■ If you were following Satan's lie(s), identify which from the chart on page 39 in step 2, and describe how you applied it to this situation:

_____

_____

_____

■ From page 39, what is God's truth and how does it apply to your situation?_____

_____

_____

_____

■ **Decide**

• What are you responsible for in this situation?_____

_____

_____

_____

• What are you not responsible for?_____

_____

_____

_____

• What would have been a healthy response to this situation?_____

_____

_____

_____

• What is your plan of action?_____

_____

_____

_____

■ **Pray.** Thank God for the insights He has given you. Claim the truth of His Word and ask Him to provide what you need to gain victory over a similar situation in the future.

Day Three

Date:_____/_____/_____

■ Identify

- Situation:_____

_____

_____

_____

- Codependent Response:_____

_____

_____

_____

■ Detach

- Were You Acting Like a savior or a Judas?_____

- Feelings:_____

_____

- Thoughts and Words:_____

_____

_____

- Actions:_____

_____

_____

■ If you were following Satan's lie(s), identify which from the chart on page 39 in step 2, and describe how you applied it to this situation:

_____

_____

_____

■ From page 39, what is God's truth and how does it apply to your situation?_____

_____

_____

_____

■ **Decide**

- What are you responsible for in this situation?_____

_____

_____

_____

- What are you not responsible for?_____

_____

_____

_____

- What would have been a healthy response to this situation?_____

_____

_____

_____

- What is your plan of action?_____

_____

_____

_____

■ **Pray.** Thank God for the insights He has given you. Claim the truth of His Word and ask Him to provide what you need to gain victory over a similar situation in the future.

Day Four

Date:_____/_____/_____

■ **Identify**

• Situation:_____

_____

_____

_____

• Codependent Response:_____

_____

_____

_____

■ **Detach**

• Were You Acting Like a savior or a Judas?_____

• Feelings:_____

_____

• Thoughts and Words:_____

_____

_____

• Actions:_____

_____

_____

■ If you were following Satan's lie(s), identify which from the chart on page 39 in step 2, and describe how you applied it to this situation:

_____

_____

_____

■ From page 39, what is God's truth and how does it apply to your situation?_____

_____

_____

_____

■ **Decide**

• What are you responsible for in this situation?_____

_____

_____

_____

• What are you not responsible for?_____

_____

_____

_____

• What would have been a healthy response to this situation?_____

_____

_____

_____

• What is your plan of action?_____

_____

_____

_____

■ **Pray.** Thank God for the insights He has given you. Claim the truth of His Word and ask Him to provide what you need to gain victory over a similar situation in the future.

Day Five

Date:_____/_____/_____

■ **Identify**

• Situation:_____

_____

_____

_____

• Codependent Response:_____

_____

_____

_____

■ **Detach**

• Were You Acting Like a savior or a Judas?_____

• Feelings:_____

_____

• Thoughts and Words:_____

_____

_____

• Actions:_____

_____

_____

■ If you were following Satan's lie(s), identify which from the chart on page 39 in step 2, and describe how you applied it to this situation:

_____

_____

_____

■ From page 39, what is God's truth and how does it apply to your situation?_____

_____

_____

_____

■ **Decide**

• What are you responsible for in this situation?_____

_____

_____

_____

• What are you not responsible for?_____

_____

_____

_____

• What would have been a healthy response to this situation?_____

_____

_____

_____

• What is your plan of action?_____

_____

_____

_____

■ **Pray.** Thank God for the insights He has given you. Claim the truth of His Word and ask Him to provide what you need to gain victory over a similar situation in the future.

Day Six

Date:_____/_____/_____

■ **Identify**

• Situation:_____

_____

_____

_____

• Codependent Response:_____

_____

_____

_____

■ **Detach**

• Were You Acting Like a savior or a Judas?_____

• Feelings:_____

_____

• Thoughts and Words:_____

_____

_____

• Actions:_____

_____

_____

■ If you were following Satan's lie(s), identify which from the chart on page 39 in step 2, and describe how you applied it to this situation:

_____

_____

_____

■ From page 39, what is God's truth and how does it apply to your situation?_____

_____

_____

_____

■ **Decide**

• What are you responsible for in this situation?_____

_____

_____

_____

• What are you not responsible for?_____

_____

_____

_____

• What would have been a healthy response to this situation?_____

_____

_____

_____

• What is your plan of action?_____

_____

_____

_____

■ **Pray.** Thank God for the insights He has given you. Claim the truth of His Word and ask Him to provide what you need to gain victory over a similar situation in the future.

Day Seven

Date:_____/_____/_____

■ **Identify**

- Situation:_____

  _____

  _____

  _____

- Codependent Response:_____

  _____

  _____

  _____

■ **Detach**

- Were You Acting Like a savior or a Judas?_____

- Feelings:_____

  _____

- Thoughts and Words:_____

  _____

  _____

- Actions:_____

  _____

  _____

■ If you were following Satan's lie(s), identify which from the chart on page 39 in step 2, and describe how you applied it to this situation:

  _____

  _____

  _____

■ From page 39, what is God's truth and how does it apply to your situation?_____

_____

_____

_____

■ **Decide**

• What are you responsible for in this situation?_____

_____

_____

_____

• What are you not responsible for?_____

_____

_____

_____

• What would have been a healthy response to this situation?_____

_____

_____

_____

• What is your plan of action?_____

_____

_____

_____

■ **Pray.** Thank God for the insights He has given you. Claim the truth of His Word and ask Him to provide what you need to gain victory over a similar situation in the future.

Day Eight

Date:_____/_____/_____

■ Identify

• Situation:_____

_____

_____

_____

• Codependent Response:_____

_____

_____

_____

■ Detach

• Were You Acting Like a savior or a Judas?_____

• Feelings:_____

_____

• Thoughts and Words:_____

_____

_____

• Actions:_____

_____

_____

■ If you were following Satan's lie(s), identify which from the chart on page 39 in step 2, and describe how you applied it to this situation:

_____

_____

_____

■ From page 39, what is God's truth and how does it apply to your situation?_____

_____

_____

_____

■ **Decide**

• What are you responsible for in this situation?_____

_____

_____

_____

• What are you not responsible for?_____

_____

_____

_____

• What would have been a healthy response to this situation?_____

_____

_____

_____

• What is your plan of action?_____

_____

_____

_____

■ **Pray.** Thank God for the insights He has given you. Claim the truth of His Word and ask Him to provide what you need to gain victory over a similar situation in the future.

Day Nine

Date:_____/_____/_____

■ Identify

- Situation:_____

_____

_____

_____

- Codependent Response:_____

_____

_____

_____

■ Detach

- Were You Acting Like a savior or a Judas?_____

- Feelings:_____

_____

- Thoughts and Words:_____

_____

_____

- Actions:_____

_____

_____

■ If you were following Satan's lie(s), identify which from the chart on page 39 in step 2, and describe how you applied it to this situation:

_____

_____

_____

■ From page 39, what is God's truth and how does it apply to your situation?_____

_____

_____

_____

■ **Decide**

• What are you responsible for in this situation?_____

_____

_____

_____

• What are you not responsible for?_____

_____

_____

_____

• What would have been a healthy response to this situation?_____

_____

_____

_____

• What is your plan of action?_____

_____

_____

_____

■ **Pray.** Thank God for the insights He has given you. Claim the truth of His Word and ask Him to provide what you need to gain victory over a similar situation in the future.

Day Ten

Date:_____/_____/_____

■ **Identify**

• Situation:_____

_____

_____

_____

• Codependent Response:_____

_____

_____

_____

■ **Detach**

• Were You Acting Like a savior or a Judas?_____

• Feelings:_____

_____

• Thoughts and Words:_____

_____

_____

• Actions:_____

_____

_____

■ If you were following Satan's lie(s), identify which from the chart on page 39 in step 2, and describe how you applied it to this situation:

_____

_____

_____

■ From page 39, what is God's truth and how does it apply to your situation?_____

_____

_____

_____

■ **Decide**

• What are you responsible for in this situation?_____

_____

_____

_____

• What are you not responsible for?_____

_____

_____

_____

• What would have been a healthy response to this situation?_____

_____

_____

_____

• What is your plan of action?_____

_____

_____

_____

■ **Pray.** Thank God for the insights He has given you. Claim the truth of His Word and ask Him to provide what you need to gain victory over a similar situation in the future.

Day Eleven

Date:_____/_____/_____

■ **Identify**

- Situation:_____

  _____

  _____

  _____

- Codependent Response:_____

  _____

  _____

  _____

■ **Detach**

- Were You Acting Like a savior or a Judas?_____

- Feelings:_____

  _____

- Thoughts and Words:_____

  _____

  _____

- Actions:_____

  _____

  _____

■ If you were following Satan's lie(s), identify which from the chart on page 39 in step 2, and describe how you applied it to this situation:

_____

_____

_____

■ From page 39, what is God's truth and how does it apply to your situation?_____

_____

_____

_____

■ **Decide**

• What are you responsible for in this situation?_____

_____

_____

_____

• What are you not responsible for?_____

_____

_____

_____

• What would have been a healthy response to this situation?_____

_____

_____

_____

• What is your plan of action?_____

_____

_____

_____

■ **Pray.** Thank God for the insights He has given you. Claim the truth of His Word and ask Him to provide what you need to gain victory over a similar situation in the future.

Day Twelve

Date:_____/_____/_____

■ **Identify**

- Situation:_____

  _____

  _____

  _____

- Codependent Response:_____

  _____

  _____

  _____

■ **Detach**

- Were You Acting Like a savior or a Judas?_____

- Feelings:_____

  _____

- Thoughts and Words:_____

  _____

  _____

- Actions:_____

  _____

  _____

■ If you were following Satan's lie(s), identify which from the chart on page 39 in step 2, and describe how you applied it to this situation:

  _____

  _____

  _____

■ From page 39, what is God's truth and how does it apply to your situation?_____

_____

_____

_____

■ **Decide**

• What are you responsible for in this situation?_____

_____

_____

_____

• What are you not responsible for?_____

_____

_____

_____

• What would have been a healthy response to this situation?_____

_____

_____

_____

• What is your plan of action?_____

_____

_____

_____

■ **Pray.** Thank God for the insights He has given you. Claim the truth of His Word and ask Him to provide what you need to gain victory over a similar situation in the future.

Day Thirteen

Date:_____/_____/_____

■ **Identify**

• Situation:_____

_____

_____

_____

• Codependent Response:_____

_____

_____

_____

■ **Detach**

• Were You Acting Like a savior or a Judas?_____

• Feelings:_____

_____

• Thoughts and Words:_____

_____

_____

• Actions:_____

_____

_____

■ If you were following Satan's lie(s), identify which from the chart on page 39 in step 2, and describe how you applied it to this situation:

_____

_____

_____

■ From page 39, what is God's truth and how does it apply to your situation?_____

_____

_____

_____

■ **Decide**

• What are you responsible for in this situation?_____

_____

_____

_____

• What are you not responsible for?_____

_____

_____

_____

• What would have been a healthy response to this situation?_____

_____

_____

_____

• What is your plan of action?_____

_____

_____

_____

■ **Pray.** Thank God for the insights He has given you. Claim the truth of His Word and ask Him to provide what you need to gain victory over a similar situation in the future.

Day Fourteen

Date:_____/_____/_____

■ **Identify**

- Situation:_____

_____

_____

_____

- Codependent Response:_____

_____

_____

_____

■ **Detach**

- Were You Acting Like a savior or a Judas?_____

- Feelings:_____

_____

- Thoughts and Words:_____

_____

_____

- Actions:_____

_____

_____

■ If you were following Satan's lie(s), identify which from the chart on page 39 in step 2, and describe how you applied it to this situation:

_____

_____

_____

■ From page 39, what is God's truth and how does it apply to your situation?_____

_____

_____

_____

■ **Decide**

• What are you responsible for in this situation?_____

_____

_____

_____

• What are you not responsible for?_____

_____

_____

_____

• What would have been a healthy response to this situation?_____

_____

_____

_____

• What is your plan of action?_____

_____

_____

_____

■ **Pray.** Thank God for the insights He has given you. Claim the truth of His Word and ask Him to provide what you need to gain victory over a similar situation in the future.

Day Fifteen

Date:_____/_____/_____

■ Identify

- Situation:_____

  _____

  _____

  _____

- Codependent Response:_____

  _____

  _____

  _____

■ Detach

- Were You Acting Like a savior or a Judas?_____

- Feelings:_____

  _____

- Thoughts and Words:_____

  _____

  _____

- Actions:_____

  _____

  _____

■ If you were following Satan's lie(s), identify which from the chart on page 39 in step 2, and describe how you applied it to this situation:

  _____

  _____

  _____

■ From page 39, what is God's truth and how does it apply to your situation?_____

_____

_____

_____

■ **Decide**

• What are you responsible for in this situation?_____

_____

_____

_____

• What are you not responsible for?_____

_____

_____

_____

• What would have been a healthy response to this situation?_____

_____

_____

_____

• What is your plan of action?_____

_____

_____

_____

■ **Pray.** Thank God for the insights He has given you. Claim the truth of His Word and ask Him to provide what you need to gain victory over a similar situation in the future.

Step Eleven

We seek to grow in our relationship with Jesus Christ through prayer, meditation and obedience, praying for wisdom and power to carry out His will.

> *But if any of you lacks wisdom, let him ask of God, who gives to all men generously and without reproach, and it will be given to him. But let him ask in faith without any doubting, for the one who doubts is like the surf of the sea driven and tossed by the wind.*
>
> James 1:5-6

Jesus Christ's primary purpose in allowing Himself to be made human, to be made sin and to be crucified on our behalf was to reconcile us to God. He desires to have a relationship with us. In John 10:1-4, 14, He said:

> *Truly, truly, I say to you, he who does not enter by the door into the fold of the sheep, but climbs up some other way, he is a thief and a robber.*
> *But he who enters by the door is a shepherd of the sheep.*
> *To him the doorkeeper opens, and the sheep hear his voice, and he calls his own sheep by name, and leads them out.*
> *When he puts forth all his own, he goes before them, and the sheep follow him because they know his voice…*
> *I am the good shepherd; and I know My own, and My own know Me. . . .*

In Scripture, Jesus is often described as the *good shepherd*, who is faithful to lead and provide for His *sheep*, those who are His. The point of this passage is clear: We can't hope to follow Jesus unless we know His voice, and we can't distinguish His voice from any other until we have cultivated an intimate relationship with Him. Such a relationship takes time, but God clearly wants it. He has taken the initiative in having a relationship with us:

> *We love because He first loved us.*
>
> 1 John 4:19

> *By this the love of God was manifested in us, that God has sent His only begotten Son into the world so that we might live through Him.*
> *In this is love, not that we loved God, but that He loved us and sent His Son to be the propitiation for our sins.*
>
> 1 John 4:9-10

Not only has God taken the initiative to have a relationship with us, He has given us the resources we need to enjoy that relationship: His Holy Spirit, His Word (the Scriptures) and prayer.

Prayer is our opportunity to communicate through the Holy Spirit to God. Scripture is God's Word (the final authority on matters of life) communicated through His Spirit to us.

Concerning the Holy Spirit's involvement in our communication with God, Scripture says:

> *And in the same way the Spirit also helps our weakness; for we do not know how to pray as we should, but the Spirit Himself intercedes for us with groanings too deep for words. . . .*
>
> Rom. 8:26

> *…for through Him we…have our access in one Spirit to the Father.*
>
> Eph. 2:18

*But know this first of all, that no prophecy of Scripture is a matter of one's own interpretation,
for no prophecy was ever made by an act of human will, but men moved by the Holy Spirit spoke
from God.*

2 Pet. 1:20-21

Prayer

As we have just read, the Holy Spirit intercedes for us in prayer. Some people hold to the premise that this means speaking to God in a *tongue*, or language that may be known only to God. But the Holy Spirit isn't limited in the ways He can speak to God on our behalf. To "pray in the Spirit" is to pray with His guidance and wisdom; with an open mind which allows Him to place on our hearts those people and things we need to speak to God about.

God's Response to Prayer

Some of us are uncomfortable with prayer. We find it difficult to concentrate on conversation with an invisible God with whom we experience no audible dialogue. Perhaps, too, we are disappointed with our prayer lives, frustrated because we can't seem to get any answers. What is God's response to prayer?

■ Read Jer. 29:11-14; 33:2-3.

• Have you been discouraged about praying? Why or why not?_____

_____

_____

• In what ways are you encouraged by these passages?_____

_____

_____

God's Reasons for Prayer

God spoke through the prophet Isaiah to tell His people: *It will come to pass that before they call, I will answer; and while they are still speaking, I will hear.* If God is in the process of answering before we call on Him, and if He hears us even before we speak, why should we pray? Does it really make a difference? Let's examine what the Scriptures say:

■ Read 1 Chron. 16:11; 2 Chron. 7:14; Ps. 50:15; Luke 18:1-8; 1 Pet. 3:12.

• From these passages, why should we pray?_____

_____

_____

■ Why do you usually pray?_____

_____

_____

■ What kinds of things do you usually ask God for when you pray?_____

_____

_____

God's Requirements for Prayer

Those of us who feel we are doing God a great service when we pray may be surprised to learn that He ha‐
requirements for prayer. After all, doesn't He *want* to hear from us? Isn't He the God of love, who freely accepts us
The answer to those questions is yes, definitely! Yet, God is holy. We hear much about the Lord being "our friend," and
this is true. Yet He is also *God*. In His holy righteousness, He has set up some ordinances for approaching Him most
effectively and has told us what He does and doesn't like to see in prayer.

■ Read Ps. 66:16-20; Matt. 5:23-24; 6:5-15; 2 Cor. 7:9-10; James 1:5-6; 1 John 1:9.

• Give as many requirements for effective prayer as you can find from the passages just read:_____

_____

_____

_____

_____

• What do these passages say about forgiveness as it affects our relationship with God?_____

_____

_____

_____

• What, according to these passages, are we to avoid?_____

_____

_____

_____

• What does Matt. 6:5-15 tell you about God's desire for you to be alone and quiet with Him?_____

_____

_____

• What are some practical ways you can meet with Him on these terms?_____

_____

God's Resources for Prayer

As already mentioned, God has given us His Holy Spirit as our Helper in prayer. He also has given us His Word, another tool we can use for communicating with Him. Sometimes our lives are in crisis, and we are simply too distraught to pray. On other occasions we may be filled with so much joy and gratitude that we are beyond words of expression. God's Word holds many promises we can take directly to His throne and claim before Him. The Lord delights in this! When we have asked the Holy Spirit to guide our prayers and are citing the truths of His Word to Him, we can be sure that we are praying in His will.

The Psalms also are an excellent resource for "prayer material." David knew the heights of ecstasy and the lonely depths of despair. The Psalms will be of great help and support to you as you pray. They also provide a marvelous example of what true communication with God can be.

Finally, God has given us His people—other Christians—as supporters in prayer. He truly honors a "network" of prayer (Matt. 18:19). This does not mean, of course, that we should rely solely on the prayers of others for our needs. God desires for each one of us to be in direct contact with Him at all times (Col. 4:2; 1 Thess. 5:17).

■ Do you have a "prayer network" of believers with whom you can pray?_____

• Whom can you enlist for prayer support?_____

_____

_____

• For what reasons might prayer support be helpful to you?_____

_____

_____

_____

_____

■ In what practical ways can you incorporate prayer into your daily activities?_____

_____

_____

_____

_____

Priority of Prayer

Many of us *know* we should be cultivating a personal relationship with God, but we often are so busy—perhaps even in Christian service—that we just don't seem to have time to pray. We may also have the perception that our prayers need to be lengthy to be effective. We will discuss the time element later in this step. For now, let's look at the priority Jesus placed on prayer.

■ Read Mark 1:34-35; 6:45-46; and Luke 5:16.

• Why do you think it was important for God the Son to spend time alone with God the Father?_____

_____

_____

_____

• What did Jesus do to ensure that He could be alone with His Father?_____

_____

_____

_____

■ Read Luke 3:21-22; 6:12-13; 9:28-31; 22:39-46.

• What significant events occurred either while Jesus was praying, or as a result of His prayers?_____

_____

_____

_____

_____

• What were the results of His prayers regarding these events?_____

_____

_____

_____

• Why did Jesus tell His disciples to pray?_____

_____

■ What practical lessons do you learn from Jesus about prayer?_____

_____

_____

_____

■ Read Ps. 5:3; Matt. 6:33; Luke 10:38-42.

• From the passage you just read in Luke, does your life reflect the activity of Martha or the quiet submission of Mary? Explain:

_____

_____

_____

• Do you gain any new insights about service—even Christian service—and its priority with God as it relates to prayer? If so, what are they?

_____

_____

_____

• Do you find any comfort in knowing that God values your time with Him even more than your dutiful service for Him? If so, explain:

_____

_____

_____

• What do you learn about prayer from Ps. 5:3?_____

_____

_____

• How can you incorporate the insights you've gained from "The Priority of Prayer" into your daily life?

_____

_____

_____

_____

Essentials of Prayer

There are many methods and varieties of prayer, and God certainly does not restrict us to any one formula! We should feel free to communicate with Him in the ways we are led by His Spirit. However, for those who may just be getting started, we offer a simple suggestion which is easily remembered by the acronym, ACTS.

A - Adoration: *Great is the Lord, and greatly to be praised...* (Ps. 48:1).

One woman has well said, "If we could better comprehend the depth of God and His love for us, our throats would ache with praise!"

Adoration is praising God for His virtues, characteristics and abilities. It is that act by which we state that *He* is the living God, *our* God, who is deserving of our single-minded worship and devotion. You may want to look at the characteristics of Christ in step 3 to help you reflect on His attributes.

■ Write some of these as praises to God, e.g., *Lord, I praise you for...*_____

_____

_____

_____

_____

C - Confession: *Behold, the Lord's hand is not so short that it cannot save; neither is His ear so dull that it cannot hear. But your iniquities have made a separation between you and your God, and your sins have hidden His face from you, so that He does not hear* (Is. 59:1-2).

By way of review, *confession* does not make us forgiven. Christ's work on the cross has already accomplished our need for forgiveness. To confess is to agree with God, to acknowledge under the Holy Spirit's leading that we have "missed the mark." In so doing, we become aware of our desperate need for God's intervention in our sinful patterns of behavior; we recognize patterns of behavior that need to be transformed by Him; we see situations that in the future may need to be avoided; we become aware of those with whom we need to make amends; and we realign our purposes with the purposes of God.

■ Is there any sinful thought or behavior you need to confess to God right now? If so, what is it?_____

_____

_____

_____

• Can you identify one or more false beliefs which prompted your sin? If so, list the belief(s):_____

_____

_____

• Which of God's truths can you substitute for the false belief(s)?_____

_____

_____

T - Thanksgiving: *In everything give thanks, for this is God's will for you in Christ Jesus* (1 Thess. 5:18).

There is something to be thankful for in *any* situation. We often miss this truth because the enemy (Satan) is making every effort to call our attention to what we are lacking in life, rather than what we have. But we can give thanks for any or all of the following:[1]

- *Spiritual blessings* (answers to prayer, salvation, forgiveness, acceptance)
- *Physical blessings* (eyes, ears, health, etc.)
- *Relational blessings* (family, friends, co-workers, etc.)
- *Material blessings* (home, job, money, car, etc.)
- *Intangible blessings* (freedom of speech, freedom of worship, freedom of choice, etc.)

■ From the above, for what are you most thankful?_____

_____

Make a habit of thanking God daily for at least one of the blessings listed in each category above.

S - Supplication: *If you abide in Me, and My words abide in you, ask whatever you wish, and it shall be done for you* (John 15:7).

There are two forms of supplication: intercession and petition. *Intercession* is praying on behalf of others; *petition* is asking God to meet our own needs.

■ **Intercession:** *Far be it from me that I should sin against the Lord by ceasing to pray for you* (1 Sam. 12:33).

Many of us may be surprised to learn that when we neglect to pray for others, it is *sin* in God's sight. Scripture continually refers to believers as the *body* of Christ (see 1 Cor. 10:16-17; 12:12-27; Eph. 5:29-30). Just as the physical body is dependent on its various parts for survival, so it is in the body of Christ. We need each other. God doesn't intend for us to do His work alone! We are therefore commanded to pray for one another, as well as for those in authority and for the "lost," or unbelievers, of the world:

> …I urge that entreaties and prayers, petitions and thanksgivings, be made on behalf of all men, for kings and all who are in authority, in order that we may lead a tranquil and quiet life in all godliness and dignity. This is good and acceptable in the sight of God our Savior, who desires all men to be saved and to come to the knowledge of the truth.
>
> 1 Tim. 2:1-4

In addition to those in positions of governing authority, we are told to pray for:

- All the *saints*, or believers (Eph. 6:18; Col. 4:3; James 5:16)
- Believers who are in sin (Gal. 6:1)
- Anyone suffering from adversity (Heb. 13:3)
- The sending forth of Christian workers (Matt. 9:38)

We can pray for these people the same blessings for which we are thankful: *spiritual* blessings (see Eph. 1:17-19); *physical* blessings (health, body, appearance); *relational* blessings (support, friendships, family); *material* blessings (jobs, home, money); and *intangible* blessings (safety if they are in another country, for example).

Ask the Holy Spirit to guide you as you answer the following, and beside each name you list, write what you think God might be asking you to pray for:

■ What political authorities may need your prayers?

Persons   **Requests**

_____   _____

_____   _____

_____   _____

_____   _____

_____   _____

■ What family members need your prayers?

Persons   **Requests**

_____   _____

_____   _____

_____   _____

_____   _____

_____   _____

■ For what other "saints" (friends, ministers, Sunday school teachers, missionaries, Christians who have fallen into sin, etc.) might God want you to pray?

Persons   **Requests**

_____   _____

_____   _____

_____   _____

_____   _____

_____   _____

■ What unbelievers (friends, family members, supervisor, co-workers, neighbors) may need your prayers?

Persons   **Requests**

_____   _____

_____   _____

_____   _____

_____   _____

■ In the space provided, write today's date: _____

You have just completed a very practical exercise in praying for other people. By writing down your requests, you have already made them known to God! You also have a list to refer back to and pray from. Making a list can be beneficial for two reasons: *it enables us to remember what it is we need to pray for and it enables us to see God's answers!*

Make it a habit to pray for one person in each of the above categories each day. As you begin to see answers to your prayers, you may want to begin your own "prayer journal" so that you can record the persons needing prayer, your requests and God's answers. This can be a very exciting way to pray!

■ Name some of the benefits you may personally receive by praying for others:

_____   _____

_____   _____

_____   _____

_____   _____

■ **Petition:** *For we do not have a high priest who cannot sympathize with our weaknesses, but one who has been tempted in all things as we are, yet without sin. Let us therefore draw near with confidence to the throne of grace, that we may receive mercy and may find grace to help in time of need* (Heb. 4:15-16).

If you abide in Me, and My words abide in you, ask whatever you wish, and it shall be done for you.

John 15:7

Many of us have a tendency to approach God with the idea of Santa Claus in mind. We may read a passage such as John 15:7 and wonder why we do not get everything we wish—like a boat, or a million dollars or healing from a spiritual or physical malady. Here, there are several things we must take into account:

When Jesus said the words we now find in John 15:7, He knew that if we would abide in Him—in His Word and in His Spirit—and if we would, by an act of our will and the power of the Holy Spirit, allow our sinful ways to be crucified (Gal. 5:24), we would pray according to His will, with a view not only to *our* best, but to what might be best in God's eyes. Because we often don't initially know what to pray for in this regard, it is wise to pray for a *knowledge of God's will and the power to carry that out.* Certainly, we can and should bring our physical, spiritual, emotional, relational and material needs before God, remembering that sometimes His answer is *no,* and sometimes, *wait.*

■ Read 2 Cor. 12:7-10.

• Are there times when God has said *no* or *wait* to your request(s)? If so, name some of those occasions:

_____   _____

_____   _____

_____   _____

• What might God have wanted to teach you through those situations?_____

_____

_____

Whether God's answer is *no* or *wait*, we must remember the words He spoke to the prophet Isaiah: "For My thoughts are not your thoughts, neither are your ways My ways," declares the Lord. "For as the heavens are higher than the earth, so are My ways higher than your ways, and My thoughts than your thoughts" (Is. 55:8-9).

God's plan and timing are perfect. As we continue to seek Him and walk with Him, we will continue to realize that He can be trusted.

■ List some of your physical needs:_____

_____

• Spiritual needs:_____

_____

• Emotional needs:_____

_____

• Relational needs:_____

_____

• Material needs:_____

_____

Make it your habit to pray for two of these each day, and then use a separate piece of paper (or a journal including intercessory prayers) to record God's answers to you.

Meditation

Having established a foundation for the importance of prayer, we are now ready to examine God's communication with us through His Word. Let's look at a few of the many reasons we need to develop a knowledge of God's Word.

■ Read Is. 40:8; 55:10-11; 2 Tim. 3:16-17; Heb. 4:12.

• From the above passages, describe some characteristics of God's Word:_____

_____

_____

_____

■ Read Matt. 7:17-19 and John 15:10.

• Why did Jesus emphasize the necessity of knowing Scripture?_____

_____

_____

_____

■ Read Ps. 119:97-105; Acts 17:11; Rom. 10:17.

• From the above, what are some benefits of knowing Scripture?_____

_____

_____

_____

■ What results can God's Word accomplish?_____

_____

_____

_____

■ What do these promises mean to you?_____

_____

_____

_____

■ Which passage about the attributes of Scripture is most meaningful to you and why?_____

_____

_____

_____

■ Read Ps. 32:8.

• Turn back to the list of personal prayer requests you made on page 251. Are there any for which you are currently seeking guidance from the Scriptures? If so, which one(s)?

_____

_____

_____

Obedience

As we mentioned earlier, we can't hope to be obedient to God without knowing His commands. While our goal in Christian living is not *perfection*, we make *progress* in our relationship with God as we practice obedience to Him in our daily affairs.

> And Samuel said, *"Has the Lord as much delight in burnt offerings and sacrifices as in obeying*
> *the voice of the Lord? Behold, to obey is better than sacrifice, and to heed than the fat of rams.*
> *For rebellion is as the sin of divination, and insubordination is as iniquity and idolatry. . . .*
> 1 Sam. 15:22-23

Jesus Christ has paid for our sins, averted the wrath of God and made us dear, beloved children of God. He is worthy of our obedience! He is Lord! He truly is excellent and He deserves our affections and our efforts. There are no political causes, persons, material goods, no fame or prestige that can compare to the One who *died and rose again on our behalf* (2 Cor. 5:15). As Christians, we have the unspeakable privilege of representing the King of kings. We can do this effectively—for eternal purposes—only as we allow the Holy Spirit to teach and guide us through prayer and personal Bible study. Let's look at some ways we can make both a part of our daily routine.

Getting Started

Many of us are eager to know the Scriptures. We may even envy those who are able to rattle off verses at the mention of any given topic. Usually, however, our jealousy doesn't propel us into action. Instead, we are often intimidated by the enormity and sometimes, complexity, of the Scriptures.

The two best tips we can give you for personal study are 1) *Get started* and 2) *Ask the Holy Spirit to teach you and help you understand the passages you are reading.*

There is no *best* place to start in the Scriptures; anywhere will do. The real key is to read on a regular basis. You may want to start with the book of Matthew and read one chapter each day until you get to Mark, and then continue through the four Gospels and the New Testament until you are finished. Then turn to Genesis and read through the Old Testament, or start again with Matthew and reread the New Testament.

There is no need to hurry or rush your way through. The point of reading is *learning*, not finishing. Why? So you can begin to apply God's truths to your life.

You may want to join a Bible study so that you will have some accountability for reading and studying. Perhaps your church, or one in your area, is offering a "Through the Bible in a Year" program. Some Bibles offer a format for reading through the Scriptures in a year.

The Bible often becomes more meaningful for us when we have something to look for. The ideas on the following page are suggested ways to study the Bible personally:

- **Find attributes of God:** We have given you some of these already. There are many others. Look for them as you read and write them down in a study notebook.
- **God's commands:** In order to fulfill God's commands, we must know them. As you read, you may want to ask the Holy Spirit to call your attention to His commands, and then ask God's help to keep them.
- **God's promises:** The Scriptures contain thousands of promises made by God to us. He is faithful. He never breaks one of His promises. Read these and underline in your Bible those that are most meaningful to you. You might even try to memorize some as you go so that you will have them in your memory when you need them.
- **God's warnings:** What warnings from God do you need to read and then heed? Watching for them and absorbing them is another way to effectively study His Word.
- **Word studies:** This is taking a word in one passage and comparing it to other passages using the same word. An example of this is the word *shepherd* in Psalm 23. How is it used in this passage? How is it used in other Scripture passages? Does it always have the same meaning?
- **Character traits:** Who were the great leaders in the Bible? What were they like? What were their assets? What were their weaknesses? What do you learn from that?
- **Topics for prayer:** The Bible is our best resource for learning how to pray in God's will. What ideas for prayer do you gain from reading? Make a list of these and place them in your prayer journal; pray them back to God.
- **Reasons to love God more:** Scripture tells us that *we love because He first loved us* (1 John 4:19). This is only one of MANY reasons why we can love God. Underline passages which cause you to love God more as you read and refer back to them in times of difficulty.
- **Asking questions:** Using a topic like the one given above, you may want to personalize your reading by asking, *In what ways has God demonstrated His love to me?* Or, in the case of a word study, *In what ways has God been a shepherd to me?* Or, *Am I acting as a shepherd to God's people?*
- **Commentaries:** Commentaries are very useful for providing background information. For example, if you studied the book of Romans, you might want to know whom specifically Paul was addressing; when the letters were written; what his primary purpose was in writing; where he was as he wrote those letters. This knowledge is very helpful in understanding the context of Scripture fully. We do, however, advise you to first read the Scriptures for yourself, ask the Holy Spirit to show you what He wants you to see, and then turn to a commentary for additional help and insight.

These are a few of the many possibilities for personal study; there are many others. Let your imagination be your guide, but above all else, *get started*!

Making Time for God

Earlier, we mentioned that a big obstacle to our personal relationship with God is T-I-M-E. Many of us resist approaching God because we feel like we owe Him a large chunk of our time. We do owe everything to God, but the truth is that He is delighted with any effort we make to spend time with Him, especially if it means having to say *no* to something else in order to keep the appointment.

These are some suggestions for pursuing time alone with God:

- **Start slowly, but be consistent.** You may want to spend ten minutes with God each day at first. You can read five verses of Scripture, and spend the rest of your time in prayer. The point is: do it *every* day.
- **Make an appointment and keep it.** Set aside one special time each day reserved specifically for you and God.
- **Find a quiet place.** Take the phone off the hook if necessary.
- **Choose a time when you'll be free of interruptions.**
- **Ask the Holy Spirit for help and guidance.**

Every relationship takes time. God knows this more than anyone else. As you continue to grow with Him, you'll find yourself *wanting* to spend more time with Him. You'll also gain a special blessing in knowing that God isn't just everyone else's God, but yours.

Step Twelve

Having had a spiritual awakening, we try to carry the message of Christ's grace and power to others who struggle with codependency, and to practice these principles in every aspect of our lives.

Brethren, even if a man is caught in any trespass, you who are spiritual, restore such a one in a spirit of gentleness; each one looking to yourself, lest you too be tempted.

Gal. 6:1

Authentic Christianity

Is recovery from codependency really just narcissism? Is it just an excuse to justify self-indulgent preoccupation? When we commit ourselves to the principles of recovery, are we really just condoning selfishness?

No. Codependency is a real problem for millions of people, resulting from the neglect, anger, denial, addictions and deep wounds prevalent in so many families today. And yes, as we become more aware of the deep hurts that stem from these family disorders, we will become more self-absorbed...for a while.

Like anything else, emotional healing requires time and attention. It doesn't happen by osmosis. Consider someone with a broken leg. Before his leg can even begin the process of healing, he needs to see a doctor, have the leg examined and x-rayed, and possibly have surgery and/or a cast for the leg. His pain will be immobilizing for at least the first several days after the break, if not longer. After some time, he will regain some of his mobility. He will become more productive. He will become less preoccupied with his leg. That doesn't mean he can forget about it, of course. After the cast comes off, he will need to work at rehabilitating his atrophied leg muscles. He may need to plan some type of training regime to continue rebuilding strength in his leg. It may be months before his leg is fully restored, if then.

Like the time and attention required for a broken leg, the time and attention required for a broken heart isn't narcissistic; it's reasonable. The initial preoccupation we all experience in recovery is only the first stage in a process that will lead to a strong sense of biblical identity, genuine love and selfless service: authentic Christianity. This process begins and continues with a growing sense of reality about life. The denial is eroded; we become more aware of our sins and the sins others commit against us. We begin to experience forgiveness for our wrongs and comfort for the hurts we have endured. Our view of God evolves from an aloof or cruel Master to a just and merciful Father. Our black-or white perspectives are more often shaded with gray as we become more comfortable with life's many ambiguities. We develop relationships that are more authentic, based increasingly on honest communication, respect for one another's separateness and genuine love.

This process of growth and change involves an interplay of spiritual, relational, physical and emotional factors. In our culture, we tend to categorize, analyze and segment these so that we can fix each one with quick, easy answers; however, these factors are inextricably related. The intense drive to rescue, for example, has its roots in the emotional pain which stems from strained relationships. Such relationships distort a person's view of God and often result in a variety of stress-related physical ailments, such as gastrointestinal problems, tension headaches, lethargy resulting from depression, etc. If one addresses only the surface symptoms of this combination, he or she may experience temporary relief...until the root problems resurface and recreate the complete, negative impact again.

One gentleman was treated symptomatically by an internist for chronic diarrhea, but the stress generated in his life by a dependent, controlling wife remained hidden from the doctor. His propensity for intestinal disorders persists even now when he is overly stressed, but he has made significant improvements physically since he started addressing the issues surrounding his codependency. A woman who came for counseling complained of loneliness and hurt, but avoided any discussion of her relationships with her parents, brothers or husband. Somehow, she hoped to resolve her emotional pain apart from relational reality, an impossible task.

Addressing the root issues of codependency in the context of spiritual, emotional, physical and relational factors may take a good bit of time and attention, and it may be somewhat complicated, but it's the key for genuine change and progress.

Our growth affects our most fundamental motivations. Instead of rescuing, giving and serving for affirmation and appreciation, our increasing strength and stability make it possible to love and give with an open hand. Jesus referred to this motivation in his Sermon on the Mount:

> "And if you love those who love you, what credit is that to you? For even sinners love those who love them.
> "And if you do good to those who do good to you, what credit is that to you? For even sinners do the same.
> "And if you lend to those from whom you expect to receive, what credit is that to you? Even sinners lend to sinners, in order to receive back the same amount.
> "But love your enemies, and do good, and lend, expecting nothing in return; and your reward will be great, and you will be sons of the Most High; for He Himself is kind to ungrateful and evil men.
> "Be merciful, just as your Father is merciful.
> "And do not judge and you will not be judged; and do not condemn, and you will not be condemned; pardon, and you will be pardoned,
> "Give, and it will be given to you; good measure, pressed down, shaken together, running over, they will pour into your lap. For by your standard of measure it will be measured to you in return."
>
> Luke 6:32-38

As rescuers, we tend to interpret the admonition to avoid judging as an excuse to avoid seeing reality (v. 37). "I shouldn't even think about my father's alcoholism," one woman told me. "That would be judging him, and that's wrong!" We also tend to view loving others, doing good and lending as cardinal virtues, without analyzing the deeper motivation that Jesus is addressing. We are prone to miss the admonition to *expect nothing in return* (v. 35) and the strength of character that godly service requires. The Scriptures *do* command us as believers to please others, but the instruction makes the motivation clear: it is for *their* good, not so we will receive appreciation. The contrast between pleasing people so that they will give us the love we want, and pleasing people for their good is seen clearly when we compare Gal. 1:10 with Rom. 15:2.

> For am I now seeking the favor of men, or of God? Or am I striving to please men? If I were still trying to please men, I would not be a bond-servant of Christ.
>
> Gal. 1:10

> Let each of us please his neighbor for his good, to his edification.
>
> Rom. 15:2

Genuine recovery from codependency doesn't make us self-indulgent and obnoxious. Far from that, the process of growing in our new identities and healthy relationships provides strength and godly character. This enables us to love and give and serve without so many of the twisted motives and deceptions common to codependency.

As our progress continues, we are better able to...

- replace our lack of objectivity with more accurate perceptions of God, other people and ourselves.
- overcome a warped sense of responsibility by gaining a better understanding of our limits of responsibility; as we live within those limits, we gradually learn to give because we *want* to, not because we feel we *have* to.
- find strength in our identities and grow to value our feelings, thoughts and decisions so that we're not so easily controlled by others.
- value others enough to let them make their own decisions, rather than attempting to control what they say and do.
- be honest about our feelings and learn how to deal with them more appropriately, instead of continuing to repress negative emotions like hurt and anger.
- move out of loneliness and grow into authentic relationships based on honesty, respect and love.

Many of us have taken various tests to help us determine our strengths, weaknesses and professional abilities. Sometimes the results of these tests reflect our emotional pathology more than our true personality. Many of us really don't know what we're like because our lives have been clouded by our compelling thirst for recognition and approval.

Several years ago I took a test which showed that I was very goal-oriented, but given to swings of emotion and perspective. (Today I would call these descriptions "driven" and "black and white!") The results also showed that I valued others' approval highly and was "malleable under pressure." (That means "easily manipulated!") I recently took the same test again to see if what I've been learning about codependency has changed my personality. I was encouraged! The results showed that I am not nearly as goal-oriented ("driven") as before, that I'm far more stable (instead of "black and white") and that I'm not nearly as easily swayed by others' opinions of me as I used to be. I'm growing! I'm in the process of recovery.

The growth that accompanies recovery frees us from the oppressive bondage of hurt, bitterness, shame and manipulation so that we can live more whole-heartedly for Christ. A deep experience of God's love has a powerful, liberating and motivating influence, as Paul wrote the believers in Corinth:

> *For the love of Christ controls us, having concluded this, that one died for all, therefore all died;*
> *and He died for all, that they who live should no longer live for themselves, but for Him who died*
> *and rose again on their behalf.*
>
> 2 Cor. 5:14-15

Authentic Christianity. Changed lives. Is this phony? No, not at all. Is it attractive? Yes, very attractive! The reason people in Christ's day were so attracted to Him—and the reason the religious establishment was so threatened by Him— was that Jesus was honest about the real issues in people's lives. He didn't mince words. He didn't offer superficial solutions and quick fixes. He offered deep solutions: authentic love, forgiveness and acceptance to meet deep needs.

If individuals became honest about their needs and if they experienced—genuinely experienced—the life-changing love and power of God in their hearts and relationships, needy people the world over would flock to Christ. They would experience deep healing from their pain. They would repent from sins of bitterness. Relationships would be restored. An awakening would break out as God's Spirit worked in countless lives.

A few weeks ago, I talked to a middle-aged friend who is growing in his perceptions and learning to experience genuine love and separateness. He said, "I wish I had learned all of this a lot earlier in my life. It surely would have prevented a lot of pain—for me and for my wife and children. But God has done so much in the past year or so. I'm very grateful! Learning this now is better than later—and it's a lot better than never at all!"

You may feel a sense of loss for not having dealt with these issues earlier in your life, but you will be glad to experience the freedom and love that you can have now. The process is hard, but it's worth it. It starts by having the courage to be honest with one other person...something to remember as you prepare (or continue) to share the news of your growth with others.

Carrying the Message

Having now arrived at step 12, you've undoubtedly met some other codependent people along the way. And in all probability, you've met some who can't wait to share their story with you. Why is that? People everywhere love to share their success stories, and in fact, such sharing is a demonstration of God's grace in our lives:

> *Blessed be the God and Father of our Lord Jesus Christ, the Father of all mercies and God of all comfort;*
> *who comforts us in all our affliction so that we may be able to comfort those who are in any affliction with the comfort with which we ourselves are comforted by God.*
>
> 2 Cor. 1:3-4

> *And we know that God causes all things to work together for good to those who love God, to those who are called according to His purpose.*
>
> Rom. 8:28

God *is* sovereign! He uses our sufferings to teach us how to comfort others—just as He has used the sorrows of others to comfort *us*! What a joy to witness the destruction and pain of codependency being used for someone else's good!

There are many other benefits of sharing such comfort with others in situations comparable to what ours used to be. It aids our own recovery, serving as a sharp reminder of our former state when we were still under the compulsions of rescuing and controlling. Such reminders make us aware of our need for humility (It is so easy to get into the habit of rescuing and controlling again) and propel us into action.

The following Scriptures remind us of our former condition, as well as the necessity of getting and receiving help through others:

> *For we also once were foolish ourselves, disobedient, deceived, enslaved to various lusts and pleasures, spending our life in malice and envy, hateful, hating one another.*
> *But when the kindness of God our Savior and His love for mankind appeared,*
> *He saved us, not on the basis of deeds which we have done in righteousness, but according to His mercy, by the washing of regeneration and renewing by the Holy Spirit,*
> *whom He poured out upon us richly through Jesus Christ our Savior,*
> *that being justified by His grace we might be made heirs according to the hope of eternal life.*
>
> Titus 3:3-7

> *Two are better than one because they have a good return for their labor.*
> *For if either of them falls, the one will lift up his companion. But woe to the one who falls when there is not another to lift him up.*
>
> Eccles. 4:9-10

Helping others is, in part, the telling of a story; the story of your progress toward health through the Twelve-Step program. In the spaces below, write:

■ How the Twelve-Step program has deepened your faith in Jesus Christ:_____

_____

_____

_____

_____

_____

■ How the power of Jesus Christ is transforming your life:

• Emotionally:_____

_____

_____

_____

• Relationally:_____

_____

_____

_____

• Spiritually:_____

_____

_____

_____

• Mentally:_____

_____

_____

_____

• Physically:_____

_____

_____

_____

■ Describe any differences in your behavior that have resulted from identifying false beliefs and replacing them with the truths of God's Word:

_____

_____

_____

_____

_____

_____

_____

■ Have other people noticed changes or improvements in your behavior? If so, describe some of these changes:

_____

_____

_____

_____

_____

By writing down some of the many changes that have occurred in your life since you entered recovery, you are gathering some good material to share with newcomers. Scripture gives us many helpful hints for successful sharing. Let's look at some of these:

■ Read Gal. 6:1.

• How would you try to restore a codependent person in a *spirit of gentleness*? Give several possible applications of this instruction:

_____

_____

_____

_____

_____

_____

• What can you do to ensure that helping newcomers won't be the cause of a downfall in your own life? List several possible safeguards:

_____

_____

_____

_____

_____

■ Read Phil. 1:27; 4:8-9.

• Is our example to others as important as what we say to them? Explain:_____

_____

_____

_____

_____

As we experience the joys of giving comfort to others who are codependent, and as we mature in our own relationship with God, we will begin to be compelled to share His transforming love and power with others. This is the work of the Holy Spirit, yet some of us shy away from this responsibility because we fear rejection. And for good reason! Christ has assured us of being rejected by at least some people when we take a stand for Him.

In John 15:18-25, Jesus said that the reason we are rejected is because, indeed, we are His: *If you belonged to the world, it would love you as its own. As it is, you do not belong to the world, but I have chosen you out of the world. That is why the world hates you* (John 15:19, NIV). Almighty God has chosen us! He has made us new, set us apart and reconciled us to Himself. We are special and precious to Him, but we should not expect the world to be thrilled with our commitment to Christ.

Sadly, we often forget that we are special and chosen. At times, we wish we belonged to the world. When faced with the choice of being rejected for taking a stand for Christ or going along with the world, we often choose the world. The fear of rejection is too great. But God has given us a solution to the fear of rejection! We no longer have to accept the opinions of others as the basis of our significance. Instead, the love and acceptance of the infinite, Almighty God frees us to live unreservedly for Him. We can step out in faith and lovingly tell people about Christ's offer of forgiveness. Billions of people are waiting to hear His message!

Appendix

Breaking the Cycle of Codependent Behavior
by Using the Truth of God's Word

...and you shall know the truth, and the truth shall make you free.
John 8:32

Replacing our codependent compulsions of rescuing and controlling with healthy patterns of behavior is a life-long process. If this is discouraging to you, consider Paul's words in 2 Cor. 12:7-10, especially v. 9: *And He* (the Lord) *has said to me, "My grace is sufficient for you, for power is perfected in weakness."*

God intends that we look to Him for the provision of strength. Our willingness to do so reflects the degree to which we are aware of our weaknesses and understand the truth about His nature.

A woman who has become acquainted with Rapha through her work in ministry broke her back several years ago in a hiking accident. That she is walking today is a miracle she attributes to God. That she is in constant pain every day and never certain that she will walk tomorrow are conditions she has accepted by trusting absolutely in the sovereignty and goodness of God.

"God knows what I need," she says. "I can be very independent. Pain is my 'short leash.' It is a constant reminder of my desperate need for God, a reminder that every step I take is because of Him.

"We tend to live as if we were in control of our lives," she says. "This is illusion. In reality, even the breath that fills our lungs is given to us by God."

This woman knows the truth about God's character. Her testimony is, in part, a helpful reminder that we interpret life's situations primarily through our belief system, and that what we believe often governs our response to those situations.

In order to respond to the situations around us in healthy ways, we must know the truth about our Lord's character. As was mentioned in step 2, we each have a tendency to transfer our concepts of human authorities to God, our ultimate authority. These erroneous concepts will govern our responses to life's situations until we replace them with the truth of God's Word.

The prophet Isaiah wrote, *The steadfast of mind Thou wilt keep in perfect peace, because he trusts in Thee* (Is. 26:3). Jesus said, *You shall know the truth and the truth shall make you free* (John 8:32). Paul wrote, *All Scripture is inspired by God and profitable for teaching, for reproof, for correction, for training in righteousness; that the man of God may be adequate, equipped for every good work* (2 Tim. 3:16).

To trust God, to be freed from unhealthy patterns of behavior and enjoy the fruits of His peace—despite our circumstances—requires that we accept as truth what Scripture says of His character. Consider using the following exercise as a tool to help you reflect on the "Characteristics of Christ" from step 3, and to help you respond to your circumstances based on what Scripture says is true about Him.

A Twenty-Day Journal

Try to set aside a specific time each day to spend with God and work on this exercise. Each time you catch yourself responding codependently to a situation, comment, thought, problem or relationship, take that condition to your meeting place. As the days pass, you will expose many thoughts that contradict the truth about God's character.

Below and on the following page is an outline to guide you through this exercise. Twenty days from now, you will have a good start on developing a new pattern for living—one which we urge you to continue indefinitely.[1]

1. *Realize:* Be objective about your situation by writing it out.

2. *Reject:* Next, use the belief systems chart on page 39 to determine the fear(s) or false belief(s) triggered by the situation.

3. *Replace:* Review the characteristics of Christ in step 3 and select one appropriate to your situation. Then select a passage of Scripture from that step (listed below) which portrays that aspect of His character. Write out the Scripture which describes this characteristic.

4. Study the passage more specifically, perhaps using the method of observation, interpretation and application.

- *Observation: Who* is portrayed in this passage? If there is a dialogue between persons, *what* are they saying? *What* are they doing? *When* are they saying or doing it? *Where* does the conversation/activity take place? *How* does the conversation/activity occur?

- *Interpretation:* What does the passage mean? What biblical principles are portrayed in this passage about God, people, relationships, goals, behavior and responses?

- *Application:* Ask yourself, *What does this mean to me? How can I specifically apply one or more of these principles today? ...this week? ...this year?* (Avoid trying to apply too much too soon, or you may become frustrated and give up on the process altogether.)

5. In prayer, affirm the application to your situation.

The following is a list of the passages you paraphrased in step 3. (Note: if you prefer going through a book of the Bible and looking for characteristics of Christ paragraph by paragraph, or if you want to work with some other passages of Scripture, feel free to do so.)

Purpose
Is. 59:1-2
Acts 4:12
Rom. 2:4-5
1 Pet. 3:18
Titus 2:11-14

Total Acceptance
Rom. 8:15-17
Rom. 15:7
Gal. 4:5-7

Unconditional Love
John 3:16-17
1 John 4:9-10
Rev. 1:5-6

Complete Forgiveness
Luke 7:36-48
Rom. 5:6-11
Col. 2:13-14
Col. 3:13

Authority and Power
Phil 2:9-11
Col. 1:15-19
Col. 2:10
Col. 2:15

Hope
Rom. 8:28
Eph. 2:12
1 Pet. 1:3

Wisdom
Is. 55:8-9
1 Cor. 1:18-27
Eph. 5:15-21
James 1:5-6

Faithfulness
1 Cor. 10:13
2 Tim. 2:11-13
Heb. 10:23

To complete this exercise, you may want to get a small notebook, or you may already have another way of keeping up with your study. Your entries on each page might look something like the following pages:

DAY ONE

Date:__/__/__

■ *Realize:* Describe your situation:

_____

_____

_____

_____

_____

■ *Reject:* Which of the four fears or false beliefs does this trigger for you?

- **The Fear of Failure:** *I must meet certain standards in order to feel good about myself.*
- **The Fear of Punishment:** *Those who fail (including me) are unworthy of love and deserve to be punished.*
- **The Fear of Rejection:** *I must be approved by certain others to feel good about myself.*
- **The Feeling of Shame:** *I am what I am. I cannot change. I am hopeless.*

■ *Replace:* What characteristic of Christ helps overcome this fear?
- Purpose
- Unconditional Love
- Complete Forgiveness
- Total Acceptance
- Authority and Power
- Faithfulness
- Hope
- Wisdom

- From the characteristics above, which passage(s) from page 264 do you find most meaningful and encouraging for this particular situation? Write it out in the spaces below:

_____

_____

_____

_____

_____

■ What are your...

- Observation(s)?

_____

_____

_____

_____

- Interpretation(s)?

_____

_____

_____

_____

_____

- Application(s)?

_____

_____

_____

_____

_____

■ Pray. Thank the Lord for the truth of His Word. Ask Him to help you apply His Word and experience His presence today.

Notes

Introduction

1. Analyses adapted from Sharon Wegscheider-Cruse, *The Family Trap*, and John Bradshaw, *The Family*.
2. Melody Beattie, *Codependent No More* (New York: Hazeldon Foundation, 1987), p. 31.
3. Sharon Wegscheider-Cruse, *Choice-Making: For Co-Dependents, Adult Children and Spirituality Seekers* (Pompano Beach, FL: Health Communications, 1985), as cited by Charles L. Whitfield, M.D., *Healing the Child Within* (Deerfield Beach, FL: Health Communications, Inc., 1987; 1989), p. 29.
4. Judith S. Wallerstein, "Bouncing Back Slowly." Excerpt. *New York Times Magazine*, 22 Jan. 1989.
5. James M. Houston, "The Independence Myth," *Christianity Today*, 15 Jan. 1990, 32.
6. Ibid, 33.

Step 1

1. Kübler-Ross, Elisabeth, *On Death and Dying* (New York: MacMillan Publishing, 1969). Adapted.

Step 2

1. Robert S. McGee, Jim Craddock and Pat Springle, *Your Parents and You* (Houston and Dallas, TX: Rapha Publishing/Word, Inc., 1990), adapted from p. 9 with permission.
2. Ibid, pp. 191-194.
3. Ibid, pp. 195-197.
4. Ibid, pp. 199-201.
5. Ibid, pp. 203-206.
6. Ibid, pp. 207-210.
7. Ibid, pp. 231-236.

Step 3

1. McGee, Craddock and Springle, *Your Parents and You*, pp. 245-272. Reprinted and adapted by permission.

Step 4

1. Claude M. Steiner, *Scripts People Live* (New York: Grove Press, 1974), as cited by Melody Beattie, *Codependent No More*, p. 77.
2. Melody Beattie, *Codependent No More*, p. 58.

Step 6

1. For an explanation of manipulative control as idolatry, see John N. Oswalt, *The Book of Isaiah* (Grand Rapids, MI: Eerdmans, 1986), pp. 82-89.

Step 9

1. *The Twelve Steps of Alcoholics Anonymous* (New York: Harper/Hazeldon, 1987), pp. 95-96.

Step 11

1. Peter M. Lord, *The 1959 Plan: A Guide to Communion with GOD* (Titusville, FL: Agape Ministries, 1976), p. 17.

Appendix

1. McGee, Craddock and Springle, *Your Parents and You*, pp. 343-347. Reprinted and adapted by permission.